SpringerBriefs in Economics

SpringerBriefs present concise summaries of cutting-edge research and practical applications across a wide spectrum of fields. Featuring compact volumes of 50 to 125 pages, the series covers a range of content from professional to academic. Typical topics might include:

- A timely report of state-of-the art analytical techniques
- A bridge between new research results, as published in journal articles, and a contextual literature review
- A snapshot of a hot or emerging topic
- An in-depth case study or clinical example
- A presentation of core concepts that students must understand in order to make independent contributions

SpringerBriefs in Economics showcase emerging theory, empirical research, and practical application in microeconomics, macroeconomics, economic policy, public finance, econometrics, regional science, and related fields, from a global author community.

Briefs are characterized by fast, global electronic dissemination, standard publishing contracts, standardized manuscript preparation and formatting guidelines, and expedited production schedules.

Fakhri J. Hasanov • Frederick L. Joutz
Jeyhun I. Mikayilov • Muhammad Javid

A Macroeconometric Model for Saudi Arabia

A Case Study on the World's Largest Oil Exporter

 Springer

Fakhri J. Hasanov
Energy Systems and Macroeconomics
King Abdullah Petroleum Studies
and Research Center
Riyadh, Saudi Arabia

Jeyhun I. Mikayilov
Energy Systems and Macroeconomics
King Abdullah Petroleum Studies
and Research Center
Riyadh, Saudi Arabia

Frederick L. Joutz
Energy Systems and Macroeconomics
King Abdullah Petroleum Studies
and Research Center
Riyadh, Saudi Arabia

Muhammad Javid
Energy Systems and Macroeconomics
King Abdullah Petroleum Studies
and Research Center
Riyadh, Saudi Arabia

ISSN 2191-5504 ISSN 2191-5512 (electronic)
SpringerBriefs in Economics
ISBN 978-3-031-12274-3 ISBN 978-3-031-12275-0 (eBook)
https://doi.org/10.1007/978-3-031-12275-0

This Springer imprint is published by the registered company Springer Nature Switzerland AG
The registered company address is: Gewerbestrasse 11, 6330 Cham, Switzerland

This book is dedicated to the memory of Frederick L. Joutz.

KGEMM: A Macroeconometric Model for Saudi Arabia

Extended Abstract

The KAPSARC Global Energy Macroeconometric Model (KGEMM) is a policy analysis tool for examining the impacts of domestic policy measures and global changes on economic, energy, and environmental variables in Saudi Arabia at both aggregate and disaggregate levels. There are nine blocks (real sector; fiscal; monetary; external sector; domestic prices; labor and wages; energy; emission; and population and age cohorts) that interact with each other to represent the Kingdom's economic, energy, and emission linkages. KGEMM can be used to analyze the current status and future paths of aggregate and sectoral economic as well as energy and environmental indicators. It can also be used to evaluate the effects of different policy options on the Kingdom. KGEMM is a hybrid model in two main senses: it combines the data-driven approach with the theory-guided approach (New Keynesian demand-side features "anchored" to medium-run equilibrium and Neoclassical long-run supply-side representations), and it incorporates input-output table representations into the macroeconometric framework.

It has flexibility and simultaneity in evaluating multiple research and policy questions. It can also be easily customized for different research and policy questions. Unlike in many other macro-models for the Kingdom, the energy (oil, natural gas, and electricity) sector is not exogenous in KGEMM as it is interlinked to non-oil activity.

KGEMM has been validated using different validation tests, such as the statistical significance and theoretical consistency of the estimated parameters, post-estimation tests for the residuals of the estimated equations, in-sample performance for the approximation of historical data, and out-of-sample performance for policy analysis. In-sample and out-of-sample simulations show that KGEMM has robust predictive and policy analysis capabilities. Indeed, the model has been used extensively since December 2015 in multi-stakeholder projects to evaluate the macroeconomic effects of the Kingdom's domestic energy and fiscal reforms, the key initiatives in Saudi Vision 2030's Fiscal Balance Program.

This book introduces the fifth version of KGEMM and briefly describes developments from the first version till this one. It also provides a detailed survey of macroeconomic modeling in Saudi Arabia. We hope that this book will be a useful information source for researchers, scholars, and practitioners as it presents econometrically estimated elasticities and other coefficients of the behavioral relationships for economic, energy, and environmental dimensions of Saudi Arabia. We also hope that this book can further enhance cooperation and collaboration between modelers, researchers, and practitioners from various government agencies and research institutions.

Riyadh, Saudi Arabia

Fakhri J. Hasanov
Frederick L. Joutz
Jeyhun I. Mikayilov
Muhammad Javid

Contents

Chapter 1
Executive Summary

The objective of this book is to introduce the KAPSARC Global Energy Macroeconometric Model (KGEMM) and to conduct a detailed survey of the existing macroeconomic models for Saudi Arabia, discussing their strengths and weaknesses. KGEMM is a policy analysis tool for examining the impacts of domestic policies and changes in global economy including energy markets on the Saudi Arabian economic, energy, and environmental variables at both aggregate and disaggregate levels.

Macroeconometric models inform policymakers about the dynamic relationships among economic indicators, how economies have performed in the past, and how their current and future behaviors might differ. Models are simplifications of actual relationships that provide analytical and empirical frameworks concentrating on important aspects of the relationships. Macroeconometric models can explain, project, and evaluate economic processes. They can be especially useful in helping policymakers to evaluate the impact of alternative policy choices. In this regard, macroeconometric models provide analytical and evidence-based foundations for policy decisions, contributing to the increased likelihood of successful policies.

A macroeconometric model for Saudi Arabia is particularly important for the country's policymakers. The Kingdom faces numerous economic, demographic, and social changes as it diversifies its economy away from oil toward a greater role for the non-oil private sector and a more efficient public sector with enhanced services. The Kingdom's economy is as responsive to international energy market dynamics as any other oil exporting economy. The future of the country's economy is based on a transformation process, outlined in the Kingdom's strategic roadmap, Saudi Vision 2030 (SV2030). SV2030 involves important initiatives such as an energy price reform to induce more rational use of the Kingdom's energy resources, fiscal reforms for more effective government spending and increasing non-oil revenues, investment projects for supporting economic growth and diversification. The role that oil exports and revenues play in Saudi Arabia's fiscal policy and economy will certainly

© The Author(s) 2023   1
F. J. Hasanov et al., *A Macroeconometric Model for Saudi Arabia*,
SpringerBriefs in Economics, https://doi.org/10.1007/978-3-031-12275-0_1

continue during the transition. Projections and assessments by international agencies suggest that global energy markets will see slower oil demand growth. Obviously, renewable transitions and environmental protection policies play a central role in this slowdown. Reforming the Kingdom's investment environment and legislation attracts more foreign direct and domestic investments. Such institutional and structural reforms could, over time, bring about changes in the country's fiscal and monetary policies and in financial markets, as highlighted in SV2030 realization programs, such as the Fiscal Sustainability Program, the National Transformation Program, and the Financial Sector Development Program. Labor market reforms are also necessary to absorb the current and coming young male and female Saudis entering the labor force. Expatriate labor's role in the workforce will change. Quantifying the effects of the above-mentioned domestic and international developments on Saudi Arabia's economic energy, and environmental dimensions requires well-designed models.

Policymakers need to know how the implementations of the above-mentioned initiatives of SV2030 coupled with global changes could influence the country's economic, energy, and environmental outlook. Macroeconometric models augmented with energy and environmental representations could provide insights about these. They could also show how the economy could be restructured and how sectoral and macroeconomic indicators should be changed to help achieve SV2030 targets.

No publicly available macroeconometric models can address the points above to the best of our knowledge. The KGEMM research project is an attempt to fill this gap and provide insights into economic-energy-environmental related policy options for the Kingdom's decision makers.

The model has nine blocks (real, fiscal, monetary, external, domestic prices, labor and wages, energy, CO_2 emissions, population and age cohorts) that interact with each other to represent the Kingdom's economic (macro and sectoral), energy, and environmental linkages.

KGEMM can address two broad sets of policies and areas of research: domestic economic-energy-environmental relationships and the effects of the rest of the world, particularly global energy markets.

The following characteristics of KGEMM show its contribution to the existing literature on macroeconomic modelling in Saudi Arabia:

- This is one of the very few macroeconometric models that incorporates an input-output table framework into its structure and, hence, can address sectoral research and policy questions through intermediate, final, and total demand relationships.
- It combines theoretical foundations with empirical coherence, including stylized facts of the Kingdom's economy and uses cutting-edge econometric methods, such as *Autometrics*, a machine-learning econometric modeling methodology.
- It has the flexibility to evaluate multiple policy and research questions simultaneously.
- It is easy to customize for different policy and research questions.

- The oil sector is not treated purely exogenously in the model as it is linked with the non-oil activities.
- Aggregate demand and aggregate supply are disaggregated into sectoral economic activities.
- It has an energy block representing detailed energy demand relationships by energy type and customer with some supply side representations, including renewable energy.
- It has an environmental block representing CO_2 emissions by energy type and customer.
- It links the export of Saudi Arabian refinery oil to 45 individual countries' refinery oil demand, allowing for comprehensive simulations of the impact of change in global oil demand due to economic activities, renewable energy transitions and climate change policies on the Saudi economy.
- A user-friendly interface and an open-box environment.

It can also contribute to economic (macro and sectoral) modeling for other open economies that are rich in natural resources, as there are similarities among these countries.

KGEMM can be used to analyze the current stance and project the future paths of economic (macro and sectoral) and energy indicators as well as CO_2 emissions. The model can also be used to evaluate the effects of different policy options (e.g., SV2030 initiatives and targets). It can further enhance effective cooperation between modelers, researchers, and practitioners from various government agencies and research institutions as it represents different aspects of the economy, energy, and environment in the Kingdom.

KGEMM has been validated using different validation tests, such as statistical significance and theoretical consistency of the estimated parameters, post-estimation tests for the residuals of the estimated equations, in-sample performance for the approximation of historical data, and out-of-sample performance for policy analysis. In this book, we run the model for an in-sample forecast to approximate the historical time path of the endogenous variables as well as an out-of-sample simulations to assess the impact of Arabian light crude oil's international price, foreign direct investments inflow, and renewable deployments on Saudi Arabia's economic, energy, and environmental indicators. In-sample and out-of-sample simulations show that KGEMM has robust predictive and policy analysis capabilities. Indeed, KGEMM has been used extensively in multi-stakeholder projects to assess the macroeconomic and sectoral effects of the Kingdom's domestic energy price and fiscal reforms, the key initiatives in SV2030's Fiscal Balance Program since December 2015.

KGEMM is a hybrid model in two senses. First, it incorporates Input-Output Table representations of intermediate, final, and total demand by economic activity sector into a typical macroeconometric modeling framework. Second, it nests the theory-guided modeling approach with the data-driven approach. The KGEMM version presented in this book has a number of developments since its third version presented in Hasanov et al. (2020). The main developments are the representations of the petrochemical sector, disaggregated imports, and CO_2 emissions. The latter one makes KGEMM a type of E3ME model (Energy-Environment-Economy Macro-Econometric model) and being similar to SEEEM (Sectoral Energy-Economic Econometric Model) and PANTA RHEI, the models that cover energy-economic-environmental dimensions.

Chapter 2
Literature Review

The history of macroeconometric model-building is comprehensively documented in Fair (1984, 1994), Bodkin et al. (1991), Hendry and Mizon (2000), Favero (2001), Pagan (2003a, b), Bårdsen et al. (2004, 2005), Valadkhani (2004), Hendry and Muellbauer (2018), Jelić and Ravnik (2021) inter alia. Also, history and macroeconometric modeling activities over the world and their classification are documented in Welfe (2013).

This section reviews only general equilibrium macroeconomic models that have been built for the Saudi Arabian economy. In other words, we do not review either partial equilibrium models built for Saudi Arabia (e.g., see Mohaddes et al. 2020) or general equilibrium models built for other resource-rich economies. The former ones are not in line with our objectives, and the latter ones are out of the scope of this book and have been reviewed by Welfe (2013) and Hasanov and Joutz (2013) to some extent, among others. Our review here is limited to models that are publicly available or available to us.[1] Table 2.1 documents these models.

As the strengths and weaknesses of each model are documented in Table 2.1, we do not discuss them again here. However, it is worth mentioning that their strengths and weaknesses are also determined by their type that they belong to among other factors. In general, structural, that is theory-guided models, such as computable general equilibrium (CGE) and dynamic stochastic general equilibrium (DSGE) models have the main strengths of being strongly consistent with textbook economic theory, useful for long-term projections and analyzing the effects of changes in policy variables. The studies listed below discuss that these models have the following main weaknesses: using micro-foundations strictly as theoretical foundations and not allowing data 'to speak freely'; they do not incorporate information about behavioral economics and information economics; they are calibrated to

---

[1] Of course, we are unable to review the models that are not publicly available, including those built and used by government agencies, international institutions, academia and research centers, and private companies. We also do not review master or dissertation theses such as Tawi (1984), Taher (1987), Aljerayed (1993) and Al-Teraiki (1999).

© The Author(s) 2023
F. J. Hasanov et al., *A Macroeconometric Model for Saudi Arabia*,
SpringerBriefs in Economics, https://doi.org/10.1007/978-3-031-12275-0_2

Table 2.1 Macroeconomic models for Saudi Arabia

Name	Period	Type	Strengths	Weaknesses	Note
Ezzati (1976)	1963–1972	Combined dynamic intertemporal, multi-sectoral, empirical linear programing model and macroeconometric model	Combination of optimization with MEM.	Insufficient theoretical underpinning (e.g., private investment and consumption equations contain only income; export, and import equations ignore relative prices or real exchange rates; production function ignores labor. The model does not capture labor and monetary markets (we could not find a consumer price inflation (CPI) or gross domestic product (GDP) deflator and exchange rate in the model).	Designed to analyze the impact of oil price and production on macroeconomic indicators in OPEC member countries including Saudi Arabia.
Looney (1986)	1980–1985	Optimal control Macroeconomic model	Macroeconomic model within the framework of optimal control can distinguish the most efficient growth path to the end target.	Stochastic properties (unit root and cointegration) of the time series variables used in the econometric estimations were ignored. Therefore, one can argue that the study might suffer from spurious regression issues. Addressing these issues is particularly important for this study, as it is designed for policy analysis. It would be informative for readers if the study reports	The Optimal Control Macroeconomic Model has been used to examine the Saudi Arabia's third Five Year Development Plan (1980–1985) for goal feasibility and tradeoffs among the plan's major goals.

				post-estimation test results, so that they can see the adequacy of the estimated relationships.	
Looney (1988)	1986–1992	Optimal control Macroeconomic model	A macroeconomic model within the framework of optimal control can distinguish the most efficient growth path to the end target.	The stochastic properties (unit root and cointegration) of the time series variables used in the econometric estimations were ignored. Therefore, one can argue that the study might suffer from spurious regression issues. Addressing these issues is particularly important for this study as it is designed for policy analysis. It would be informative for readers if the study reports post-estimation test results so that they can see adequacy of the estimated relationships.	This model has been developed to examine the socio-economic planning dilemmas confronting Saudi Arabian policy during an era of falling oil revenue.
Johansen and Magnussen (1996)	1980–1991	Combination of MEM and IOT	Combination of MEM and IOT. Accounts for the stylized facts of Saudi Arabia. Employs ECM specifications in the model.	The model does not capture the monetary aspects of the economy. The empirical analysis does not consider the integration and cointegration properties of the data used. So, the risk of spurious results and consequently misleading recommendations exist.	Developed by the Research Department, Statistics Norway for the Kingdom of Saudi Arabia's Ministry of Economy and planning. Its main purpose is to assist in the Kingdom's five-year development plans by analyzing fiscal and monetary

(continued)

Table 2.1 (continued)

Name	Period	Type	Strengths	Weaknesses	Note
				There are some assumptions which are hard to believe can hold in reality in Saudi Arabia. E.g., export categories are treated as exogenous; coefficients in the linear expenditure system are not estimated but calibrated using studies on other countries; the real oil price is included in the private consumption equation along with disposable income, which may cause double accounting of the oil effect; neither consumption nor investment equations include interest rates.	policies and shocks from the oil sector and abroad.
Cappelen and Magnussen (1996)	1989	CGE model	Well-established theoretical foundation combined with the stylized facts of Saudi Arabia. Very disaggregate representation of the Kingdom's economy.	The modelling of production sectors and capital stock data are based on weak data foundations and strong assumptions. Some rough assumptions of the labor market (e.g., wage rate and foreign workers are exogenous). The governmental sector is aggregated in the model;	Designed for the preparation of five-year development plans, especially to explore the outcome of investment programs.

| Bjerkholt (1993) | NR | MEM | | | there is no breakdown of government consumption.
The model does not capture monetary, labor, and energy aspects of the economy.
It does not have an explicit price block (Johansen and Magnussen 1996).
The model's equations do not consider the integration and cointegration properties of the data used. So, the risk of spurious results and consequently, misleading recommendations exist.
Important linkages are ignored. For example, changes in government consumption and private consumption do not affect GDP.
Lack of theoretical foundation. For example, non-oil GDP is only the function of its own lag and non-oil investment; some sectors' production capacities are modeled as only the function of the time trend.
The model does not account for simultaneity. | Designed as a planning model for the fifth development plan of the Ministry of Economy and planning. |
| Bjerkholt (1993) | NR | AGE | | | Very disaggregate representation of the economy | Given the level of granularity, it was very difficult to |

(continued)

Table 2.1 (continued)

Name	Period	Type	Strengths	Weaknesses	Note
			(model contains 36 production sectors, 14 household types, 5 labor skill categories, 31 consumption groups).	handle, maintain, update, and upgrade the model due to (a) the technical capacity of the Ministry of Economy and planning employees, and (b) periodic surveys had to be conducted to obtain the required data, which was not resourceful and cost effective.	Coopers & Lybrand built the model for the Ministry of Economy and Planning.
Bjerkholt (1993)	1969–1989	MEM	Very disaggregate representation of the economy (model contains 36 production sectors, 14 household types, 5 labor skill categories, and 31 consumption groups).	The model does not capture monetary, labor, and energy aspects of the economy. The model's equations do not consider the integration and cointegration properties of the data used. So, the risk of spurious results and consequently, misleading recommendations exist. Important linkages are ignored. For example, spillover from the oil sector to the non-oil sector is only through oil revenues, not via intermediate consumption and investment. The exogeneity assumptions are overly set. For example, non-oil export and oil	Designed as a planning model for the sixth development plan of the Ministry of Economy and Planning By The Research Department of Economic and Social Development as part of a technical cooperation project to strengthen the planning capabilities of the Kingdom of Saudi Arabia's Ministry of Economy and planning.

				refining are exogenous. Very weak theoretical foundation. E.g., government consumption is a residual of GDP identity; production capacity depends only on investment; private consumption is a function of income only; the deflator is only dependent on wages. The model does not account for simultaneity and fine-tunings.	
Laxton et al. (1998)	1998	IMF MULTIMOD Mark III	The long-run properties of the MULTIMOD III have solid theoretical foundations and dynamic equations. The dynamic equations in MULTIMOD Mark III have a steady-state analogue equation.	IMF-MULTIMOD Mark III includes explicit country sub-models for each of the seven largest industrial countries. The remaining countries are then aggregated into separate blocks of developing and transition economies.	MULTIMOD is a dynamic multicounty macro model of the world economy that has been designed to study the transformation of shocks across countries and the short-run and medium-run consequences of alternative monetary and fiscal policies.
De Santis (2003)	1990	Static multisector CGE model	Theoretically well-established foundation combined with the stylized facts of Saudi Arabia.	The model does not capture labor market aspects of the economy. The energy sector is represented mainly by crude oil. Exogeneity assumptions are overly set. For example, investments and the current	The model is designed to analyze the impact of the crude oil price, demand and supply shocks on prices, output, profits, and welfare in Saudi Arabia.

(continued)

Table 2.1 (continued)

Name	Period	Type	Strengths	Weaknesses	Note
				account deficit are exogenous. There are a few assumptions, which are hard to believe can hold in reality in Saudi Arabia. E.g., the sources of private income are wages and returns to capital; the budget balance is always in equilibrium.	
Alam (1982)	NA	GE model	Theoretically well-established foundation combined with the stylized facts of an oil-dependent economy.	This is a theoretical model and not simulated using data for Saudi Arabia. The model has very limited coverage as it includes only tradable and non-tradable goods, reserves, and prices of non-tradable goods.	This is a theoretical model designed to investigate the impact of oil revenue-financed government expenditure on the indicators included in the model.
Bayoumi et al. (2004)	2004	IMF-global economy model	The main advantage of GEM is that it can provide evaluations of policies in a general equilibrium setting, allowing for the full range of effects across equations. The model is based on explicit microeconomic foundations; changing one of the deep parameters in the model can affect a wide range of relationships.	Calibrating GEM is time-consuming because the concepts in the model often do not match the existing data. Moving to a model with a tight theoretical structure also imposes limitations, at least in the short term.	GEM is a large-scale version of a micro-based open economy model. It primarily focuses on creating a unifying framework for the analysis of international interactions.

Nakov and Nuno (2013)	Average of January 1973–April 2009	GE model	Theoretically well-established	This is a very specific (oil-focused) model. There are a few assumptions, which are hard to believe can hold in reality. E.g., there is no labor and wage in production function and profit maximization of oil exporters, respectively; the oil-exporters maximize their profits only through oil production.	*It is built to investigate the impacts of oil production options, taxes, and subsidies mainly on oil importers' welfare and oil-exporters' oil production and oil revenues.
Blazquez et al. (2017)	1995–2014*	DSGE model	Theoretically well-established	This is a very specific (renewable-focused) model**. Hence, it covers only three sectors, i.e., a representative household, firms producing energy and aggregate non-energy products, and a restricted government. Again, since this is a very specific model, it has some restrictive assumptions. E. g., government revenues are only from energy sales; government expenditures only comprise of investment and transfers to households; natural gas is utilized only in electricity generation.	* This is the model calibration period not the estimation period. ** Designed to investigate the effects of renewables penetration and a reduction in energy subsidies on some macroeconomic indicators in Saudi Arabia.

(continued)

Table 2.1 (continued)

Name	Period	Type	Strengths	Weaknesses	Note
Gonand et al. (2019)	1980–2016*	GE model	The OLG model takes a finite lifetime into account and offers a more realistic approach to the study of long-run effects. The OLG model deals with the life cycle behavior of human capital, and the implication of the allocation of resources across generations.	Economic interaction takes place between agents belonging to many different age groups. Competitive equilibria may be Pareto suboptimal.	* This is the model calibration period not the estimation period. The authors developed an energy sector augmented dynamic macroeconomic model with overlapping generations for Saudi Arabia. This is a bespoke model for Saudi Arabia that builds on and develops the overlapping generation (OLG) model of Gonand and Jouvet (2015) by including the characteristics of the Saudi economy.
Soummane et al. (2019)*	2013, 2014–2017**	CGE model	Theoretically well-established foundation. Compared to other CGE models for KSA it has the following merits: (i) Uses original dataset That reconciles national accounting and energy balance data; (ii) performs a dynamic exploration; (iii) considers exogenous energy consumption pathways backed by a bottom-up mode; (iv) considers	Does not have monetary sector Behavioral specifications of the model are limited to non-energy trade-offs as all dimensions of energy trade, supply, and demand are treated as exogenous. It has some restrictive assumptions, such as foreign and domestic price ratio is unity; labor is only the function on unemployment.	* The CGE models in Soummane et al. (2022) and Soummane and Ghersi (2022) are very similar to the one in Soummane et al. (2019). ** This is the model calibration period not the estimation period.

Blazquez et al. (2017)	1997–2016*	DSGE model	imperfections of primary factor markets. Theoretically well-established foundation combined with some stylized facts of Saudi Arabia.	This is a stylized model.** hence, it focuses mainly on the real economic activities and does not cover the entire economy (e.g., monetary sector is missing). Again, since this is a stylized model, it has some restrictive assumptions, such as international trade is represented by net exports, not exports and imports separately.	* This is the model calibration period not the estimation period. ** Designed to investigate the effects of renewables deployment, domestic energy price reform and VAT on some macroeconomic indicators in Saudi Arabia.
OEGEM (2022)	1980–2019	Combination of MEM and IOT	Global coverage. Large database with historical and projected values. Combination of MEM and IOT. Accounts for the stylized facts of Saudi Arabia at some extent. Has energy and environmental components.	Insufficient theoretical foundation. In most cases, quarterly data is converted from annual data. Not enough attention paid to the Saudi MEM module as OEGEM has very wide global coverage*.	Commercial model available on a subscription basis. *OEGEM has 80 countries and 13 regional blocks. Saudi MEM is just one country module.
KGEMM (2022)*	1980–2019	Combination of MEM and IOT	Well-established theoretical foundation coupled with the empirical coherence, stylized facts of the Saudi economy and cutting-edge econometric methods. Flexible and simultaneous	Heavily data-intensive. Data updates and revision issues require re-estimation of behavioral equations. Data and model maintain and update requires a mid-size team.	* The model presented in this paper. The model has been built at KAPSARC and is currently in use at KAPSARC and the Ministry of Energy.

(continued)

Table 2.1 (continued)

Name	Period	Type	Strengths	Weaknesses	Note
			evaluation of different research/policy-related questions.		
			Customizable model to address different research/policy questions.		
			User-friendly interface and open box environment.		
			Disaggregated sectoral demand using an input-output framework and sectoral productions from the production functions.		
			Detailed energy block representing 14 energy demand relationships by energy type and customer.		
			CO_2 block reflecting emissions from energy products.		

Notes: MEM = macroeconometric model, *IOT* = input output table, *NR* = not reported, *NA* = not applicable, *ECM* = error correction model, *CPI* = consumer price index, *GDP* = gross domestic product, *OEGEM* = Oxford economics' global economic model, *GE* = general equilibrium, *AGE* = applied general equilibrium, *KEM-SA* = KAPSARC energy model for Saudi Arabia. Calibrated models include computable general equilibrium (CGE), dynamic stochastic general equilibrium (DSGE), and hybrid, among others capture only equilibrium positions with none to limited information about short-run dynamics, and they do not provide information about the errors that they make in their representations and simulations; they rely on many assumptions, restrictions, parametrizations that are not always true in reality (see Romer 2016; Stiglitz 2018; Blanchard 2017, 2018; Hendry and Muellbauer 2018; Wren-Lewis 2018; Fair 2019; Colander et al. 2008; Colander 2006; Hara et al. 2009; Pagan 2003a; Gürkaynak and Tille 2017; Crump et al. 2021; Wickens 1995 inter alia). Additionally, Giacomini (2015), Gürkaynak et al. (2013), among others, show that DSGEs, pure structural models produce very poor forecasting performance compared to econometric models in the empirical analyses. Moreover, Wickens (1995), Pesaran and Smith (2011), Blanchard (2017), inter alia, discuss that for DSGE models to survive in the future, they should account for data and hence switch from calibration of the deterministic relationships to estimation of the stochastic specifications, they should estimate well-specified long-run relationships rather than trend approximations and consider more dynamic short-run specifications to possibly account for habits, expectational errors, learning, and the costs and frictions of search and matching, and they should relax the assumptions made, such as optimal behavior, homogenous agent, symmetric information about market conditions, etc. Furthermore, Nikas et al. (2019, p. 37–38) discuss that standard structural models assume that markets clear in the short-run and, hence, they ignore disequilibrium and short-run relationships. For example, they usually assume that there is no unemployment in their representation of an economy. This obviously is not a relevant assumption even in the long-run and, hence, leads to drawbacks in their performances. Most likely due to the above-mentioned issues, the government agencies such as central banks recently prefer hybrid type macroeconometric models, which are built using equilibrium correction equations, in their policy analyses, forecasting, and projections. Because hybrid macroeconometric models perform better than purely theory-based models (e.g., CGE, DSGE, optimal growth models) and purely data-based models (e.g., unrestricted vector autoregression models) since they are the combination of theory-guided and data-driven approaches as the literature discusses (see discussions in Ballantyne et al. 2020, Cusbert and Kendall 2018, Hendry 2018, Hendry and Muellbauer 2018, Bulligan et al. 2017; Jelić and Ravnik 2021; Giacomini 2015; Pagan 2019; Gervais and Gosselin 2014). Moreover, the behavioral representations of economic agents in the macroeconometric models are based on their historical evolution, whereas in the theory-guided models, they are usually based on the optimization of a representative agent, imposed parameters, and calibration using data from a single year or an average of years (e.g., see Lutz 2011; Lehr et al. 2012).

Jelić and Ravnik (2021) and Pagan (2019), among other studies, discuss four generations of macroeconometric models that are coexisted for the last more than 80 years and recent hybrid models incorporate the insights derived from the third- and fourth-generation models into the second-generation models. The main strengths of the hybrid types of macroeconometric models (MEMs) over the other types of macroeconomic models are that they have theoretical coherence to represent long-run equilibrium relationships (like CGE and DSGE models and unlike VAR models). They also possess empirical coherence, i.e., they allow the data 'to speak freely' (unlike CGE and DSGE models and like VAR models) to represent short-run dynamics and disequilibrium. In other words, they bring together 'theory-guided' and 'data-driven' approaches (e.g., see Hendry 2018). They can represent the behavioral aspects of economic relationships based on the statistical time series properties of national data. Other advantages of MEMs are that they can be modified or customized to accommodate different policy questions and various simulations can be done in one model simultaneously, making them user-friendly for policy analyses. Their main weaknesses are, as mentioned in the Table 2.1, being data-dependent, data updates and revision issues require a reconsideration of all the behavioral equations, require a large team for data and model maintenance and update. For detailed strengths and weaknesses of different kinds of models, interested readers can refer to the above-listed references as well as Ackerman (2002), Pagan (2003b), Hoover et al. (2008), Herbst et al. (2012), Arora (2013), Hurtado (2014), and Oxford Economics (2022).

KGEMM is a hybrid model, i.e., it combines an economic theory-guided modeling approach with empirical data-driven evidence.[2] This is performed through statistical estimations and testing, not by imposing theory on the model. Practically, it attempts to adjust for econometric weaknesses in earlier models built for Saudi Arabia. KGEMM also incorporates detailed demand-side representations and CO_2 emissions of the main energy products by customer type. In this regard, KGEMM is a type of E3ME model (Energy-Environment-Economy Macro-Econometric model, see Econometrics, Cambridge 2019; Nikas et al. 2019; Gramkow and Anger-Kraavi 2019; Lee et al. 2018; Dagoumas and Barker 2010, inter alia). And it is similar to SEEEM (Sectoral Energy-Economic Econometric Model, see Blazejczak et al. 2014a, b) and PANTA RHEI (see Lutz et al. 2014a, b; Flaute et al. 2017; Lehr and Lutz 2016; Lehr et al. 2012; Lutz 2011), which both cover energy-economic-environmental representations.

---

[2]In the view of Pagan (2019) classification, KGEMM is a type I hybrid model, i.e., the long run paths are not articulated, leaving equilibrium correction mechanisms to ensure convergence.

Chapter 3
Theoretical Framework and Stylized Facts

In a very broad sense, KGEMM is a demand-side macroeconometric model augmented with several supply-side representations. The fifth version of KGEMM, presented in this book, has more supply-side augmentation compared to earlier versions. Welfe (2011), among others discuss that for macroeconometric models to be used for policy analysis and projections they should represent both the demand- and supply-side relationships.

The demand-side relationships are mainly represented using Keynesian and new-Keynesian schools of thought. This is true for many relationships modeled in the blocks of the model that we discuss in Chaps. 6 and 7. Therefore, we do not discuss equation-by-equation application of the theory here.

Supply-side representations are mainly in the real and price blocks of the model using Neoclassical theory. For example, modeling the supply side of the economic activities using the production function framework from the Neoclassical theory. Supply- and demand-side determinants have also been considered in modeling the price indexes for the consumer basket sub-groups, GDP deflators for sectoral economic activities, and non-oil exports. In general, the model brings together demand-side factors, such as consumption, investment, exports and imports, and supply-side factors, such as potential output, capital stock, employment, and prices.

As mentioned earlier, one of the characteristics of KGEMM is that it takes into consideration stylized facts of the Saudi Arabian economy. The stylized facts originate from a number of characteristics of Saudi Arabia, some of which are listed below:

Saudi Arabia is an oil-based economy. In 1970–2019, oil constituted on average 59% of the total economy, 79% of budget revenues, and 93% of total exports (SAMA 2020).

Saudi Arabia, like other Gulf Cooperation Council countries, has a substantial foreign labor force. Foreign nationals, particularly from East and Southeast Asian countries, account for 37% of its total population and more than 81% of the country's private sector employment (e.g., see Hasanov et al. 2021).

© The Author(s) 2023
F. J. Hasanov et al., *A Macroeconometric Model for Saudi Arabia*,
SpringerBriefs in Economics, https://doi.org/10.1007/978-3-031-12275-0_3

Historically, policymakers did not consider taxes as the main sources of fiscal revenue and, thus, they did not use taxes as key fiscal policy variables in economic adjustments (e.g., see Looney 1988).

The country is the custodian of the two holiest cities of the Islamic world, Makkah Al-Mukarramah and Al-Madīnah Al-Munawwarah. As such, there is great potential for religious tourism to be one of the main sources of the country's fiscal revenues (SV2030).

Chapter 4
KGEMM Methodology

This chapter briefly describes the methodological framework KGEMM uses. KGEMM is a hybrid model, i.e., it brings together theoretical and empirical coherences at some degree. Put differently, KGEMM nests "theory-driven" and "data-driven" approaches suggested by Hendry (2018), among others, and employed by many modelers in building semi-structural, that is, hybrid macroeconometric models (e.g., see Jelić and Ravnik 2021; Gervais and Gosselin 2014; Bulligan et al. 2017). For this purpose, it uses an equilibrium correction modeling (ECM) framework, in which the long-run relationships follow economic theories, and the short-run relationships are mainly data-driven (see Pagan 2003a, b inter alia). Hara et al. (2009) and Yoshida (1990), among others, note that ECM-based MEMs provide realistic results as their equilibrium correction mechanisms help stabilize long-term projections and capture short-term fluctuations more than other models while Engle et al. (1989) find the forecast performance of ECM more accurate.

KGEMM's methodological framework for estimating the behavioral equations is based on three pillars: cointegration and ECM, the general-to-specific modeling strategy (*Gets*) with *Autometrics*, a machine-learning econometric modeling method (Ericsson 2021), and the encompassing test (Fig. 4.1). This chapter briefs the methodological framework to save space and details of it will be described later in Appendix A.

The econometric methods are employed (i) to estimate behavioral equations, which represent behavioral aspects of the economic and energy linkages of Saudi Arabia and (ii) to test the existence of relationships and hypotheses. The following is the "road map" that we use in our empirical estimations and testing.

Because we use annual time series data, the first step is to check the stochastic properties of the data using unit-root tests. For the unit-root analysis, we use the conventional tests, that is, Augmented Dickey–Fuller (ADF) (Dickey and Fuller 1981), Phillips–Perron (PP) (Phillips and Perron 1988), and Kwiatkowski et al. (1992). Additionally, we use unit root tests with structural breaks where it seems reasonable to do so based on the nature of the data. We employ the ADF with a structural break (ADFBP hereafter) developed by Perron (1989), Perron and

© The Author(s) 2023
F. J. Hasanov et al., *A Macroeconometric Model for Saudi Arabia*,
SpringerBriefs in Economics, https://doi.org/10.1007/978-3-031-12275-0_4

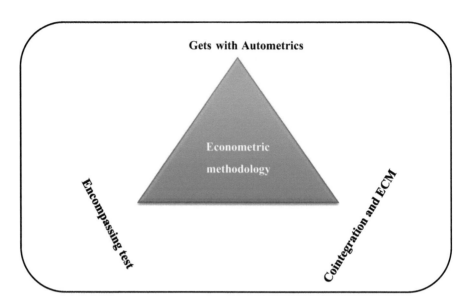

Fig. 4.1 KGEMM's methodological framework

Vogelsang (1992a, b), and Vogelsang and Perron (1998). We also use the Fourier ADF developed by Enders and Lee (2012a, b) and extended by Furuoka (2017), where there are multiple breaks in a given series and the conventional tests do not produce commonly accepted results. We do not describe these tests here as they are widely used in the literature. Readers interested in these tests can refer to the above-given references as well as Enders (2015), Perron (2006), Zivot and Andrews (1992), and Banerjee (1992).

If the variables are non-stationary, we perform cointegration tests to check whether they are cointegrated. For this purpose, we use Johansen's (1988) trace and maximum eigenvalue tests, the Pesaran's bounds test (Pesaran and Shin 1999; Pesaran et al. 2001), Engle and Granger (1987) test, Phillips–Ouliaris test (Phillips and Ouliaris 1990), and variable addition test by Park (1990). If more than two variables are involved in the analyses, which is mostly the case, then we first apply Johansen's cointegration test since it can reveal the number of cointegrating relationships if there is more than one, while the other tests above assume only one or no cointegrating relationship. We also use Hansen's (2000) cointegration test, which considers the break in the cointegration relationship. If there is a need to include level shift or trend break dummies in the Johansen cointegration test procedure, then we conduct our analysis in OxMetrics, as this software automatically calculates critical values that account for dummy variables.

If cointegration exists between the variables, then we estimate numerical parameters such as long-run coefficients. For this, we employ the following estimation methods to get robust results. Vector error correction (VEC) maximum likelihood estimation (Johansen 1988; Johansen and Juselius 1990), autoregressive distributed lags (ADL) (Hendry et al. 1984a, b; Pesaran and Shin 1999), fully modified ordinary least squares (FMOLS) (Phillips and Hansen 1990), dynamic ordinary least squares (DOLS) (Saikkonen 1992; Stock and Watson 1993), and canonical cointegration regression (CCR) (Park 1992) methods. After the estimation, we perform post-estimation tests, such as residuals diagnostics for serial correlation, non-normality, heteroscedasticity, parameter stability, misspecification, and other tests where possible.

In the last part of the chain, we employ an ECM to conduct a short-run analysis, that is, estimating short-run coefficients, including the speed of adjustment. We utilize the *Gets* with *Autometrics*, following the London School of Economics, or the Hendry, modeling approach (Ericsson 2021). *Gets* first includes contemporaneous and lagged values of all the relevant variables, based on the related economic theory and evidence of modeler to the specification called the general unrestricted model (GUM). Then it chooses the final specification based on a range of econometric tests for diagnostics, stability, and misspecification. Further details of the *Gets* can be found in Davidson et al. (1978), Hendry et al. (1984a, b), Ericsson et al. (1990), de Brouwer and Ericsson (1995), and Campos et al. (2005), among others. We usually perform *Gets* using *Autometrics* in the OxMetrics software (Doornik 2009; Doornik and Hendry 2018). *Autometrics* is a cutting-edge machine-learning multi-block search algorithm of modern econometrics. It performs *Gets* automatically to select a final specification from a GUM using the tests indicated above. One of the advantages of *Autometrics* is that it can also account for structural breaks and other extraordinary changes observed in data using the *impulse indicator saturation* technique (e.g., see Doornik 2009; Hendry and Doornik 2009, 2014). Another key advantage of *Autometrics* is that it addresses the time invariance of the estimated coefficients and hence, super exogeneity properties of variables remained in the final ECM specification can be tested (Castle et al. 2021; Hendry and Santos 2010). These features of *Autometrics* allows to address the so-called Lucas critique (Ericsson and Irons 1995). It is shown that *Autometrics* outperforms other model selection methods, such as, Stepwise regression, the least absolute shrinkage and selection operator (LASSO), and the adaptive LASSO (e.g., see Epprecht et al. 2021; Desboulets 2018; Castle et al. 2011 inter alia).

The short-run growth equation is estimated if there is no cointegrating relationship between the variables under consideration. The procedure is the same as in the ECM analysis above, but the equilibrium correction term (ECT) is absent as the variables are not cointegrated. *Gets* with *Autometrics* is also applied to growth equations.

We use encompassing tests to compare, choose, and combine different estimated specifications for analysis and forecasting purposes. The encompassing tests compare the predictive ability of alternative specifications and select the best one. Although this is part of our econometric methodology, we have not used this test frequently, primarily because there are not enough previously estimated specifications for Saudi Arabian energy-macroeconomic relations to compare with ours. Details of the tests can be found in Mizon (1984), Mizon and Richard (1986), Harvey et al. (1998), Harvey and Newbold (2000), Ericsson (1992, 1993), Bontemps and Mizon (2008), and Clements and Hendry (2011).

As part of the KGEMM methodology, we also use various tests to validate the estimated behavioral equations and the entire model as a whole (including in-sample and out-of-sample testing for predictive ability). These include post-estimation tests for the residuals of the estimated equations, testing the statistical significance and theoretical consistency of the estimated parameters, as well as in-sample performance test and out-of-sample performance test for the entire model. Detailed discussions of these methods can be found in Fair (1984), Klein et al. (1999), Fair (2004), Bardsen and Nymoen (2008), Clements and Hendry (2011), Hendry and Mizon (2014), Beenstock et al. (1986), Calzolari and Corsi (1977), and Welfe (2011).

The KGEMM model has been built in the EViews software package, as it provides a number of advanced features for building and simulating MEMs compared to other programs. Different stages of the empirical estimations and testing are conducted in EViews and OxMetrics, which includes *Autometrics*. The final specifications of the equations estimated in OxMetrics are then transferred to EViews to include in the model.

Interested readers can refer to Appendix A for a detailed discussion of KGEMM's methodological framework and philosophy, including the use of *Gets* and *Autometrics*. Appendix A also discusses addressing the endogeneity issue and the Lucas critique using invariance and super exogeneity tests.

Chapter 5
Database

One of the heaviest resource-consuming tasks of KGEMM, as with all MEMs, is the collection, update, revision, and maintenance of data. In econometric modeling, data are the key elements in determining the statistical properties of relationships. In this regard, data availability plays an important role in establishing linkages between the variables in time series-based MEMs. As discussed in the literature review, MEMs are heavily data-intensive, and obtaining comprehensive results is conditional upon the accuracy and time span of the data. MEMs are also data-dependent, with data updates and revisions resulting in re-estimation of the behavioral equations.

The fifth version of KGEMM has 828 annual time-series variables. In total, 397 of them are endogenous, expressed by behavioral equations and identities. There are 96 behavioral equations, and the rest endogenous variables are represented by identities. The endogenous variables are those on which we are interested in examining the impacts of other variables including domestic policy variables, as well as variables from the rest of the world. There are two main types of identities across the blocks of the model: System of National Accounting identities (e.g., total demand is the sum of private and government consumption, investments, and net exports) and definitional identities (e.g., nominal value added is obtained by multiplying real value added and the respective price deflator). The other 431 variables are exogenous in KGEMM. Many of the exogenous variables are dummy variables that capture permanent and temporary changes in relationships (that cannot be explained by the data)[1] and discrepancy or error terms that are used to balance relationships. The rest of the world variables, which provide a comprehensive picture of the global economic and energy ties of Saudi Arabia, are also treated as exogenous variables.[2] The remaining exogenous variables are policy-related variables and energy prices.

---

[1] For numerical interpretation of different types of dummy variables, see Roberto (2013), Kennedy (1981), and Halvorsen and Palmquist (1980).

[2] For example, the identity for the world trade index for refined oil demand variable (WTREF) contains 45 countries' demand for refined oil products and thus 45 exogenous variables (see identity # 228 in Sect. 7.4).

© The Author(s) 2023
F. J. Hasanov et al., *A Macroeconometric Model for Saudi Arabia*,
SpringerBriefs in Economics, https://doi.org/10.1007/978-3-031-12275-0_5

The data were collected from various domestic and external sources. Most of the domestic data come from the General Authority of Statistics (GaStat), formerly the Central Department of Statistics (CDSI) and the Saudi Arabian Monetary Agency (SAMA). These two sources provide a crucial portion of the country's data. Some domestic data are collected from the Ministry of Energy (MoE), and Saudi Aramco, the Ministry of Economy and Planning (MEP), the Ministry of Finance (MoF). External data mainly come from the databases of Oxford Economics Global Economic Model, the World Bank, the United Nations, the International Monetary Fund, and the International Energy Agency. The KGEMM database includes aggregated and disaggregated sector-level data. The KGEMM database contains nominal, real (usually at 2010 prices), index, ratio, and other user-calculated variables data for the real, monetary, fiscal, external, energy sectors, as well as consumer and producer prices, labor market, and population. The mnemonics and descriptions of the variables used in the fifth version of KGEMM are documented in Appendix B.

Chapter 6
A Brief History and Structure of KGEMM

It is useful to provide a brief overview of the development stages of KGEMM, as these stages shaped the structure of the current version of the model. As mentioned previously, KGEMM has been developed to have a better representation of the Saudi Arabian economic (sectoral and macro) and energy relationships. The main motivation for developing it was that there was no available model (including subscription based) that properly represented the Saudi Arabian economy and could comprehensively inform the policy decision-making process.

The model presented in this book is the fifth version of KGEMM. The first version of the model was built in early 2014 by Frederick L. Joutz, Fakhri J. Hasanov, and John Qualls, researchers of the KGEMM team at KAPSARC. It was built upon the Saudi Arabian module of the Oxford Economics Global Economic Model (OEGEM). KGEMM enhanced the OEGEM's Saudi Arabian module by addressing its key limitations, including its oversimplified representation of the Saudi economy, which would prevent it from being used to comprehensively inform the policymaking process.[1] KGEMM differs from the Saudi Arabian module of

---

[1]The details of the oversimplification of the module were documented by the KGEMM team in 2014–2015 and are available on request. The oversimplification mainly resulted from shortcomings such as numerical unification across the sectors, its limitation to non-theoretical underpinning, and the inconsistency between its reported data and estimated parameters. This is understandable from the perspective of Oxford Economics as they serve more than 1500 clients of international corporations, financial institutions, government organizations, and universities (https://www.oxfordeconomics.com/about-us). The Saudi Arabia module is just one out of 80 countries' and 13 regional modules in OEGEM and enhancing modules require additional time and resources. The KGEMM team at KAPSARC cooperated with Oxford Economics in 2017–2018 and communicated the shortcomings of OEGEM Saudi Arabia module and the developed characteristics of KGEMM so that Oxford Economics could take them (shortcomings and developed characteristics) into account in their revision of the Saudi Arabian module. For this, Oxford Economics acknowledges KAPSARC's cooperation in their each release.

© The Author(s) 2023
F. J. Hasanov et al., *A Macroeconometric Model for Saudi Arabia*,
SpringerBriefs in Economics, https://doi.org/10.1007/978-3-031-12275-0_6

OEGEM considerably.[2] The main feature of the second version of KGEMM was the development of a detailed energy block representing 14 energy demand relationships by energy type and customer. The third version of KGEMM had estimated production function relationships for economic activity sectors, and thus derived sectoral output gaps feeding into consumer price index (CPI) equations for 12 household consumption basket items. It also had employment demand equations for economic activity sectors estimated as a function of output and wage (see Hasanov et al. 2021). Finally, it had more detailed external sector representations. For example, it linked the export of Saudi Arabian refinery oil to 45 individual countries' refinery oil demand, which offers the opportunity to simulate the impact of the global demand for oil and thus, environmental implementations and energy transitions on the Saudi economy. The third version of KGEMM was published as Hasanov (2020). In the fourth version of KGEMM, sectoral wage relationships were econometrically estimated as a function of the labor productivity and output price mainly. Additionally, sectoral investment relationships were developed using econometrically estimated investment demand equations, as a function of output, interest rate, and exchange rate (see Javid et al. 2022). That version also considered substitution effects in energy demand equations. Finally, the fifth version of KGEMM has a number of developments that considerably differentiates it from the previous versions. These developments include but are not limited to the following: CO_2 block, which assesses carbon emissions of the energy block, that is, each of 15 energy products; more detailed external sector represented by enhanced non-oil export equation (Hasanov et al. 2022c), developed oil refinery export equation, and outflow remittances equation (Javid and Hasanov 2022); representations of the supply-side of energy, that is, fuel mix components for electricity generation as well as renewable energy represented by solar energy (Elshurafa et al. 2022; Hasanov et al. 2022a); representations of the petrochemical sector through mainly estimated output, investment, employment, energy demand, and feedstock (ethane, methane, naphtha, liquified petroleum gases) demand equations; imports of goods disaggregated into capital, intermediate, and consumer goods, each estimated econometrically as a function of domestic demand and real exchange rate. Details of the developments in the fifth version of KGEMM can be noticed in the description of each block below in this section as well as in behavioral equations and identities given in the following section. Figure 6.1 illustrates the structure of the fifth version of KGEMM.

---

[2]Since the first version of KGEMM has been built on the OEGEM's Saudi Arabia module to overcome limitations of the module, the notations of the variables in these two models are quite similar. The main points that differentiate KGEMM from the OEGEM' Saudi Arabia module are the well-established theoretical foundation and consistency between data and the estimated parameters. Moreover, KGEMM has a detailed energy block, CO_2 block, a number of newly developed sectoral and aggregated relationships, and uses cutting edge econometric tools, such as *Autometrics*, a machine-learning econometric methodology.

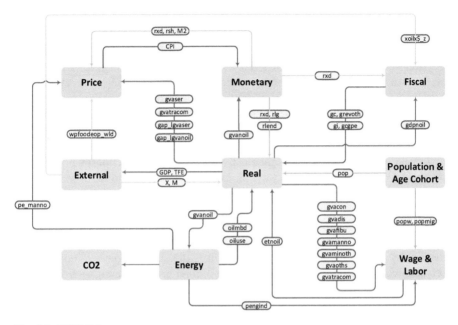

Fig. 6.1 KGEMM structure

The model has nine blocks interacting with each other to represent the Saudi Arabian energy–economic–environment relationships. What follows is a brief block-by-block description of KGEMM's structure.

6.1 Real Block

This block can be broadly divided into demand-side and supply-side representations.

6.1.1 Real Block: Demand Side

Conventional MEMs, many of them for the Saudi Arabian economy, treat demand on an aggregate level. However, as mentioned earlier, aggregate demand in KGEMM is broken down into intermediate demand, final demand, and total demand for 13 economic activity sectors. The intermediate demand is modeled as the demand of all these economic activities for each other's goods and services using coefficients derived from the input–output table for Saudi Arabia. Also, the final demand components of gross domestic product (GDP), such as private consumption, government consumption, investment, and exports are disaggregated into the economic activities using the coefficients derived from the input–output table. In addition, the investments are further broken into government, oil sector, and non-oil sector investments. While exports are represented by non-oil, oil, and service exports. The total demand for a given economic activity sector is the sum of its intermediate demand and final demand. Such a detailed framework makes the model able to distinguish intermediate, final, and total demand effects in different sectors of the economy. For example, the effects of government investment in the construction and transportation sectors are not identical, but sector-specific, each represented by its own coefficient. This allows a modeler to quantify sector-specific effects of the government policies.

Private consumption is econometrically estimated as a function of private disposable income, interest rate, and wealth using cointegration and ECM methods by Hasanov et al. (2022b) and incorporated into KGEMM. Note that the private disposable income data is not available from official agencies and hence has been constructed by the authors using the System of National Accounts framework.

Investment is the sum of oil and non-oil private and government investments as mentioned above. Non-oil private investment is the sum of domestic and foreign private investments. The latter one is the sum of foreign direct, foreign portfolio, and foreign other investments—all coming from the external block. The domestic private investments are the sum of private investment in eight non-oil economic activity sectors. Sectoral private investments are econometrically modeled as a function of sectoral output, interest rate, and exchange rate by Javid et al. (2022) over the period 1989–2017. Later, the KGEMM team updated estimations till 2019 and expanded the estimation coverage by modeling petrochemical sector investment.

The other final demand components, i.e., government consumption, exports and imports, will be discussed in their respective blocks later. These indicators link the real block to the fiscal and external blocks.

The economic activities are econometrically estimated, using the demand-side approach, where demand for a given economic activity sector is a function of total demand for this sector and the sector's demand for energy. This approach comes from the input–output framework and additionally includes energy demand. This is very similar to the modeling approach taken by Bradley et al. (1995) for the European countries. The purpose of including energy demand variable in the estimations is to measure the explicit effects of energy on economic activities. This makes it possible to use the model to analyze the impact of the domestic energy sector-related reforms on various economic activities. These estimations link the real sector to the energy and price blocks.

6.1.2   Real Block: Supply Side

The supply side of the real block mainly contains production functions for the economic activities, which estimate the potential outputs of the activities as functions of capital stocks and employment mainly, alongside technological change proxied by the time trend and other explanatory variables. This is consistent with the theory of production (Cobb and Douglas 1928; Douglas 1976). We use the Cobb–Douglas type as the form of the production function because it has been recommended and widely used in macroeconometric modeling (e.g., see Welfe 2011).

The capital stock for a given economic activity sector has been constructed using investment in the sector, the sector-specific depreciation rate, and assumed initial capital stock in the perpetual inventory method framework (Collins et al. 1996; Nehru and Dhareshwar 1993; Hall and Jones 1999; Arezki and Cherif 2010). The relationships representing employment for economic activity sectors, used in the production function estimations, will be discussed in the wage and labor block.

The output gaps of the economic activities have been calculated using the identities, which express the differences between the actual outputs and potential outputs coming from the estimated production functions. The gaps feed into the behavioral equations for the CPIs of the different household consumption basket items, as discussed in the price block.

Demand-side and supply-side breakdowns of the entire economy into economic activity sectors can provide useful information about sectoral compositions and changes in the structure of the economy. This is very important for diversification and local content purposes, key targets of SV2030, as articulated in the National Transformation Program (SV2030 2019b).

Section 7.1 provides additionally definitional relationships for disposable income and wealth of households, total final expenditure, and domestic demand. The sub-section also presents the nominal value added of the economic activity sectors and the aggregation of the economic activity sectors into large sectors, such as the service sector, the industry sector, the oil sector, and the non-oil sector.

6.2   Fiscal Block

Total government expenditure is the sum of government capital and current expenditure in KGEMM. The former is a function of the one-period lagged capital expenditure, the relative increase in government investment, and the remainder of capital expenditure. The government current expenditure is the sum of the government's five current spending items, namely, wages, salaries, and allowances; administrative expenses; maintenance and operational costs; transfers to the private sector; and other current expenses. Government consumption is the sum of the first three current spending items above. Each of these five current spending items alongside government investment spending is econometrically estimated using government revenues as an explanatory variable.

Total government revenue is the sum of the government's oil and non-oil revenues. The former is linked to oil exports from the external block. The government's non-oil revenues are the sum of revenues from energy sales, value added tax (VAT), the expatriate levy, the Umrah and Hajj visa fees, other visa fees, tax on international trade and transactions (which is effectively customs duty fees on imports as Saudi Arabia does not apply tax or fee on exports), taxes on income, profits, and capital gains, and other non-oil revenues. The latter is the balancing item and includes collections such as traffic fines, the idle land tax, the luxury good tax, government investment returns, other non-oil sector related fees, tariffs, and collections. Energy sales are linked to the economy's total energy consumption in monetary measure coming from the energy block. VAT revenues is formed by the final consumption, VAT rate, and VAT collection efficiency ratio. The last two are policy variables for the fiscal authority. The Umrah and Hajj visa fees and other visa fees are linked to developments in the exports travel service, while the expatriate levy is tied to developments in the migrant population. The taxes on income, profits, and capital gains are linked to the changes in the non-oil sector's activity. The total government revenue in the model has been structured according to the stylized facts of the Saudi Arabian economy. This allows us to model the impacts of oil market changes, which are mostly exogenous, as well as the impacts of internal policy decisions for the energy prices reform, VAT, expatriate fees, and other revenue components—the key initiatives of the Fiscal Balance Program (FBP) of SV2030 (2019a)—on the Kingdom's economy.

Lastly, the block contains the government's budget balance: the difference between its total revenues and total expenditures. It also contains the government's non-oil budget balance: the difference between the government's non-oil revenues and its total expenditure. The latter is another stylized fact of the economy, and its purpose in the model is to show to what extent non-oil sector revenues can finance government spending. The government can then take measures to increase the efficiency of both its spending and revenue collection and fiscal consolidation— the key objectives of the FBP (SV2030 2019a). The block also has general government debt, which is econometrically modeled as being dependent on government balance. General government gross debt is the sum of its past value and general government debt. Section 7.2 expresses the relationship described above.

6.3   Monetary Block

The monetary block of the model is fairly small, mainly because of the nature of monetary policy in Saudi Arabia, another stylized fact of the economy. The exchange rate of the Saudi riyal (SAR) is pegged to the US dollar . Hence, Saudi Arabia's interest rate follows the US Federal Reserve interest rate and, therefore, monetary policy does not have much to do with economic growth, employment, and price stability.

The block contains definitional identities for all monetary aggregates, i.e., cash held outside banks, cash with demand deposits, a broad monetary aggregate, and a broad monetary aggregate with foreign currency deposits. It also has identities for interest rates, namely, the interest rate on lending, the effective interest rate on external debt, the interest rate on 10-year government bonds, and spread between the foreign and domestic interest rates. The block uses the definitional identity for the real exchange rate the real effective exchange rate. The latter one is determined by the ratio of domestic and foreign prices, together with the nominal effective SAR exchange rate against a basket of currencies of its main trading partners. This identity links the monetary block to the external and prices blocks. Real effective exchange rates are considered as a measurement of international price competitiveness in many theoretical and empirical studies. Therefore, we have econometrically modeled the impacts of the key theoretically predicted and Saudi-specific determinants, such as relative productivity in the oil and non-oil sectors, government consumption, net foreign assets on the real effective exchange rate, which allows us to calculate the equilibrium trajectory of the real effective exchange rate. (This equation is the slightly modified version of the equation estimated in Hasanov and Razek 2022) In this regard, the model can simulate how changes in domestic and foreign markets can shape Saudi Arabia's international competitiveness. Such simulations might be important for policy making as SV2030 targets to increase Saudi Arabia's position up to among the 15 most competitive economies over the world by 2030. Finally, the block contains another behavioral equation for broad money demand, M2 aggregate, which estimates it in real terms as a function of the interest rate differential between the domestic and foreign interest rates, GDP from the real sector, real oil price from the external sector, real effective exchange rate, and financial innovation proxied by time trend (This equation was borrowed from Hasanov et al. (2022) and slightly modified.) Section 7.3 provides details of the relationships of the monetary block.

6.4   External Block

The external sector in KGEMM is classified into exports, imports, and other balance of payment components.

Total exports are the sum of exports of goods and services. The exports of goods are broken down into oil exports and non-oil goods exports as stylized facts of the Saudi economy. The former is the sum of the exports of crude oil and oil refinery products. Crude oil exports are represented by an identity, which links it to domestic oil production minus domestic oil use, multiplied by the global price of Arabian light. It is one of the most important relationships in the block, as it links the external block to the real block, the energy block, and to the rest of the world. Thus, one can simulate the model to see how energy price reform could increase crude oil export revenues by lowering domestic oil use and freeing up more oil for export. Alternatively, one can look at the impact of international oil price dynamics and the impact of OPEC oil production agreements and exports on Saudi Arabia's oil export revenues. The behavioral equation for the exports of refined oil products includes, alongside other variables, the world trade index for refined oil products. This index combines 45 individual countries' demand for refined oil products. This enables the model to simulate how changes in the demand for refined oil products in a given country caused by renewable energy transitions or environmental policies influence Saudi Arabia's refinery oil exports. The Kingdom's oil exports feed into the government's oil revenues in the fiscal block. The non-oil goods exports are estimated as being dependent on the real effective exchange rate, domestic production capacity, and demand from the rest of the world. Put differently, the equation brings together demand and supply-side factors and links the external sector to the real sector, and the monetary sector and the rest of the world. The total exports of services are the sum of the exports of services from the following nine activities: oil, investment income, other services, transportation, travel, communications, freight and insurance, financial services, and government. This detailed breakdown allows a modeler to simulate each service activity's role in total exports and in overall economic performance.

Total imports are the sum of the imports of goods and services, broken down into the same categories as total exports. The imports of goods in turn broken into three categories, imports of capital goods, imports of intermediate goods, and imports of consumer goods. Each category is econometrically modeled as a function of domestic demand and the real effective exchange rate, which reflects the nominal effective exchange rate and differences in domestic and foreign prices. The imports of services are also estimated as a function of domestic demand and the real exchange rate. Such breakdown allows a modeler to examine the role of various imported goods and services in domestic demand which may provide insights about import substitutions and local content implications being important for the diversification of the Saudi economy. The block also contains overall and non-oil trade balance both determined as identities, that is, the difference between exports and imports as well as non-oil exports and imports, respectively.

As with other balance of payment components in the model, we have identities for foreign direct investments outflows and net foreign direct investment. Outflows are linked to the development of the Saudi economy and the net is the difference between the inflows and outflows. As mentioned above, the world trade index for refined oil products is represented by an identity combining 45 individual countries' demand for refined oil products. KSA tourism demand indicator is also represented by an identity, which reflects the kingdom's tourism demand for 10 countries, including developed and developing economies. Additionally, the block has an outflow of remittances econometrically estimated as a function of domestic economic activity measured by Saudi GDP, employed foreigners, living costs in Saudi Arabia measured by domestic price level, and expatriate levy. (The equation is borrowed from Javid and Hasanov 2022 and modified slightly.) This equation can provide insights about the main determinants of the outflow remittances, which is a leakage from the Kingdom and thereby diminishes the magnitude of its fiscal multipliers. Such insights are quite important given that fiscal policy-related economic development initiatives are dominant in the Saudi economy, and the Kingdom is one of the top countries globally in terms of outflow remittances. Lastly, the KGEMM team is examining the inflow of foreign direct investment using its theoretically predicted determinants such as productivity, macroeconomic stability, openness, and business costs, including the unit labor cost, infrastructure, and institutional development. This is the work under progress and not completed yet. Section 7.4 details the external sector relationships.

6.5 Domestic Prices Block

This block comprises three sub-blocks in a broader classification: consumer price indexes (CPIs), GDP deflators or producer price indexes, and aggregated energy prices. We discuss them briefly below.

The model has all 12 consumer basket prices as given by GaStat, estimated using behavioral equations. In forming the specifications for the CPIs we considered mainly supply-side factors using the markup and purchasing power parity approaches (e.g., see Brouwer and Ericsson 1998; Juselius 1992). This is because we assume that Saudi inflation is primarily cost-push inflation. The markup approach factors we considered were unit labor cost or just wages, domestic energy prices, producer prices, and VAT rate. In this framework, a modeler to simulate the effects of policy interested variables (such as VAT rate, domestic energy prices) and foreign prices on domestic consumer prices. As the Saudi economy undergoes a transformation process in line with SV2030, future versions of the KGEMM could also incorporate the money market and output gap approaches in inflation modeling. In addition to the 12 estimated equations, the sub-block contains an identity for overall CPI, which is a weighted average of the 12 CPI components. The weight variable of each of 12 components contains two values, old weights from 1970 to 2012 and new weights for 2013–2019 as documented in Appendix E.

GDP deflators, considered as the producer prices, sub-block, estimates GDP deflators for economic activity sectors, considering the respective overall price (i.e., deflators for non-oil GDP, oil GDP, and GDP) as a catch-up factor and domestic energy prices, foreign/import prices among other control variables. This setup allows a modeler to simulate the model to investigate the impact of the ongoing energy price reforms on the production costs, and thus the competitiveness of the economic activities.

The aggregated energy prices sub-block mainly contains weighted average domestic prices of energy products by customer type for several economic activity sectors, if a given sector uses more than one energy product. For example, the aggregate energy price for the utility sector is the weighted average price of natural gas, crude oil, diesel, and heavy fuel oil. The weighted average domestic energy price was calculated for the following economic activity sector as well: distribution, agriculture, financial and banking services, other services, transportation and communication, construction, and government services. Such a weighted average price allows us to simulate the model for both the price and demand effects of different energy products on a given economic activity sector under consideration. It should be noted, however, that with the exception of the utility sector (and electricity consumption to some extent), we do not have data on the consumption of energy products in the economic activity sectors. Therefore, the calculated weighted average prices for the economic activity sectors other than the utility sector are only rough approximations. A detailed description of the domestic prices block is documented in Sect. 7.5.

6.6 Labor and Wages Block

This block contains relationships for employment, wages, and unit labor cost for economic activity sectors. The block also comprises definitional identities for labor force, unemployment, and its rate.

Total employment is broken into oil sector and non-oil sector employment. Employment in the oil sector is the sum of employment of oil mining and oil refinery. Employment in the non-oil sector is the sum of employment in 11 non-oil economic activities. Employment of each non-oil economic activity is econometrically estimated as a function of wage and output in a given activity sector (see Hasanov et al. 2021). We also have employment in the private sector and it is the sum of nationals and foreigners.

The wage equations for some economic activity sectors are econometrically estimated using output price and labor productivity as main determinants. However, they have not yet been completed for all sectors at the time of writing and, hence, cover seven economic activity sectors. Employment and wage equations establish links with the real block and domestic prices block.

The block contains identities that represent the unit labor costs for 12 economic activity sectors (and three aggregated sectors, that is, service, oil and non-oil). The identities use the conventional definition for unit labor cost, that is, each sector's unit labor cost is the sector-specific average wage rate multiplied by the sector-specific employment divided by the sector-specific value added. Also, the block has economy-wide labor compensation. This is the sum of labor compensation (wage rate times employment) in 11 non-oil activities and two oil activities. This variable links this block to the real block of the model as the variable feeds into the identity for disposable income. In addition, it provides the capability to simulate the model for the impact of different wage rates and employment in various sectors on households' disposable income.

Lastly, considering the stylized facts of the Saudi economy, the labor force is linked to working age population groups of Saudis and non-Saudis, both broken into the sum of males and females coming from the population and age cohorts block. This allows one to differentiate the role of each group and their male and female components in the labor force and, thus, also in the unemployment. A detailed description of the labor market and wages block is documented in Sect. 7.6.

6.7 Energy Block

The energy block differentiates KGEMM from conventional (semi-)structural macroeconomic models. The block comprises demand for different energy products in volume and value (monetary) measures as well as the supply of electricity.

The block has econometrically estimated 15 behavioral equations for energy demand in volume terms. As a volume term, we use million tons of oil equivalent

(MTOE) for all the energy products to make them comparable with each other. There are nine energy products (crude oil, diesel, heavy fuel oil [HFO], natural gas, electricity, liquefied petroleum gas [LPG], kerosene, gasoline, and other oil products) and six customer types (residential, industry, commercial, government, transport, agriculture and forestry). In addition to this, the first four energy products are used in the utility sector, but they are not econometrically estimated as the sector is mostly government-owned, that is, exogenous. However, not all six customers consume all 15 energy products (e.g., electricity is consumed by all customers except transport, whereas only industry and utility consume HFO and crude oil). The equations have been estimated using the conventional energy demand framework, where demand for a given energy product is a function of its own price and customer-specific income, both in real terms. For some energy products, we extended the conventional framework with other explanatory variables as deemed reasonable. For instance, we had real prices of substitutable energy products, where they became theoretically interpretable and statistically significant alongside own price and income in the estimations (see estimated equations for the industrial demand for crude oil, HFO, natural gas; for the transport demand for diesel; for the residential demand for kerosene and LPG). Also, we included cooling degree days in the residential electricity demand equation and accounted for the population effect. The latter effect was also accounted for in the gasoline demand estimation. Moreover, we had a working age group population in the industrial electricity demand estimations following the theoretical framework developed in Hasanov et al. (2021). Furthermore, we found that the investments are statistically significant and have a negative sign, indicating efficiency gains in the electricity demand equations for commercial and agricultural sectors. The customer-specific price deflators have been used to calculate energy prices in real terms, as suggested by the energy demand literature. The estimated equations mainly link this block to the domestic prices block and real block. Recall that energy consumption also feeds into the demand-side estimation of the economic activities in the real block.

The block also represents the above-mentioned 15 energy products consumption in value terms, that is, their volumes in MTOE are multiplied by their prices in Saudi riyals for per TOE. This monetary representation is for the purpose of calculating government energy sale revenues by product, customer, and by total economy. Recall that total energy consumption in monetary terms feeds into the government's non-oil revenues in the fiscal block.

The supply of electricity is broken into two generation sources: fossil fuels and renewable. Fossil fuels-based generation accounts for four main energy products used in the electricity generation in Saudi Arabia, namely, crude oil, diesel, HFO, and natural gas. The sum of these fossil fuels is multiplied by the efficiency ratio to calculate the amount of electricity generated. The second part of the electricity generation is coming from solar energy sources. We did not consider renewable energy sources other than solar, as they are very negligible historically. Even solar power generation has an average share of 0.1% of total electricity generation over the 2010–2021 period. The good news is that this share has increased significantly in recent years. Saudi Arabia plans to increase the share of renewables in total electricity generation demanded to 50% by 2030, with the other 50% coming from natural gas. This implies excluding the other fossil fuels from the power generation. Having total electricity generation coming from fossil fuels and solar sources makes KGEMM unique in simulating the economic, energy, and environmental effects of different scenarios for displacing fuels with renewables as it was done in Elshurafa et al. (2022) and Hasanov et al. (2022a). The above discussed behavioral equations and identities in addition to others are represented in Sect. 7.7.

6.8 CO_2 Emissions Block

This is another block that makes KGEMM different from conventional (semi-) structural macroeconometric models. The literature on environmental pollution shows that usually, energy-related CO_2 emissions are around 90% of the total CO_2 emissions. Therefore, this block was constructed using the energy block above. It is calculated as volume of a given energy product consumed (e.g., crude oil) multiplied by the product-specific conversion factor to reach up to the amount of CO_2 emissions. We used each product-specific emission conversion factor in the calculation. The conversion factors are retrieved from various reputed sources such as the International Energy Agency, US Energy Information Administration, US Environmental Protection Agency. Appendix E documents conversion factors and their sources while Sect. 7.8 reports calculations, i.e., constructed identities. We grouped product-based CO_2 emissions by customer type—industry, transport, residential, commercial, government, agriculture, but other classifications can be considered as well. As mentioned at the beginning of this section, CO_2 emissions are one of the new developments in the fifth version of KGEMM meaning that it has room for extension. We plan to expand the block by incorporating other emission indicators into it. For example, a carbon price or carbon tax is one of the considerations for future work. The block allows a modeler to assess the impacts of different CO_2 emissions reduction options on energy consumption and economic indicators.

6.9   Population and Age Cohorts Block

The total population in the block is the sum of the 12 age groups: 0–14, 15–19, 20–24, 25–29, 30–34, 35–39, 40–44, 45–49, 50–54, 55–59, 60–64, 65 and above. Each age cohort is determined as the sum of males and females. The block represents the total Saudi population as the sum of Saudi males and females. The same formula is applied to the non-Saudi population. The working age population is the sum of males and females. Both male and female working age population groups are the sum of age cohorts 15–19 through 60–64. The population of Saudis and non-Saudis feeds into the labor force in the wages and labor block as mentioned above. One can simulate the model to assess the impacts of changes in each of the 12 age cohorts broken into females and males on the on various relationships and the total economy, as well as the Saudi and non-Saudi impacts on the labor force and unemployment. Details of the block can be found in Sect. 7.9

Chapter 7
KGEMM Behavioral Equations and Identities

This chapter reports the estimated long-run equations and identities in Sects. 7.1, 7.2, 7.3, 7.4, 7.5, 7.6, 7.7, 7.8, and 7.9 while the estimated short-run equations, i.e., final ECM specifications associated with the long-run equations are reported in Appendix B to save space in the main text.[1] Note that the long-run and ECM equations are estimated till 2019 in the fifth version of KGEMM. Starting years of the estimations range from the 1970s to the 1990s dictated by the data availability. For the readers ease, we describe one of the long-run equations below and the rest equations here follow the same context. As an example, we select the first appeared long-run equation, i.e., Eq. (7.43).

$$LOG(IFDIS) = 1.00^* LOG\ (GVADIS) - 0.03^* RRLEND1 - 2.33 + ECT\_IFDIS$$

Where LOG indicates the natural logarithmic transformation of a given variable. IFDIS, GVADIS, RRLEND1 are the variables (see Appendix B for the definitions and notations of the variables). ECT_IFDIS is the residuals of the long-run equation of the retail, wholesale, hotels, and catering sector's investment, i.e., equilibrium correction term. In general, ECT_X denotes the equilibrium correction term for the variable X (Its one period lagged series enters the short run, i.e., ECM equation of the variable X as reported in Appendix B).

The long-run equation shows that private investment in the retail, wholesale, hotels, and catering sector (IFDIS) increases by 1% when the sector's output (GVADIS) increases by 1%, while it decreases by 3% if the real lending rate (RRLEND1) rises by 1 percentage point, holding other factors constant. A detailed

---

[1] The long-run and short-run relationships among the variables are estimated using the cointegration and ECM frameworks, respectively. Therefore, there are two versions of the model: the long- and short-run versions. The former one uses the estimated long-run (cointegrated) equations (e.g., such as Musila, 2002; Fair 1979, 1993), while the latter one uses the estimated final ECM equations (e.g., such as Buenafe and Reyes 2001; Welfe 2013) alongside identities. A detailed description of both, short-run and long-run, versions of the model are available from the authors upon request.

© The Author(s) 2023
F. J. Hasanov et al., *A Macroeconometric Model for Saudi Arabia*,
SpringerBriefs in Economics, https://doi.org/10.1007/978-3-031-12275-0_7

discussion of this and other estimated long- and short-run equations of investments for economic activity sectors can be found in Javid et al. (2022).

To save space, we do not report the significance levels of the estimated coefficients as well as pre-estimation (e.g., unit root and cointegration) and post-estimation (e.g., diagnostics, stability) test results for the long- and short-run equations because they number 192. They are available from the authors on request. Note, however, that all the estimated coefficients (reported below in the tables and in Appendix B) are statistically significant and the cointegration tests indicate long-run relationships among the variables at different conventional significance levels.

7.1   Real Block Equations and Identities (Demand-Side and Supply-Side)

7.1.1   Demand-Side

7.1.1.1   Identities for Intermediate, Final and Total Demand by Economic Activity Sector

Intermediate Demand

$$
\begin{aligned}
IDAGR = {} & A1^* \text{ GVAOIL} + A2^* \text{ GVAMINOTH} + A3^* \text{ GVAPETCH} \\
& + A4^* \text{ GVAMANNOLPC} + A5^* \text{ GVAU} + A6^* \text{ GVACON} \\
& + A7^* \text{ GVADIS} + A8^* (\text{GVATRACOM} - \text{GVATRAPIPE}) \\
& + A9^* \text{ GVAAGR} + A10^* \text{ GVAFIBU} + A11^* \text{ GVAGOV} \\
& + A12^* \text{ GVAOTHS} + \text{DIS\_IDAGR}
\end{aligned}
\tag{7.1}
$$

$$
\begin{aligned}
IDCON = {} & B1^* \text{ GVAOIL} + B2^* \text{ GVAMINOTH} + B3^* \text{ GVAPETCH} \\
& + B4^* \text{ GVAMANNOLPC} + B5^* \text{GVAU} + B6^* \text{ GVACON} \\
& + B7^* \text{ GVADIS} + B8^* (\text{GVATRACOM} - \text{GVATRAPIPE}) \\
& + B9^* \text{GVAAGR} + B10^* \text{ GVAFIBU} + B11^* \text{ GVAGOV} \\
& + B12^* \text{ GVAOTHS} + \text{DIS\_IDCON}
\end{aligned}
\tag{7.2}
$$

$$
\begin{aligned}
IDDIS = {} & C1^* \text{GVAOIL} + C2^* \text{GVAMINOTH} + C3^* \text{GVAPETCH} \\
& + C4^* \text{ GVAMANNOLPC} + C5^* \text{GVAU} + C6^* \text{ GVACON} \\
& + C7^* \text{ GVADIS} + C8^* (\text{GVATRACOM} - \text{GVATRAPIPE}) \\
& + C9^* \text{GVAAGR} + C10^* \text{ GVAFIBU} + C11^* \text{ GVAGOV} \\
& + C12^* \text{ GVAOTHS} + \text{DIS\_IDDIS}
\end{aligned}
\tag{7.3}
$$

$$\begin{aligned}
IDFIBU = {} & D1^* \, GVAOIL + D2^* \, GVAMINOTH + D3^* \, GVAPETCH \\
& + D4^* \, GVAMANNOLPC + D5 * \, GVAU + D6^* \, GVACON \\
& + D7^* \, GVADIS + D8^* (GVATRACOM - GVATRAPIPE) \\
& + D9^* GVAAGR + D10^* \, GVAFIBU + D11^* \, GVAGOV \\
& + D12^* \, GVAOTHS + DIS\_IDFIBU \qquad\qquad (7.4)
\end{aligned}$$

$$\begin{aligned}
IDGOV = {} & E1^* \, GVAOIL + E2^* \, GVAMINOTH + E3^* \, GVAPETCH \\
& + E4^* \, GVAMANNOLPC + E5^* GVAU + E6^* \, GVACON \\
& + E7^* \, GVADIS + E8^* (GVATRACOM - GVATRAPIPE) \\
& + E9^* GVAAGR + E10^* \, GVAFIBU + E11^* \, GVAGOV \\
& + E12^* \, GVAOTHS + DIS\_IDGOV \qquad\qquad (7.5)
\end{aligned}$$

$$\begin{aligned}
IDMANNOLPC = {} & F1^* \, GVAOIL + F2^* \, GVAMINOTH + F3^* \, GVAPETCH \\
& + F4^* \, GVAMANNOLPC + F5^* \, GVAU + F6^* \, GVACON \\
& + F7^* \, GVADIS + F8^* (GVATRACO \ GVATRAPIPE) \\
& + F9^* GVAAGR + F10^* \, GVAFIBU + F11^* \, GVAGOV \\
& + F12^* \, GVAOTHS + DIS\_IDMANNOLPC \qquad (7.6)
\end{aligned}$$

$$\begin{aligned}
IDMINOTH = {} & G1^* \, GVAOIL + G2^* \, GVAMINOTH + G3^* \, GVAPETCH \\
& + G4^* \, GVAMANNOLPC + G5^* \, GVAU + G6^* \, GVACON \\
& + G7^* \, GVADIS + G8^* (GVATRACOM - GVATRAPIPE) \\
& + G9^* GVAAGR + G10^* \, GVAFIBU + G11^* \, GVAGOV \\
& + G12^* \, GVAOTHS + DIS\_IDMINOTH \qquad\qquad (7.7)
\end{aligned}$$

$$\begin{aligned}
IDOIL = {} & H1^* \, GVAOIL + H2^* \, GVAMINOTH + H3^* \, GVAPETCH \\
& + H4^* \, GVAMANNOLPC + H5^* GVAU + H6^* \, GVACON \\
& + H7^* \, GVADIS + H8^* (GVATRACOM - GVATRAPIPE) \\
& + H9^* GVAAGR + H10^* \, GVAFIBU + H11^* \, GVAGOV \\
& + H12^* \, GVAOTHS + DIS\_IDOIL \qquad\qquad (7.8)
\end{aligned}$$

$$
\begin{aligned}
IDOILREF = {} & I1^* \, GVAAGR + I2^* \, GVACON + I3^* \, GVADIS \\
& + I4^* \, GVAFIBU + I5^* \, GVAFIBUOTH + I6^* \, GVAREAL \\
& + I7^* \, GVAMANNO + I8^* \, GVAMINOTH + I9^* \, GVAOILMIN \\
& + I10^* \, GVAOILREF + I11^* \, GVAOTHS + I12^* \, GVAGOV \\
& + I13^* \, GVATRACOM + I14^* \, GVAU
\end{aligned} \tag{7.9}
$$

$$
\begin{aligned}
IDOTHS = {} & J1^* \, GVAOIL + J2^* \, GVAMINOTH + J3^* \, GVAPETCH \\
& + J4^* \, GVAMANNOLPC + J5^* GVAU + J6^* \, GVACON \\
& + J7^* \, GVADIS + J8^*(GVATRACOM - GVATRAPIPE) \\
& + J9^* \, GVAAGR + J10^* \, GVAFIBU + J11^* \, GVAGOV \\
& + J12^* \, GVAOTHS + DIS\_IDOTHS
\end{aligned} \tag{7.10}
$$

$$
\begin{aligned}
IDPETCH = {} & K1^* \, GVAOIL + K2^* \, GVAMINOTH + K3^* \, GVAPETCH \\
& + K4^* \, GVAMANNOLPC + K5^* \, GVAU + K6^* \, GVACON \\
& + K7^* \, GVADIS + K8^*(GVATRACOM - GVATRAPIPE) \\
& + K9^* GVAAGR + K10^* \, GVAFIBU + K11^* \, GVAGOV \\
& + K12^* \, GVAOTHS + DIS\_IDPETCH
\end{aligned} \tag{7.11}
$$

$$
\begin{aligned}
IDTRACOM = {} & L1^* \, GVAOIL + L2^* \, GVAMINOTH + L3^* \, GVAPETCH \\
& + L4^* \, GVAMANNOLPC + L5^* \, GVAU + L6^* \, GVACON \\
& + L7^* \, GVADIS + L8^*(GVATRACOM - GVATRAPIPE) \\
& + L9^* GVAAGR + L10^* \, GVAFIBU + L11^* \, GVAGOV \\
& + L12^* \, GVAOTHS + DIS\_IDTRACOM
\end{aligned} \tag{7.12}
$$

$$
\begin{aligned}
IDU = {} & M1^* \, GVAOIL + M2^* \, GVAMINOTH + M3^* \, GVAPETCH \\
& + M4^* \, GVAMANNOLPC + M5^* GVAU + M6^* \, GVACON \\
& + M7^* \, GVADIS + M8^*(GVATRACOM - GVATRAPIPE) \\
& + M9^* GVAAGR + M10^* \, GVAFIBU + M11^* \, GVAGOV \\
& + M12^* \, GVAOTHS + DIS\_IDU
\end{aligned} \tag{7.13}
$$

Here, the coefficients from A1 to M12 are Input-Output coefficients. We do not report numerical values of them due to the data confidentiality issue as they obtained from OEGEM.

Final Demand

$$FDAGR = N1^* CONS + N2^* GC + N3^* IFOIL + N4^* IFNOILP + N5^* GI$$
$$+ N6^* XGOIL + N7^* XGNOIL + N8^* XS + DIS\_FDAGR \qquad (7.14)$$

$$FDCON = O1^* CONS + O2^* GC + O3^* IFOIL + O4^* IFNOILP + O5^* GI$$
$$+ O6^* XGOIL + O7 * XGNOIL + O8^* XS + DIS\_FDCON \qquad (7.15)$$

$$FDDIS = P1^* CONS + P2^* GC + P3^* IFOIL + P4^* IFNOILP + P5^* GI$$
$$+ P6^* XGOIL + P7^* XGNOIL + P8^* XS + DIS\_FDDIS \qquad (7.16)$$

$$FDFIBU = Q1^* CONS + Q2^* GC + Q3^* IFOIL + Q4^* IFNOILP + Q5^* GI$$
$$+ Q6^* XGOIL + Q7 * XGNOIL + Q8^* XS + DIS\_FDFIBU \qquad (7.17)$$

$$FDGOV = R1^* CONS + R2^* GC + R3^* IFOIL + R4^* IFNOILP + R5^* GI$$
$$+ R6^* XGOIL + R7^* XGNOIL + R8^* XS + DIS\_FDGOV \qquad (7.18)$$

$$FDMANNOLPC = S1^* CONS + S2^* GC + S3^* IFOIL + S4^* IFNOILP$$
$$+ S5^* GI + S6^* XGOIL + S7^* XGNOIL + S8^* XS$$
$$+ DIS\_FDMANNOLPC \qquad (7.19)$$

$$FDMINOTH = T1^* CONS + T2^* GC + T3^* IF + T4^* X + T5^* IS \qquad (7.20)$$

$$FDOIL = U1^* CONS + U2^* GC + U3^* IFOIL + U4^* IFNOILP + U5^* GI$$
$$+ U6^* XGOIL + U7^* XGNOIL + U8^* XS \qquad (7.21)$$

$$FDOILREF = V1^* CONS + V2^* GC + V3^* IF + \quad V4^* X + V5^* IS \qquad (7.22)$$

$$FDOTHS = W1^* CONS + W2^* GC + W3^* IFOIL + W4^* IFNOILP$$
$$+ W5^* GI + W6^* XGOIL + W7^* XGNOIL + W8^* XS$$
$$+ DIS\_FDOTHS \qquad (7.23)$$

$$FDPETCH = X1^* CONS + X2^* GC + X3^* IFOIL + X4^* IFNOILP$$
$$+ X5^* GI + X6^* XGOIL + X7 * XGNOIL + X8^* XS$$
$$+ DIS\_FDPETCH \qquad (7.24)$$

$$FDTRACOM = Y1^* CONS + Y2^* GC + Y3^* IFOIL + Y4^* IFNOILP$$
$$+ Y5^* GI + Y6^* XGOIL + Y7^* XGNOIL + Y8^* XS$$
$$+ DIS\_FDTRACOM \qquad (7.25)$$

$$FDU = Z1^* \, CONS + Z2^* \, GC + Z3^* \, IFOIL + Z4^* \, IFNOILP + Z5^* \, GI$$

$$+ \, Z6^* \, XGOIL + Z7^* XGNOIL + Z8^* \, XS + DIS\_FDU \qquad (7.26)$$

Here, the coefficients from N1 to Z8 are Input-Output coefficients. We do not report numerical values of them due to the data confidentiality issue as they obtained from OEGEM.

Total Demand

$$TDAGR = IDAGR + FDAGR \qquad\qquad\qquad\qquad\qquad (7.27)$$

$$TDPETCH = IDPETCH + FDPETCH \qquad\qquad\qquad\qquad (7.28)$$

$$TDCON = IDCON + FDCON \qquad\qquad\qquad\qquad\qquad (7.29)$$

$$TDDIS = IDDIS + FDDIS \qquad\qquad\qquad\qquad\qquad\quad (7.30)$$

$$TDFIBU = IDFIBU + FDFIBU \qquad\qquad\qquad\qquad\qquad (7.31)$$

$$TDGOV = IDGOV + FDGOV \qquad\qquad\qquad\qquad\qquad (7.32)$$

$$TDMANNOLPC = IDMANNOLPC + FDMANNOLPC \qquad\quad (7.33)$$

$$TDMINOTH = IDMINOTH + FDMINOTH \qquad\qquad\qquad (7.34)$$

$$TDOIL = IDOIL + FDOIL \qquad\qquad\qquad\qquad\qquad\quad (7.35)$$

$$TDOILREF = IDOILREF + FDOILREF \qquad\qquad\qquad\qquad (7.36)$$

$$TDOTHS = IDOTHS + FDOTHS \qquad\qquad\qquad\qquad\qquad (7.37)$$

$$TDTRACOM = IDTRACOM + FDTRACOM \qquad\qquad\qquad (7.38)$$

$$TDU = IDU + FDU \qquad\qquad\qquad\qquad\qquad\qquad\quad (7.39)$$

7.1.1.2   Identities for Total Final Expenditure and Domestic Demand

$$TFE = CONS + IF + GC + IS + X \qquad\qquad (7.40)$$

$$DOMD = CONS + IF + IS + GC \qquad\qquad (7.41)$$

$$DOMD\_Z = CONS\_Z + IF\_Z + IS\_Z + GC\_Z \qquad (7.42)$$

Equations for Investments by Economic Activity Sector

$$\text{LOG (IFDIS)} = 1.00^* \text{ LOG (GVADIS)} - 0.03^* \text{ RRLEND1} - 2.33 \\ + \text{ECT\_IFDIS} \tag{7.43}$$

$$\text{LOG (IFCON)} = 0.82^* \text{ LOG (GVACON)} - 0.02^* \text{ RRLEND1} + 0.30 \\ + \text{ECT\_IFCON} \tag{7.44}$$

$$\text{LOG (IFFIBU)} = 2.32^* \text{LOG(GVAFIBU)} + 0.94^* \text{ LOG (REER)} - 21.98 \\ - 0.54^* \text{ DSH2010} + \text{ECT\_IFFIBU} \tag{7.45}$$

$$\text{LOG (IFMANNOLPC)} = 0.69^* \text{ LOG (GVAMANNOLPC)} - 0.03^* \text{ RRLEND1} \\ + 0.86^* \text{ LOG (RER)} + 1.40 + \text{ECT\_IFMANNOLPC} \tag{7.46}$$

$$\text{LOG (IFOTHS)} = 2.65^* \text{ LOG (GVAOTHS)} - 0.13^* \text{ RRLEND1} \\ - 2.75^* \text{ LOG (RER)} - 14.26 + \text{ECT\_IFOTHS} \tag{7.47}$$

$$\text{LOG (IFPETCH)} = 2.72^* \text{ LOG (GVAPETCH)} + 2.24^* \text{ LOG (RER)} \\ - 0.13^* \text{ RRLEND1} - 20.72 + \text{ECT\_IFPETCH} \tag{7.48}$$

$$\text{LOG (IFTRACOX)} = 0.81^* \text{ LOG (GVATRACOM)} - 0.06^* \text{ RRLEND1} \\ + 1.09 + \text{ECT\_IFTRACOM} \tag{7.49}$$

$$\text{LOG (IFU)} = 0.79^* \text{ LOG(GVAU)} - 0.05^* \text{ RRLEND1} - 0.37^* \text{ LOG (RER)} \\ + 2.54 + \text{ECT\_IFU} \tag{7.50}$$

$$\text{LOG (IFAGR)} = 3.25^* \text{ LOG(GVAAGR)} + 3.26^* \text{ LOG (RER)} - 33.17 \\ + 2.54^* \text{ DST1012} + \text{ECT\_IFAGR} \tag{7.51}$$

7.1.1.3   Identities for Investments

$$\text{IF} = \text{IFOIL} + \text{IFNOIL} + \text{DIS\_IF} \tag{7.52}$$

$$\text{IF\_Z} = \text{IF}^* \text{ PIF}/100 \tag{7.53}$$

$$\text{IFNOIL} = \text{IFNOILP} + \text{GI} + \text{ISP} \tag{7.54}$$

$$\text{IFNOILP} = \text{IFDOMP} + \\ 100^*(((\text{FI\$IN\_Z}^* \text{ RXD})/(\text{WPMF\$\_WLD}/111.4992^* 100))) \\ + \text{DIS\_IFNOILP} \tag{7.55}$$

$$FI\$IN\_Z = FDI\$IN\_Z + FPI\$IN\_Z + FOI\$IN\_Z \tag{7.56}$$

$$
\begin{aligned}
IFDOMP = \; & IFAGR + IFCON + IFDIS + IFFIBU + IFMANNO \\
& + IFMINOTH + IFOTHS + IFTRACOX + IFU \\
& + DIS\_IFDOM
\end{aligned}
\tag{7.57}
$$

$$IFMANNO = IFMANNOLPC + IFPETCH \tag{7.58}$$

$$IFNOIL\_Z = IFNOILP\_Z + GI\_Z \tag{7.59}$$

$$GI = GI\_Z/PIF^*100 + DIS\_GI \tag{7.60}$$

Equations for Gross Value Added by Economic Activity Sector

$$
\begin{aligned}
LOG(GVAAGR) = \; & 0.14^* \, LOG(DELE\_AGR) + 0.07^* \, LOG(TDAGR) \\
& + 0.08^* \, LOG(DDIS\_IND) + 9.85 + 0.01^* @TREND \\
& - 0.07^* \, DP2008 - 0.11^* \, DP2009 + 0.01^* \, DBT2010 \\
& + ECT\_GVAAGR
\end{aligned}
\tag{7.61}
$$

$$
\begin{aligned}
LOG(GVACON) = \; & 0.28^* LOG(TDCON) + 0.63^* LOG(DELE\_COMM \\
& + DEN\_TOT\_TRA) + 5.68 + ECT\_GVACON
\end{aligned}
\tag{7.62}
$$

$$
\begin{aligned}
LOG(GVADIS) = \; & 1.22^* \, LOG(TDDIS) + 0.18^* \, LOG(DELE\_COMM) \\
& - 3.07 + ECT\_GVADIS
\end{aligned}
\tag{7.63}
$$

$$
\begin{aligned}
LOG(GVAFIBU) = \; & 0.16^* \, LOG(DELE\_COMM) + 0.71^* \, LOG(TDFIBU) \\
& + 3.57 + ECT\_GVAFIBU
\end{aligned}
\tag{7.64}
$$

$$
\begin{aligned}
LOG(GVAGOV) = \; & 0.25^* LOG(TDGOV) + 0.29^* LOG(DELE\_GOV) + 0.13^* \\
& LOG(DEN\_TOT\_TRA) + 8.72 - 0.06^* DP2008 + \\
& ECT\_GVAGOV
\end{aligned}
\tag{7.65}
$$

$$
\begin{aligned}
LOG(GVAMANNOLPC) = \; & 0.91^* \, LOG(TDMANNOLPC) \\
& + 0.19^* \, LOG(DNGA\_IND) \\
& + 0.12^* LOG(DDIS\_IND) \\
& + 0.24^* \, LOG(DHFO\_IND) \\
& + 0.05^* \, LOG(DCOIL\_IND) - 0.92 \\
& + 0.18^* \, DP1997 + ECT\_GVAMANNOLPC
\end{aligned}
\tag{7.66}
$$

$$\text{LOG(GVAOILMIN)} = 0.98^* \text{LOG(OILMBD)} + 11.44 + 0.002^* \text{@TREND}$$
$$+ \text{ECT\_GVAOILMIN} \tag{7.67}$$

$$\text{LOG(GVAOILREF)} = 1.01^* \text{LOG(TDOIL)} + 0.56^* \text{LOG} \Big(\text{OILUSE}^* 365^*$$
$$0.1486 - \text{DCOIL\_U}) - 0.36^* \text{LOG(DNGA\_IND}$$
$$+ \text{DNGA\_IND\_NEU} + \text{DNGA\_EOU} \Big) - 4.41$$
$$- 0.21^* \text{DP2013} + \text{ECT\_GVAOILREF} \tag{7.68}$$

$$\text{LOG(GVAOTHS)} = 0.47^* \text{LOG(TDOTHS)} + 0.19^* \text{LOG(DELE\_COMM)}$$
$$+ 5.43 + 0.03^* \text{DBT2015} + \text{ECT\_GVAOTHS} \tag{7.69}$$

$$\text{LOG(GVAPETCH)} = 0.31^* \text{LOG(TDPETCH)}$$
$$+ 0.54^* \text{LOG(DETH\_IND\_NEU}$$
$$+ \text{DLPG\_IND\_NEU} + \text{DNAP\_IND\_NEU}$$
$$+ \text{DNGA\_IND\_NEU}) + 0.38^* \text{LOG(DELE\_IND)}$$
$$+ 4.70 - 0.20^* \text{DSH2008} + \text{ECT\_GVAPETCH} \tag{7.70}$$

$$\text{LOG(DETH\_IND\_NEU)} = -0.14^* \text{LOG(PETH\_IND\_NEU/PGDPPETCH}^* 100)$$
$$+ 0.71^* \text{LOG(GVAPETCH)} - 4.19$$
$$- 0.21^* \text{DSH000102} - 0.19^* \text{DP2008}$$
$$+ \text{ECT\_DETH\_IND\_NEU} \tag{7.71}$$

$$\text{LOG(DLPG\_IND\_NEU)} = -0.14^* \text{LOG(PLPG\_IND\_NEU/PGDPPETCH}^* 100)$$
$$+ 0.53^* \text{LOG(GVAPETCH)} - 2.93$$
$$+ 0.17^* \text{DTB9501} - 0.47^* \text{DSH2003}$$
$$+ \text{ECT\_DLPG\_IND\_NEU} \tag{7.72}$$

$$\text{LOG(DNAP\_IND\_NEU)} = -0.31^* \text{LOG(PNAP\_IND\_NEU/PGDPPETCH}^* 100)$$
$$+ 3.47^* \text{LOG(GVAPETCH)} - 24.81$$
$$- 0.14^* \text{@TREND} - 1.35^* \text{DP1991}$$
$$+ \text{ECT\_DNAP\_IND\_NEU} \tag{7.73}$$

$$\text{LOG(DNGA\_IND\_NEU)} = -0.08^* \text{LOG(PNGA\_IND\_NEU/PGDPPETCH}^* 100)$$
$$+ 0.35^* \text{LOG(GVAPETCH)} - 1.76$$
$$+ 0.06^* \text{TI2009} + 0.12^* \text{S12001}$$
$$+ \text{ECT\_DNGA\_IND\_NEU} \tag{7.74}$$

$$LOG(GVATRACOM) = 1.40^* LOG(TDTRACOM)$$
$$+ 0.38^* LOG(DELE\_COMM)$$
$$+ 0.65^* LOG(DGAS\_TRA)$$
$$+ 0.14^* LOG(DEOTH\_TRA) - 4.21$$
$$- 0.06^* @TREND + 0.07^* DBT2016$$
$$+ ECT\_GVATRACOM \qquad (7.75)$$

$$LOG(GVAU) = 0.14^* LOG(TDU) + 0.46^* LOG(DNGA\_U)$$
$$+ 0.17^* LOG(DCOIL\_U) + 0.49^* LOG(DDIS\_U + DHFO\_U)$$
$$+ 5.16 - 0.07^* DP2008 + ECT\_GVAU \qquad (7.76)$$

7.1.1.4 Identities for Gross Value Added

Sectoral Aggregations

$$GVAREAL = GVAFIBU - GVAFIBUOTH \qquad (7.77)$$

$$GVAIND = GVAU + GVAMAN + GVAMINOTH + GVAOILMIN \qquad (7.78)$$

$$GVAMIN = GVAMINOTH + GVAOILMIN \qquad (7.79)$$

$$GVAMANNO = GVAMANNOLPC + GVAPETCH \qquad (7.80)$$

$$GVAMAN = GVAMANNO + GVAOILREF \qquad (7.81)$$

$$GVAOIL = GVAOILMIN + GVAOILREF + DIS\_GVAOIL \qquad (7.82)$$

$$GVANOIL = GVAAGR + GVACON + GVAU + GVAMANNO$$
$$+ GVAMINOTH + GVADIS + GVATRACOM$$
$$+ GVAFIBU + GVAOTHS + GVAGOV$$
$$- GVAFISIM + DIS\_GVANOIL \qquad (7.83)$$

$$GDP = GVANOIL + GVAOIL + GVANIT \qquad (7.84)$$

Value Added in Nominal Terms by Economic Activity Sector

$$GVACON\_Z = GVACON^* \, PGDPCON/100 \tag{7.85}$$

$$GVAFIBU\_Z = GVAFIBUOTH\_Z + GVAREAL\_Z \tag{7.86}$$

$$GVAFIBUOTH\_Z = GVAFIBUOTH^* \, PGDPFIBUOTH/100 \tag{7.87}$$

$$GVASER = GVADIS + GVATRACOM + GVAFIBU + GVAOTHS \\ + GVAGOV \tag{7.88}$$

$$GVASER\_Z = GVADIS\_Z + GVATRACOM\_Z + GVAFIBU\_Z \\ + GVAOTHS\_Z + GVAGOV\_Z \tag{7.89}$$

$$GVADIS\_Z = GVADIS^* \, PGDPDIS/100 \tag{7.90}$$

$$GVATRACOM\_Z = GVATRACOM^* \, PGDPTRACOM/100 \tag{7.91}$$

$$GVAGOV\_Z = GVAGOV^* \, PGDPGOV/100 \tag{7.92}$$

$$GVAIND\_Z = GVAU\_Z + GVAMAN\_Z + GVAMINOTH\_Z \\ + GVAOILMIN\_Z \tag{7.93}$$

$$GVAU\_Z = GVAU^* \, PGDPU/100 \tag{7.94}$$

$$GVAMAN\_Z = GVAMAN^* \, PGDPMAN/100 \tag{7.95}$$

$$GVAMINOTH\_Z = GVAMINOTH^* \, PGDPMINOTH/100 \tag{7.96}$$

$$GVAOILMIN\_Z = GVAOILMIN^* \, PGDPOILMIN/100 \tag{7.97}$$

$$GVAMIN\_Z = GVAMINOTH\_Z + GVAOILMIN\_Z \tag{7.98}$$

$$GVAMANNO\_Z = GVAMAN\_Z - GVAOILREF\_Z \tag{7.99}$$

$$GVAOILREF\_Z = GVAOILREF^* \, PGDPOILREF/100 \tag{7.100}$$

$$GVAAGR\_Z = GVAAGR^* \, PGDPAGR/100 \tag{7.101}$$

$$GVANOIL\_Z = GVAAGR\_Z + GVACON\_Z + GVAU\_Z \\ + GVAMANNO\_Z + GVAMINOTH\_Z + GVADIS\_Z \\ + GVATRACOM\_Z + GVAFIBU\_Z + GVAOTHS\_Z \\ + GVAGOV\_Z - GVAFISIM\_Z + DIS\_GVANOIL\_Z \tag{7.102}$$

$$GVAFISIM\_Z = GVAFISIM^* \, PGDPFISIM/100 \tag{7.103}$$

$$\text{GVAOIL\_Z} = \text{GVAOILMIN\_Z} + \text{GVAOILREF\_Z} + \text{DIS\_GVAOIL\_Z} \quad (7.104)$$

$$\text{GDP\_Z} = \text{GVANOIL\_Z} + \text{GVAOIL\_Z} + \text{GVANIT\_Z} \quad (7.105)$$

$$\text{GDP\$\_Z} = \text{GDP\_Z/RXD} \quad (7.106)$$

$$\text{GVANIT\_Z} = \text{GVANIT}^* \text{ PGDPNIT}/100 + \text{DIS\_GVANIT\_Z} \quad (7.107)$$

Disposable Income, Private Consumption and Wealth

$$\text{DI\_T\_Z} = \text{NNSA\_Z} + \text{CONS\_Z} + \text{GC\_Z} \quad (7.108)$$

$$\text{DI\_Z} = \text{LABCOMP} + \text{GCGPE} - \text{REMOF} + \text{DIS\_DI\_Z} \quad (7.109)$$

$$\text{DI} = \text{DI\_Z/CPI}^* \text{ 100} \quad (7.110)$$

$$\text{LOG(CONS)} = 1.00^* \text{ LOG(DI)} - 0.03^*(\text{RCB} - \text{@PCH(CPI)} * 100)$$
$$- 0.54^* \text{ LOG(WEALTH)} + 5.97 + \text{ECT\_CONS} \quad (7.111)$$

$$\text{PCONS} = \text{CONS\_Z/CONS}^* \text{ 100} \quad (7.112)$$

$$\text{WEALTH} = ((\text{M3} - \text{M0}) - \text{LIABP})/\text{CPI}^* \text{ 100} \quad (7.113)$$

7.1.2   Supply-Side

7.1.2.1   Identities for Capital Stocks by Economic Activity Sector

$$\text{CAPAGR} = \text{CAPAGR}(-1)^* \text{ 0.95} + \text{IFAGR} + \text{DIS\_CAPAGR} \quad (7.114)$$

$$\text{CAPCON} = \text{CAPCON}(-1)^* \text{ 0.95} + \text{IFCON} + \text{DIS\_CAPCON} \quad (7.115)$$

$$\text{CAPDIS} = \text{CAPDIS}(-1)^* \text{ 0.95} + \text{IFDIS} + \text{DIS\_CAPDIS} \quad (7.116)$$

$$\text{CAPFIBU} = \text{CAPFIBU}(-1)^* \text{ 0.95} + \text{IFFIBU} + \text{DIS\_CAPFIBU} \quad (7.117)$$

$$\text{CAPGOV} = \text{CAPGOV}(-1)^* \text{ 0.95} + \text{GI} + \text{DIS\_CAPGOV} \quad (7.118)$$

$$\text{CAPMANNOLPC} = \text{CAPMANNOLPC}(-1)^* \text{ 0.95} + \text{IFMANNOLPC}$$
$$+ \text{DIS\_CAPMANNOLPC} \quad (7.119)$$

$$CAPNOIL = CAPNOIL(-1)^* \, 0.95 + IFNOIL + DIS\_CAPNOIL \qquad (7.120)$$

$$CAPOILREF = CAPOILREF(-1)^* \, 0.95 + IFOIL + DIS\_CAPOILREF \quad (7.121)$$

$$CAPOTHS = CAPOTHS(-1)^* \, 0.95 + IFOTHS + DIS\_CAPOTHS \qquad (7.122)$$

$$\begin{aligned} CAPPETCH = CAPPETCH(-1)^* \, 0.788 + IFPETCH \\ + DIS\_CAPPETCH \end{aligned} \qquad (7.123)$$

$$CAPU = CAPU(-1)^* \, 0.95 + IFU + DIS\_CAPU \qquad (7.124)$$

$$KOILREF = IFREF + KOILREF(-1)^* \, 0.9500000 + DIS\_KOILREF \quad (7.125)$$

7.1.2.2 Identities for the Estimated Potential Output Equations by Economic Activity Sector

$$\begin{aligned} POT\_GVAAGR = EXP\Big(0.21^* \, LOG(CAPAGR) + 0.19^* \, LOG(ETAGR) \\ + 0.56^* \, LOG(AGRLANDSH) + 4.82 \\ + 0.003^* \, DSH2010^*@TREND\Big) \end{aligned} \qquad (7.126)$$

$$\begin{aligned} POT\_GVACON = EXP\Big(0.28^* \, LOG(CAPCON) + 0.72^* \, LOG(ETCON) \\ + 3.09 + 0.10^* \, DP2011\Big) \end{aligned} \qquad (7.127)$$

$$\begin{aligned} POT\_GVADIS = EXP\Big(0.73^* \, LOG(CAPDIS) + 0.56^* \, LOG(ETDIS) - 0.98 \\ - 0.14^* \, DP2003 - 0.07^* \, DP2011\Big) \end{aligned} \qquad (7.128)$$

$$\begin{aligned} POT\_GVAFIBU = EXP\Big(0.36^* \, LOG(CAPFIBU) + 0.51^* \, LOG(ETFIBU) \\ + 4.96 + 0.41^* \, DP2013\Big) \end{aligned} \qquad (7.129)$$

$$\begin{aligned} POT\_GVAGOV = EXP\Big(0.09^* \, LOG \, (CAPGOV) \\ + 0.66^* \, LOG \, (ETGOV) + 6.74\Big) \end{aligned} \qquad (7.130)$$

$$\begin{aligned} POT\_GVAMANNOLPC = EXP\Big(0.82^* \, LOG(CAPMANNOLPC) \\ + 0.46^* \, LOG(ETMANNO) - 0.24\Big) \end{aligned} \qquad (7.131)$$

$$\text{POT\_GVANOIL} = \text{EXP}(0.40^* \text{ LOG(CAPNOIL)} + 0.59^* \text{ LOG(ETNOIL)} + 2.51) \quad (7.132)$$

$$\text{POT\_GVAOILREF} = \text{EXP}\Big(0.86^* \text{ LOG(CAPOILREF)}$$
$$+ 0.44^* \text{ LOG(ETOILREF)} + 1.23\Big) \quad (7.133)$$

$$\text{POT\_GVAOTHS} = \text{EXP}\Big(0.11^* \text{ LOG(CAPOTHS)} + 0.71^* \text{ LOG(ETOTHS)}$$
$$+ 4.19 + 0.04^* \text{ DBT2015}\Big) \quad (7.134)$$

$$\text{POT\_GVAPETCH} = \text{EXP}\Big(0.43^* \text{ LOG(CAPPETCH)}$$
$$+ 0.31^* \text{ LOG(ETPETCH)} + 3.96 + 0.24^* \text{ DST0312}$$
$$- 0.29^* \text{ DP2012}\Big) \quad (7.135)$$

$$\text{POT\_GVATRACOM} = \text{EXP}\Big(1.23^* \text{ LOG(CAPNOIL} - \text{CAPMANNO)}$$
$$+ 0.40^* \text{ LOG(ETTRACOM)} - 8.93\Big) \quad (7.136)$$

$$\text{POT\_GVAU} = \text{EXP} (0.78^* \text{ LOG(CAPU)} + 0.35^* \text{ LOG(ETU)} - 1.11) \quad (7.137)$$

$$\text{POT\_GVAMANNO} = \text{POT\_GVAMANNOLPC} + \text{POT\_GVAPETCH} \quad (7.138)$$

7.1.2.3   Identities for Output Gaps by Economic Activity Sector

$$\text{GAP\_GVAAGR} = \text{GVAAGR} - \text{POT\_GVAAGR} \quad (7.139)$$

$$\text{GAP\_GVACON} = \text{GVACON} - \text{POT\_GVACON} \quad (7.140)$$

$$\text{GAP\_GVADIS} = \text{GVADIS} - \text{POT\_GVADIS} \quad (7.141)$$

$$\text{GAP\_GVAFIBU} = \text{GVAFIBU} - \text{POT\_GVAFIBU} \quad (7.142)$$

$$\text{GAP\_GVAGOV} = \text{GVAGOV} - \text{POT\_GVAGOV} \quad (7.143)$$

$$\text{GAP\_GVAMANNOLPC} = \text{GVAMANNOLPC}$$
$$- \text{POT\_GVAMANNOLPC} \quad (7.144)$$

$$\text{GAP\_GVANOIL} = \text{GVANOIL} - \text{POT\_GVANOIL} \quad (7.145)$$

$$\text{GAP\_GVAOILREF} = \text{GVAOILREF} - \text{POT\_GVAOILREF} \tag{7.146}$$

$$\text{GAP\_GVAOTHS} = \text{GVAOTHS} - \text{POT\_GVAOTHS} \tag{7.147}$$

$$\text{GAP\_GVAPETCH} = \text{GVAPETCH} - \text{POT\_GVAPETCH} \tag{7.148}$$

$$\text{GAP\_GVATRACOM} = \text{GVATRACOM} - \text{POT\_GVATRACOM} \tag{7.149}$$

$$\text{GAP\_GVAU} = \text{GVAU} - \text{POT\_GVAU} \tag{7.150}$$

7.2 Fiscal Block Behavioral Equations and Identities

7.2.1 Equations for Government Expenditure Items

$$\text{LOG(GWSA\_Z)} = 0.86^* \, \text{LOG(GREV)} + 1.18 + \text{ECT\_GWSA\_Z} \tag{7.151}$$

$$\text{LOG(GAE\_Z)} = 0.87^* \, \text{LOG(GREV)} - 0.96 + \text{ECT\_GAE\_Z} \tag{7.152}$$

$$\text{LOG(GMO\_Z)} = 0.68^* \, \text{LOG(GREV)} + 2.05 + \text{ECT\_GMO\_Z} \tag{7.153}$$

$$\begin{aligned}\text{LOG(GCGPE)} = {}& 0.72^* \, \text{LOG(GREV)} - 5.57 + 6.21^* \, \text{DSH1981} \\ & + \text{ECT\_GCGPE}\end{aligned} \tag{7.154}$$

$$\text{LOG(GC\_Z\_OTH)} = 1.03^* \, \text{LOG(GREV)} - 2.28 + \text{ECT\_GC\_Z\_OTH} \tag{7.155}$$

$$\text{LOG(GI\_Z)} = 0.81^* \, \text{LOG(GREV)} + 0.80 + \text{ECT\_GI\_Z} \tag{7.156}$$

7.2.2 Identities for Government Expenditures

$$\text{GEXP} = \text{PSCE} + \text{PSCAPE} \tag{7.157}$$

$$\text{PSCE} = \text{GWSA\_Z} + \text{GAE\_Z} + \text{GMO\_Z} + \text{GCGPE} + \text{PSCE\_OTH} \tag{7.158}$$

$$\begin{aligned}\text{LOG(PSCE\_OTH)} = {}& 0.45^* \, \text{LOG(GREVOIL)} + 0.65^* \, \text{LOG(GREVNOIL)} \\ & - 1.70 - 2.29^* \, \text{DP1986} + \text{ECT\_PSCE\_OTH}\end{aligned} \tag{7.159}$$

$$\text{PSCAPE} = \text{PSCAPE}(-1)^* \, \text{GI\_Z/GI\_Z}(-1) + \text{DIS\_PSCAPE} \tag{7.160}$$

$$\text{GC\_Z} = \text{GWSA\_Z} + \text{GAE\_Z} + \text{GMO\_Z} + \text{GC\_Z\_OTH} \tag{7.161}$$

$$\text{GC} = \text{GC\_Z/PGC}^* \, 100 \tag{7.162}$$

7.2.3 Identities for Government Revenues

$$GREV = GREVOIL + GREVNOIL \tag{7.163}$$

$$GREVOIL = 0.80^* \, XGOIL\$\_Z^* \, RXD + DIS\_GREVOIL \tag{7.164}$$

$$GREVNOIL = 0.85^* \, CEN\_TOT\_KSA + VAT\_REV + EXPL + HUVF$$
$$+ OVF + TOITT + TOIPC + DIS\_GREVNOIL \tag{7.165}$$

$$VAT\_REV = VAT\_RATE/100^* \, C\_RATIO^* \left(0.90^* \, GC\_Z \right.$$
$$\left. + 0.90^*(CONS^* \, PCONS/100) \right)^* VAT\_REV\_DUMMY$$
$$+ DIS\_VAT\_REV \tag{7.166}$$

$$EXPL = EXPL(-1)^* \, POPNS/POPNS(-1) + DIS\_EXPL \tag{7.167}$$

$$HUVF = HUVF(-1)^* \, XSTRAV\_Z/XSTRAV\_Z(-1) + DIS\_HUVF \tag{7.168}$$

$$OVF = OVF(-1)^* \, XSTRAV\_Z/XSTRAV\_Z(-1) + DIS\_OVF \tag{7.169}$$

$$TOITT = TOITT(-1)^* \, M\_Z/M\_Z(-1) + DIS\_TOIT \tag{7.170}$$

$$TOIPC = TOIPC(-1)^* \, GVANOIL/GVANOIL(-1) + DIS\_TOIPC \tag{7.171}$$

7.2.4 Identities for Total and Non-oil Budget Balance

$$GB = GREV - GEXP \tag{7.172}$$

$$GBNOIL = GB - GREVOIL \tag{7.173}$$

$$DEBT\_GOV = -0.44^* \, GB + 17290.59 + 225653.47^* \, DP2008$$
$$+ ECT\_DEBT\_GOV \tag{7.174}$$

$$DEBTG\_GOV = DEBTG\_GOV(-1) + DEBT\_GOV \tag{7.175}$$

7.3   Monetary Block Equations and Identities

$$
\begin{aligned}
\text{LOG(M2)} = {}& 1.00^* \text{ LOG(PGDP)} + 0.82^* \text{ LOG(GDP)} - 0.02^* \text{ IRD} + 0.10^* \\
& \text{LOG(WPO\_AL\_R)} + 0.624835^* \text{ LOG(REER)} \\
& + 0.03^* @\text{TREND(50)} - 3.21 + \text{ECT\_MD\_UR}
\end{aligned}
\tag{7.176}
$$

$$
\text{M0} = \text{M2} - \text{DTS} - \text{DD}
\tag{7.177}
$$

$$
\text{M1} = \text{M2} - \text{DTS}
\tag{7.178}
$$

$$
\text{M3} = \text{M2} + \text{DQM}
\tag{7.179}
$$

$$
\text{LIABP} = (\text{LIABP}(-1)^* \, (\text{DD} + \text{DTS})/(\text{DD}(-1) + \text{DTS}(-1)) + \text{DIS\_LIABP})
\tag{7.180}
$$

$$
\text{RLEND} = \text{RLEND}(-1) + (\text{RSH} - \text{RSH}(-1))
\tag{7.181}
$$

$$
\text{RRLEND} = \text{RLEND} - \text{DLOG(CPI)}^* \, 100
\tag{7.182}
$$

$$
\text{RLG} = \text{RLG}(-1) + (\text{RSH} - \text{RSH}(-1)) + \text{DIS\_RLG}
\tag{7.183}
$$

$$
\text{IRD} = \text{IR\_UK} - \text{RLEND}
\tag{7.184}
$$

$$
\text{RDEBT} = \text{RDEBT}(-1) + \text{RLEND} - \text{RLEND}(-1)
\tag{7.185}
$$

$$
\text{RRXD} = (\text{RXD}/3.75*100)*(\text{CPI\_USA}/\text{CPI})
\tag{7.186}
$$

$$
\text{REER} = \text{NEER}^* \, \text{CPI}/\text{CPI\_USA} + \text{DIS\_REER}
\tag{7.187}
$$

$$
\begin{aligned}
\text{REERE} = {}& \text{EXP}(1.28^* \text{LOG}((((\text{GVANOIL}/\text{RXD})/(\text{POP}^*10^3))/ \\
& (\text{GDPPC\_WLD}) * 100) + 0.20^* \text{LOG}(((\text{GVAOIL}/\text{RXD})/ \\
& (\text{POP}^*10^3))/(\text{GDPPC\_WLD}) * 100) - 0.24^* \text{LOG(NFA}/ \\
& \text{GDP\_Z}^* \, 100) + 0.68^* \text{ LOG(GC\_Z}/\text{GDP\_Z}^* \, 100) - 3.28)
\end{aligned}
\tag{7.188}
$$

$$
\text{PRODDN} = \big((\text{GVANOIL}/\text{RXD})/\big(\text{POP}^*10^3\big)\big)/(\text{GDPPC\_WLD}) * 100
\tag{7.189}
$$

$$
\text{PRODDO} = \big((\text{GVAOIL}/\text{RXD})/\big(\text{POP}^*10^3\big)\big)/(\text{GDPPC\_WLD}) * 100
\tag{7.190}
$$

7.4   External Block Equations and Identities

7.4.1   *Exports Related Equations and Identities*

$$X = XG + XS + DIS\_X \tag{7.191}$$

$$XG = XGNOIL + XGOIL \tag{7.192}$$

$$
\begin{aligned}
LOG\ (XGNOIL) = {} & -1.17^* \ LOG\ (REER) \\
& + 0.82^* \ LOG\ (GDP\_MNA^* \ RXD) \\
& + 1.08^* \ LOG\ (GVANOIL) - 10.30 \\
& + ECT\_XGNOIL
\end{aligned}
\tag{7.193}
$$

$$
\begin{aligned}
LOG(XOILREF) = {} & 2.68^* \ LOG(WTREF) + 1.49^* \ LOG(GVAOILREF) \\
& - 0.18^* \ LOG(WPO\_AL\_R) - 20.52 - 0.12^*@TREND \\
& - 0.21^* \ DP2001 + ECT\_XOILREF
\end{aligned}
\tag{7.194}
$$

$$WPO\_AL\_R = WPO\_AL/CPI\_USA^* \ 100 + DIS\_WPO\_AL\_R \tag{7.195}$$

$$XGOIL = XGOIL\_Z/PGDPOIL^* \ 100 \tag{7.196}$$

$$XGOIL\_Z = XGOIL\$\_Z^* \ RXD \tag{7.197}$$

$$
\begin{aligned}
XGOIL\$\_Z = {} & XOILC^* \ 365^* \ WPO\_AL + XOILREF^* \ 1.2^* \ WPO\_AL \\
& + DIS\_XGOIL\$\_Z
\end{aligned}
\tag{7.198}
$$

$$XOILC = OILMBD - OILUSE \tag{7.199}$$

$$XGNOIL\_Z = XGNOIL^* \ PGDPNOIL/100 \tag{7.200}$$

$$X\_Z = X^* \ PX/100 \tag{7.201}$$

$$X\$\_Z = XG\$\_Z + XS\$\_Z \tag{7.202}$$

$$XG\$\_Z = XGOIL\$\_Z + XGNOIL\$\_Z \tag{7.203}$$

$$XGNOIL\$\_Z = XGNOIL\_Z/RXD \tag{7.204}$$

$$XS\$\_Z = XS\_Z/RXD \tag{7.205}$$

$$XS = XS\_Z/PX^* \ 100 \tag{7.206}$$

$$
\begin{aligned}
XS\_Z = {} & (XSOIL\_Z + XSII\_Z + XSTRAN\_Z + XSTRAV\_Z \\
& + XSIP\_Z + XSFIN\_Z + XSCOM\_Z + XSOBS\_Z + XSGOV\_Z)
\end{aligned}
\tag{7.207}
$$

7.4.2 Imports Related Equations and Identities

$$M = MG + MS + DIS\_M \tag{7.208}$$

$$MG = MGCAP + MGCONS + MGINTER + DIS\_MG \tag{7.209}$$

$$\begin{aligned}
LOG(MGCAP) = \; & 1.03^* \, LOG(DOMD) + 0.84^* \, LOG(NEER) \\
& - 0.31^* \, LOG(PGDP\_US/PGDP) - 7.16 \\
& + 0.37^* \, DSH2003 - 0.15^* \, DBT2018 + ECT\_MGCAP
\end{aligned} \tag{7.210}$$

$$\begin{aligned}
LOG(MGCONS) = \; & 0.86^* \, LOG(DOMD) + 1.08^* \, LOG(REER) - 7.07 \\
& + 0.02^* @TREND - 0.12 * DBT2018 + 0.32^* \, DSH2003 \\
& + ECT\_MGCONS
\end{aligned} \tag{7.211}$$

$$\begin{aligned}
LOG(MGINTER) = \; & 2.56^* \, LOG(GVANOIL + GVAOIL) \\
& + 0.56^* \, LOG(NEER) - 0.86^* LOG(PGDP\_US/PGDP) \\
& - 25.62 - 0.04^* @TREND - 0.09^* \, DBT2018 \\
& - 0.14^* \, DSH2010 + ECT\_MGINTER
\end{aligned} \tag{7.212}$$

$$MG\_Z = MGCAP\_Z + MGCONS\_Z + MGINTER\_Z + DIS\_MG\_Z \tag{7.213}$$

$$MGCAP\_Z = MGCAP^* \, PMG \tag{7.214}$$

$$MGCONS\_Z = MGCONS^* \, PMG \tag{7.215}$$

$$MGINTER\_Z = MGINTER^* \, PMG \tag{7.216}$$

$$\begin{aligned}
LOG(MS) = \; & 0.44^* \, LOG(DOMD) - 1.61^* \, LOG(RRXD) + 12.60 \\
& + ECT\_MS
\end{aligned} \tag{7.217}$$

$$\begin{aligned}
MOILREF = \; & DOILREF\_T + XOILREF^* \, 0.14 - QOILREF \\
& + DIS\_MOILREF
\end{aligned} \tag{7.218}$$

$$M\_Z = M^* \, PM/100 \tag{7.219}$$

7.4.3   Overall and Non-oil Trade Balance

$$TB = X - M \tag{7.220}$$

$$TBNOIL = XGNOIL - M \tag{7.221}$$

7.4.4   Other BOP Related Equations and Identities

$$
\begin{aligned}
LOG(100* REMOF* RXD/PGDP) = {} & 1.70* LOG\ (GDP) \\
& + 1.00* LOG\ (ETNS) \\
& + 1.43* LOG\ (PGDP) \\
& - 0.09* LOG((EXPL/PGDP* 100) + 1) \\
& + ECT\_REMOF
\end{aligned}
\tag{7.222}
$$

$$
\begin{aligned}
FDI\$OUT\_Z = {} & FDI\$OUT\_Z(-1)^* (GDP\$\_Z/GDP\$\_Z(-1)) \\
& + DIS\_FDI\$OUT
\end{aligned}
\tag{7.223}
$$

$$FDI\$ = FDI\$IN\_Z - FDI\$OUT\_Z + DIS\_FDI\$ \tag{7.224}$$

$$
\begin{aligned}
WTOUR = {} & (WTOUR(-1)^* (AA1^* MS\$\_ZAF/MS\$\_ZAF(-1)+ \\
& AA2^* MS\$\_USA/MS\$\_USA(-1) + AA3^* MS\$\_CAN/MS\$\_CAN(-1)+ \\
& AA4^* (MS\$\_MEX)/(MS\$\_MEX(-1)) + AA5^* MS\$\_JPN/MS\$\_JPN(-1)+ \\
& AA6^* (MS\$\_TUR)/(MS\$\_TUR(-1)) + AA7^* MS\$\_DEU/MS\$\_DEU(-1)+ \\
& AA8^*MS\$\_FRA/MS\$\_FRA(-1) + AA9^* MS\$\_ITA/MS\$\_ITA(-1)+ \\
& AA10^* MS\$\_GBR/MS\$\_GBR(-1))) + DIS\_WTOUR
\end{aligned}
\tag{7.225}
$$

$$
\begin{aligned}
\text{WTREF} = 100^* \, (&\text{AB1}^* \, \text{DOILREF\_ARGENTIN/AB2} \\
&+ \text{AB3}^* \, \text{DOILREF\_AUSTRALI/AB4} \\
&+ \text{AB5}^* \, \text{DOILREF\_AUSTRIA/AB6} \\
&+ \text{AB7}^* \, \text{DOILREF\_BELGIUM/AB8} \\
&+ \text{AB9}^* \, \text{DOILREF\_BRAZIL/AB10} \\
&+\text{AB11}^* \, \text{DOILREF\_BULGARIA/AB12} \\
&+ \text{AB13}^* \, \text{DOILREF\_CANADA/AB14} \\
&+ \text{AB15}^* \, \text{DOILREF\_CHILE/AB16} \\
&+ \text{AB17}^* \, \text{DOILREF\_CHINA/AB18} \\
&+ \text{AB19}^* \, \text{DOILREF\_CROATIA/AB20} \\
&+ \text{AB21}^* \, \text{DOILREF\_CZECH/AB22} \\
&+ \text{AB23}^* \, \text{DOILREF\_DENMARK/AB24} \\
&+ \text{AB25}^* \, \text{DOILREF\_FINLAND/AB26} \\
&+ \text{AB27}^* \, \text{DOILREF\_FRANCE/AB28} \\
&+ \text{AB29}^* \, \text{DOILREF\_GERMANY/AB30} \\
&+ \text{AB31}^* \, \text{DOILREF\_GREECE/AB32} \\
&+ \text{AB33}^* \, \text{DOILREF\_HK/AB34} \\
&+\text{AB35}^* \, \text{DOILREF\_HUNGARY/AB36} \\
&+ \text{AB37}^* \, \text{DOILREF\_INDIA/AB38} \\
&+ \text{AB39}^* \, \text{DOILREF\_INDONESI/AB40} \\
&+ \text{AB41}^* \, \text{DOILREF\_IRELAND/AB42} \\
&+ \text{AB43}^* \, \text{DOILREF\_ITALY/AB44} \\
&+ \text{AB45}^* \, \text{DOILREF\_JAPAN/AB46} \\
&+ \text{AB47}^* \, \text{DOILREF\_KOREA/AB48} \\
&+ \text{AB49}^* \, \text{DOILREF\_MALAYSIA/AB50} \\
&+ \text{AB51}^* \, \text{DOILREF\_MEXICO/AB52} \\
&+ \text{AB53}^* \, \text{DOILREF\_NETH/AB54} \\
&+ \text{AB55}^* \, \text{DOILREF\_NORWAY/AB56} \\
&+ \text{AB57}^* \, \text{DOILREF\_PHILIPPI/AB58} \\
&+ \text{AB59}^* \, \text{DOILREF\_POLAND/AB60} \\
&+ \text{AB61}^* \, \text{DOILREF\_PORTUGAL/AB62} \\
&+ \text{AB63}^* \, \text{DOILREF\_ROMANIA/AB64} \\
&+ \text{AB65}^* \, \text{DOILREF\_RUSSIA/AB66}
\end{aligned}
$$

$$+ \text{AB67}^* \text{ DOILREF\_SAFRICA/AB68}$$
$$+ \text{AB69}^* \text{ DOILREF\_SINGPORE/AB70}$$
$$+ \text{AB71}^* \text{ DOILREF\_SLOVAKIA/AB72}$$
$$+ \text{AB73}^* \text{ DOILREF\_SPAIN/AB74}$$
$$+ \text{AB75}^* \text{ DOILREF\_SWEDEN/AB76}$$
$$+ \text{AB77}^* \text{ DOILREF\_SWITZ/AB78}$$
$$+ \text{AB79}^* \text{ DOILREF\_TAIWAN/AB80}$$
$$+ \text{AB81}^* \text{ DOILREF\_THAILAND/AB82}$$
$$+ \text{AB83}^* \text{ DOILREF\_TURKEY/AB84}$$
$$+ \text{AB85}^* \text{ DOILREF\_UAEMOD/AB86}$$
$$+ \text{AB87}^* \text{ DOILREF\_UK/AB88}$$
$$+ \text{AB89}^* \text{ DOILREF\_US/AB90)} \tag{7.226}$$

Here, the coefficients from AA1 to AA10 and from AB1 to AB90 are obtained from OEGEM. We do not report numerical values of them due to the data confidentiality issue.

7.5 Domestic Prices Block Equations and Identities

7.5.1 Consumer Prices

7.5.1.1 Equations for Sectoral CPI

$$\begin{aligned}
\text{LOG (CPIU)} = {} & 0.44^* \text{ LOG (PGDPREAL)} + 0.13^* \text{ LOG (PE\_RES)} \\
& + 0.69^* \text{ LOG (PGDPSER)} - 1.47 - 0.20^* \text{ DP2018} \\
& - 0.26^* \text{ DP2019} + \text{LOG ((VAT\_RATE} + 100)/100) + \text{ECT\_CPIU}
\end{aligned} \tag{7.227}$$

$$\begin{aligned}
\text{LOG (CPIFOOD)} = {} & 1.67^* \text{ LOG (PGDPAGR)} + 0.50^* \text{ LOG (PMG)} \\
& + 0.16^* \text{ LOG (WDIS)} + 0.08^* \text{LOG (PELE\_COMM)} \\
& - 7.55 + \text{LOG ((VAT\_RATE} + 100)/100) + \text{ECT\_CPIFOOD}
\end{aligned} \tag{7.228}$$

$$\begin{aligned}
\text{LOG (CPITRA)} = {} & 0.18^* \text{ LOG (WSER)} + 0.19^* \text{ LOG (PE\_TRACOM)} \\
& + 0.30^* \text{ LOG (PMG)} + 0.25 + \text{LOG((VAT\_RATE} + 100)/100) \\
& + \text{ECT\_CPITRA\_ULC}
\end{aligned} \tag{7.229}$$

$$\begin{aligned}
\text{LOG (CPIHH)} = {}& 0.21^* \text{ LOG (WDIS)} + 0.71^* \text{ LOG (PGDPMANNO)} \\
& + 0.25^* \text{ LOG (PM)} - 1.20 - 0.01^* @\text{TREND} \\
& - 0.08^* \text{ DP2008} + \text{LOG ((VAT\_RATE} + 100)/100) \\
& + \text{ECT\_CPIHH\_ULC}
\end{aligned}$$

(7.230)

$$\begin{aligned}
\text{LOG (CPICOMM)} = {}& 0.25^* \text{ LOG (WTRACOM)} + 0.57^* \text{ LOG (PGDPTRACOM)} \\
& + 0.49^* \text{ LOG (PM)} - 0.03^* (@\text{TREND}) \\
& + \text{LOG ((VAT\_RATE} + 100)/100) + \text{ECT\_CPICOM\_ULC}
\end{aligned}$$

(7.231)

$$\begin{aligned}
\text{LOG (CPIHTL)} = {}& 1.36 + 0.63^* \text{ LOG (PGDPDIS)} + 0.06^* \text{ LOG (PMS)} \\
& + \text{LOG ((VAT\_RATE} + 100)/100) \\
& + \text{ECT\_CPIHTL\_ULC}
\end{aligned}$$

(7.232)

$$\begin{aligned}
\text{LOG (CPICLOTH)} = {}& 0.50^* \text{ LOG (PGDPMANNO)} + 0.16^* \text{ LOG (PM)} \\
& + 0.14^* \text{ LOG (WDIS)} - 0.02^* @\text{TREND} \\
& + 0.09^* \text{ DP2016} + 1.58 + \text{LOG ((VAT\_RATE} + 100)/100) \\
& + \text{ECT\_CPICLOTH\_ULC}
\end{aligned}$$

(7.233)

$$\begin{aligned}
\text{LOG (CPIMISC)} = {}& 0.52^* \text{ LOG (PGDPMANNO)} + 0.34^* \text{ LOG (PGDPSER)} \\
& + 0.21^* \text{ LOG (PMG)} - 0.07 - 0.004^* @\text{TREND} \\
& + \text{LOG((VAT\_RATE} + 100)/100) + \text{ECT\_CPIMISC\_ULC}
\end{aligned}$$

(7.234)

$$\begin{aligned}
\text{LOG (CPIEDU)} = {}& 0.12^* \text{ LOG (W)} + 0.24^* \text{ LOG (PGDPSER)} \\
& + 0.05^* \text{ LOG (PMS)} + 2.13 + \text{LOG ((VAT\_RATE} + 100)/100) \\
& + \text{ECT\_CPIEDU\_ULC}
\end{aligned}$$

(7.235)

$$\begin{aligned}
\text{LOG (CPIART)} = {}& 0.60^* \text{ LOG (PGDPSER)} + 0.51^* \text{ LOG (WSER)} \\
& + 0.55^* \text{ LOG (PM)} - 0.05^* (@\text{TREND}) \\
& + \text{LOG((VAT\_RATE} + 100)/100) + \text{ECT\_CPIART\_ULC}
\end{aligned}$$

(7.236)

$$\begin{aligned}
\text{LOG (CPIHEAL)} = {}& 0.16^* \text{ LOG (PGDPSER)} + 0.09^* \text{ LOG (PMS)} + 3.45 \\
& + 0.05^* \text{ DP2003} + 0.05 * \text{ DB1617} + \text{LOG((VAT\_RATE} + 100)/100) \\
& + \text{ECT\_CPIHEAL\_ULC}
\end{aligned}$$

(7.237)

$$\begin{aligned}
\text{LOG (CPITOBC)} = {}& 1.61^* \text{ LOG (PGDPMANNO)} + 0.71^* \text{ LOG (WDIS)} + 0.15^* \\
& \text{LOG (PELE\_COMM)} + 0.01^* (@\text{TREND}) + \text{LOG ((VAT\_RATE} + 100)/100) \\
& + \text{ECT\_CPITOBC\_ULC}
\end{aligned}$$

(7.238)

7.5.1.2   Identity for Total CPI

$$\begin{aligned}
\text{CPI} = {} & \text{CPIU\_W}^* \text{ CPIU} + \text{CPIFOOD\_W}^* \text{ CPIFOOD} \\
& + \text{CPITRA\_W}^* \text{ CPITRA} + \text{CPIHH\_W}^* \text{CPIHH} \\
& + \text{CPICOMM\_W}^* \text{ CPICOMM} + \text{CPIHTL\_W}^* \text{ CPIHTL} \\
& + \text{CPICLOTH\_W}^* \text{ CPICLOTH} + \text{CPIMISC\_W}^* \text{ CPIMISC} \\
& + \text{CPIEDU\_W}^* \text{ CPIEDU} + \text{CPIART\_W}^* \text{ CPIART} \\
& + \text{CPIHEAL\_W}^* \text{CPIHEAL} + \text{CPITOBC\_W}^* \text{ CPITOBC} \\
& + \text{DIS\_CPI}
\end{aligned} \tag{7.239}$$

7.5.2   Producer Prices

7.5.2.1   Equations for Sectoral Producer Prices

$$\begin{aligned}
\text{LOG(PGDPAGR)} = {} & 0.05^* \text{ LOG(WAGR)} + 0.24^* \text{ LOG(PELE\_AGR)} \\
& + 0.34^* \text{ LOG(PMG)} + 0.82 + 0.09^* \text{ DP2017} \\
& + \text{ECT\_PGDPAGR}
\end{aligned} \tag{7.240}$$

$$\begin{aligned}
\text{LOG(PGDPCON)} = {} & 0.09^* \text{ LOG(ULCCON)} + 0.09^* \text{ LOG(PE\_CON)} \\
& + 0.59^* \text{ LOG(PM)} + 0.20 + 0.01^* \text{@TREND} \\
& + \text{ECT\_PGDPCON}
\end{aligned} \tag{7.241}$$

$$\begin{aligned}
\text{LOG(PGDPDIS)} = {} & 0.22^* \text{ LOG(WDIS)} + 0.50^* \text{ LOG(PMG)} - 0.67 \\
& + 0.01^* \text{@TREND} + 0.16^* \text{DP2017} + \text{ECT\_PGDPDIS}
\end{aligned} \tag{7.242}$$

$$\begin{aligned}
\text{LOG(PGDPFIBU)} = {} & 0.14^* \text{ LOG(ULCFIBU)} + 0.63^* \text{ LOG(PELE\_COMM)} \\
& + 0.51^* \text{ LOG(PMG)} - 3.08 + \text{ECT\_PGDPFIBU}
\end{aligned} \tag{7.243}$$

$$\begin{aligned}
\text{LOG(PGDPGOV)} = {} & 0.30^* \text{ LOG(ULCGOV)} + 0.12^* \text{ LOG(PE\_GOV)} \\
& + 1.74^* \text{ LOG(PM)} - 5.65 + \text{ECT\_PGDPGOV}
\end{aligned} \tag{7.244}$$

$$\begin{aligned}
\text{LOG(PGDPMANNO)} = {} & 0.04^* \text{ LOG(WMAN)} + 0.14^* \text{ LOG(PE\_MANNO)} \\
& + 0.97^* \text{ LOG(PM)} - 1.08 + \text{ECT\_PGDPMANNO}
\end{aligned} \tag{7.245}$$

$$\text{LOG(PGDPOILREF)} = 0.11^* \text{ LOG(ULCOILREF)}$$
$$+ 0.69^* \text{ LOG(PGDPOIL)} + 0.75^* \text{LOG(PCOIL\_IND)}$$
$$- 2.52 + \text{ECT\_PGDPOILREF} \qquad (7.246)$$

$$\text{LOG(PGDPOTHS)} = 0.12^* \text{ LOG(ULCSER)} + 0.04^* \text{ LOG(PE\_OTHS)}$$
$$+ 0.62^* \text{ LOG(PM)} + 0.96 + \text{ECT\_PGDPOTHS}$$
$$(7.247)$$

$$\text{LOG(PGDPTRACOM)} = 0.14^* \text{ LOG(ULCTRACOM)}$$
$$+ 0.07^* \text{ LOG(PE\_TRACOM)} + 0.32^* \text{LOG(PM)}$$
$$+ 2.04 + \text{ECT\_PGDPTRACOM} \qquad (7.248)$$

$$\text{LOG(PGDPSER)} = 0.07^* \text{ LOG(WSER)} + 0.75^* \text{ LOG(PM)}$$
$$+ 0.12^* \text{ LOG(PELE\_COMM)} - 1.27 + 0.01^* @\text{TREND}$$
$$- 0.06^* \text{ DP2008} + \text{ECT\_PGDPSER} \qquad (7.249)$$

$$\text{LOG(PGDPU)} = 0.22^* \text{ LOG(ULCU)} + 0.80^* \text{ LOG(PE\_U)}$$
$$+ 0.92^* \text{ LOG(PMG)} - 4.73 - 0.20^* \text{DP2008} + \text{ECT\_PGDPU}$$
$$(7.250)$$

7.5.2.2 Identities for Producer Prices

$$\text{PGDP} = (\text{GVANOIL/GDP})^* \text{ PGDPNOIL} + (\text{GVAOIL/GDP})^* \text{ PGDPOIL}$$
$$+ (\text{GVANIT/GDP})^* \text{PGDPNIT} + \text{DIS\_PGDP} \qquad (7.251)$$

$$\text{PGDPNOIL} = (\text{GVAAGR/GVANOIL})^* \text{ PGDPAGR}$$
$$+ (\text{GVAMINOTH/GVANOIL})^* \text{PGDPMINOTH}$$
$$+ (\text{GVAMANNO/GVANOIL})^* \text{ PGDPMANNO}$$
$$+ (\text{GVAU/GVANOIL})^* \text{ PGDPU}$$
$$+ (\text{GVACON/GVANOIL})^* \text{ PGDPCON}$$
$$+ (\text{GVADIS/GVANOIL})^* \text{ PGDPDIS}$$
$$+ (\text{GVATRACOM/GVANOIL})^* \text{ PGDPTRACOM}$$
$$+ (\text{GVAFIBU/GVANOIL})^* \text{ PGDPFIBU}$$
$$+ (\text{GVAOTHS/GVANOIL})^* \text{ PGDPOTHS}$$
$$+ (\text{GVAGOV/GVANOIL})^* \text{ PGDPGOV} + \text{DIS\_PGDPNOIL} \quad (7.252)$$

7.5.2.3 Identities for Aggregated Energy Prices

$$
\begin{aligned}
\text{PE\_AGR} = \ & (\text{DELE\_AGR}/(\text{DELE\_AGR}+\text{DGAS\_TRA}+\text{DDIS\_TRA} \\
& + \text{DKER\_TRA}))^{*}\text{PELE\_AGR} \\
& +(\text{DGAS\_TRA}/(\text{DELE\_AGR}+\text{DGAS\_TRA} \\
& + \text{DDIS\_TRA}+\text{DKER\_TRA}))^{*}\text{PGAS\_TRA} \\
& +(\text{DDIS\_TRA}/(\text{DELE\_AGR}+\text{DGAS\_TRA} \\
& + \text{DDIS\_TRA}+\text{DKER\_TRA}))^{*}\text{PDIS\_TRA} \\
& +(\text{DKER\_TRA}/(\text{DELE\_AGR}+\text{DGAS\_TRA} \\
& + \text{DDIS\_TRA}+\text{DKER\_TRA}))^{*}\text{PKER\_TRA}
\end{aligned} \tag{7.253}
$$

$$
\begin{aligned}
\text{PE\_CON} = \ & (\text{DGAS\_TRA}/(\text{DEN\_TOT\_TRA} \\
& + \text{DELE\_COMM})) * \text{PGAS\_TRA} \\
& +(\text{DDIS\_TRA}/(\text{DEN\_TOT\_TRA} \\
& + \text{DELE\_COMM})) * \text{PDIS\_TRA} \\
& +(\text{DKER\_TRA}/(\text{DEN\_TOT\_TRA} \\
& + \text{DELE\_COMM})) * \text{PKER\_TRA} \\
& +(\text{DELE\_COMM}/(\text{DEN\_TOT\_TRA} \\
& + \text{DELE\_COMM})) * \text{PELE\_COMM}
\end{aligned} \tag{7.254}
$$

$$
\begin{aligned}
\text{PE\_DIS} = \ & (\text{DELE\_COMM}/(\text{DELE\_COMM} \\
& +\text{DGAS\_TRA} + \text{DDIS\_TRA}))^{*}\text{PELE\_COMM} \\
& +(\text{DGAS\_TRA}/(\ \text{DELE\_COMM} \\
& +\text{DGAS\_TRA} + \text{DDIS\_TRA}))\ ^{*}\text{PGAS\_TRA} \\
& +(\text{DDIS\_TRA}/(\text{DELE\_COMM} \\
& +\text{DGAS\_TRA} + \text{DDIS\_TRA}))\ ^{*}\text{PDIS\_TRA}
\end{aligned} \tag{7.255}
$$

$$
\begin{aligned}
\text{PE\_FIBU} = \ & (\text{DELE\_COMM}/(\text{DELE\_COMM} + \text{DGAS\_TRA} \\
& + \text{DDIS\_TRA} + \text{DKER\_TRA}))^{*}\text{PELE\_COMM} \\
& +(\text{DGAS\_TRA}/(\text{DELE\_COMM} + \text{DGAS\_TRA} \\
& + \text{DDIS\_TRA} + \text{DKER\_TRA}))^{*}\text{PGAS\_TRA} \\
& +(\text{DDIS\_TRA}/(\text{DELE\_COMM} + \text{DGAS\_TRA} \\
& + \text{DDIS\_TRA} + \text{DKER\_TRA}))^{*}\text{PDIS\_TRA} \\
& +(\text{DKER\_TRA}/(\text{DELE\_COMM} + \text{DGAS\_TRA} \\
& + \text{DDIS\_TRA} + \text{DKER\_TRA}))^{*}\text{PKER\_TRA}
\end{aligned} \tag{7.256}
$$

$$
\begin{aligned}
\text{PE\_GOV} = \ & (\text{DELE\_GOV}/(\text{DELE\_GOV} + \text{DGAS\_TRA} + \text{DDIS\_TRA} \\
& + \text{DKER\_TRA}))^* \text{PELE\_GOV} \\
& + (\text{DGAS\_TRA}/(\text{DELE\_GOV} + \text{DGAS\_TRA} \\
& + \text{DDIS\_TRA} + \text{DKER\_TRA}))^* \text{PGAS\_TRA} \\
& + (\text{DDIS\_TRA}/(\text{DELE\_GOV} + \text{DGAS\_TRA} \\
& + \text{DDIS\_TRA} + \text{DKER\_TRA}))^* \text{PDIS\_TRA} \\
& + (\text{DKER\_TRA}/(\text{DELE\_GOV} + \text{DGAS\_TRA} \\
& + \text{DDIS\_TRA} + \text{DKER\_TRA}))^* \text{PKER\_TRA}
\end{aligned}
$$

$$(7.257)$$

$$
\begin{aligned}
\text{PE\_OTHS} = \ & (\text{DELE\_COMM}/(\text{DELE\_COMM} + \text{DGAS\_TRA} \\
& + \text{DDIS\_TRA} + \text{DKER\_TRA}))^* \text{PELE\_COMM} \\
& + (\text{DGAS\_TRA}/(\text{DELE\_COMM} + \text{DGAS\_TRA} \\
& + \text{DDIS\_TRA} + \text{DKER\_TRA}))^* \text{PGAS\_TRA} \\
& + (\text{DDIS\_TRA}/(\text{DELE\_COMM} + \text{DGAS\_TRA} \\
& + \text{DDIS\_TRA} + \text{DKER\_TRA}))^* \text{PDIS\_TRA} \\
& + (\text{DKER\_TRA}/(\text{DELE\_COMM} + \text{DGAS\_TRA} \\
& + \text{DDIS\_TRA} + \text{DKER\_TRA}))^* \text{PKER\_TRA}
\end{aligned}
$$

$$(7.258)$$

$$
\begin{aligned}
\text{PE\_TRACOM} = \ & (\text{DELE\_COMM}/(\text{DELE\_COMM} + \text{DGAS\_TRA} \\
& + \text{DDIS\_TRA} + \text{DKER\_TRA}))^* \text{PELE\_COMM} \\
& + (\text{DGAS\_TRA}/(\text{DELE\_COMM} + \text{DGAS\_TRA} \\
& + \text{DDIS\_TRA} + \text{DKER\_TRA}))^* \text{PGAS\_TRA} \\
& + (\text{DDIS\_TRA}/(\text{DELE\_COMM} + \text{DGAS\_TRA} \\
& + \text{DDIS\_TRA} + \text{DKER\_TRA}))^* \text{PDIS\_TRA} \\
& + (\text{DKER\_TRA}/(\text{DELE\_COMM} + \text{DGAS\_TRA} \\
& + \text{DDIS\_TRA} + \text{DKER\_TRA}))^* \text{PKER\_TRA}
\end{aligned}
$$

$$(7.259)$$

$$PE\_U = (DNGA\_U/(DNGA\_U + DCOIL\_U + DDIS\_U + DHFO\_U))^*$$
$$PNGA\_IND + (DCOIL\_U/(DNGA\_U + DCOIL\_U + DDIS\_U$$
$$+ DHFO\_U))^* PCOIL\_IND + (DDIS\_U/(DNGA\_U$$
$$+ DCOIL\_U + DDIS\_U + DHFO\_U))^* PDIS\_IND$$
$$+(DHFO\_U/(DNGA\_U + DCOIL\_U + DDIS\_U$$
$$+ DHFO\_U))^* PHFO\_IND$$

$$(7.260)$$

$$PE\_MANNO = (DNGA\_IND/(DNGA\_IND + DNGA\_IND\_NEU$$
$$+DHFO\_IND + DDIS\_IND + DCOIL\_IND$$
$$+DELE\_IND + DOTH\_IND))^* PNGA\_IND$$
$$+(DNGA\_IND\_NEU/(DNGA\_IND + DNGA\_IND\_NEU$$
$$+DHFO\_IND + DDIS\_IND + DCOIL\_IND + DELE\_IND$$
$$+DOTH\_IND))^*PNGA\_IND + (DDIS\_IND/(DNGA\_IND$$
$$+DNGA\_IND\_NEU + DHFO\_IND + DDIS\_IND$$
$$+DCOIL\_IND + DELE\_IND + DOTH\_IND))^* PDIS\_IND$$
$$+(DHFO\_IND/(DNGA\_IND + DNGA\_IND\_NEU$$
$$+DHFO\_IND + DDIS\_IND + DCOIL\_IND + DELE\_IND$$
$$+DOTH\_IND))^*PHFO\_IND + (DCOIL\_IND/(DNGA\_IND$$
$$+ DNGA\_IND\_NEU + DHFO\_IND + DDIS\_IND$$
$$+DCOIL\_IND + DELE\_IND + DOTH\_IND))^* PCOIL\_IND$$
$$+ (DELE\_IND/(DNGA\_IND + DNGA\_IND\_NEU$$
$$+DHFO\_IND + DDIS\_IND + DCOIL\_IND + DELE\_IND$$
$$+ DOTH\_IND))^*PELE\_IND + (DOTH\_IND/(DNGA\_IND$$
$$+ DNGA\_IND\_NEU + DHFO\_IND + DDIS\_IND$$
$$+DCOIL\_IND + DELE\_IND$$
$$+ DOTH\_IND))^* POTH\_IND$$

$$(7.261)$$

$$PE\_OILREF = (DCOIL\_IND/(DCOIL\_IND + DELE\_EOU$$
$$+ DNGA\_EOU))^* PCOIL\_IND$$
$$+(DELE\_EOU/(DCOIL\_IND + DELE\_EOU$$
$$+ DNGA\_EOU))^* PELE\_IND$$
$$+(DNGA\_EOU/(DCOIL\_IND + DELE\_EOU$$
$$+ DNGA\_EOU))^* PNGA\_IND \qquad (7.262)$$

$$PE\_AGR = (DELE\_AGR/(DELE\_AGR + DGAS\_TRA + DDIS\_TRA$$
$$+ DKER\_TRA))^*PELE\_AGR$$
$$+ (DGAS\_TRA/(DELE\_AGR + DGAS\_TRA$$
$$+ DDIS\_TRA + DKER\_TRA))^*PGAS\_TRA$$
$$+ (DDIS\_TRA/(DELE\_AGR + DGAS\_TRA$$
$$+ DDIS\_TRA + DKER\_TRA))^*PDIS\_TRA$$
$$+ (DKER\_TRA/(DELE\_AGR + DGAS\_TRA$$
$$+ DDIS\_TRA + DKER\_TRA))^*PKER\_TRA$$

$$(7.263)$$

7.6   Labor and Wages Block Equations and Identities

7.6.1   Equations for Sectorial Employment

$$LOG\,(ETAGR) = 0.92^*\,LOG\,(GVAAGR) - 0.86^*\,LOG\,(WAGR/PGDPAGR^*\,100)$$
$$+ 1.36 + 0.04^{*}@TREND + 0.18^*\,DP2018$$
$$+ ECT\_ETAGR$$

$$(7.264)$$

$$LOG(ETCON) = 0.94^*\,(GVACON) - 0.21^*\,LOG(WCON/PGDPCON^*\,100)$$
$$- 1.68 - 0.24 * DP200708 + ECT\_ETCON$$

$$(7.265)$$

$$LOG(ETDIS) = 0.13^*\,LOG(GVADIS) - 0.72^*\,LOG(WDIS/PGDPDIS^*\,100)$$
$$+ 12.87 + 0.13^*DBT2016 - 0.13^*\,DP2003 + ECT\_ETDIS$$

$$(7.266)$$

$$LOG(ETFIBU) = 0.93^*\,LOG(GVAFIBU)$$
$$- 0.16^*\,LOG(WFIBU/PGDPFIBU^*\,100)$$
$$- 3.50 - 0.35 * DP201314 + 0.38^*\,DP201718$$
$$+ ECT\_ETFIBU$$

$$(7.267)$$

$$\text{LOG (ETGOV)} = 1.12^* \text{LOG (GVAGOV)}$$
$$-0.14^* \text{LOG (GWSA\_Z/PGDPGOV}^* 100)$$
$$-5.42 + \text{ECT\_ETGOV} \qquad (7.268)$$

$$\text{LOG(ETMANNO)} = 0.74^* \text{LOG(GVAMANNO)}$$
$$+0.13^* \text{LOG(WMAN}^* 100/\text{PGDPMAN)}$$
$$-6.21 - 0.36^* \text{DP2010} + \text{ECT\_ETMANNO} \quad (7.269)$$

$$\text{LOG(ETMINOTH)} = 0.28^* \text{LOG(GVAMINOTH)}$$
$$-0.58^* \text{LOG(WMIN/PGDPMINOTH}^* 100) + 9.21$$
$$-0.15^* \text{DP2009} + 0.19^* \text{DP2014} + \text{ECT\_ETMINOTH}$$
$$(7.270)$$

$$\text{LOG(ETOTHS)} = 1.00^* \text{LOG(GVAOTHS)}$$
$$-0.53^* \text{LOG(W\_CEIC/PGDPOTHS}^* 100)$$
$$+1.94 + 0.16^* \text{DP2014} - 0.09^* \text{DP2009} + \text{ECT\_ETOTHS}$$
$$(7.271)$$

$$\text{LOG(ETPETCH)} = 1.65^* \text{LOG(GVAPETCH)} - 1.21^* \text{LOG(WPETCH)}$$
$$-3.85 + 0.05^* \text{@TREND} + \text{ECT\_ETPETCH}$$
$$(7.272)$$

$$\text{LOG(ETTRACOM)} = 0.47^* \text{LOG(GVATRACOM)}$$
$$-0.54^* \text{LOG(WTRACOM/PGDPTRACOM}^* 100)$$
$$-6.29 + \text{ECT\_ETTRACOM}$$
$$(7.273)$$

$$\text{LOG(ETU)} = 0.42^* \text{LOG(GVAU)} - 0.48^* \text{LOG(WU/PGDPU}^* 100)$$
$$+5.63 + \text{ECT\_ETU} \qquad (7.274)$$

7.6.1.1   Identities for Labor Market

$$\text{ET} = \text{ETNOIL} + \text{ETOIL} + \text{DIS\_ET} \qquad (7.275)$$

$$\text{ETNOIL} = \text{ETAGR} + \text{ETCON} + \text{ETDIS} + \text{ETFIBU} + \text{ETGOV}$$
$$+ \text{ETMANNO} + \text{ETPETCH} + \text{ETMINOTH} + \text{ETOTHS}$$
$$+ \text{ETTRACOM} + \text{ETU} + \text{DIS\_ETNOIL} \qquad (7.276)$$

$$ETOIL = ETOILREF + ETOILMIN \tag{7.277}$$

$$ETMIN = ETMINOTH + ETOILMIN \tag{7.278}$$

$$ETP = ETPS + ETPNS \tag{7.279}$$

$$ETSER = ETDIS + ETTRACOM + ETFIBU + ETOTHS + ETGOV \tag{7.280}$$

$$LF = PART/100.00^* (POPS + POPNS - POP014) + DIS\_LF \tag{7.281}$$

$$U = LF - ET + DIS\_U \tag{7.282}$$

$$UR = U/LF^* 100 \tag{7.283}$$

$$UR\_C = UR - UR\_N \tag{7.284}$$

7.6.2 Equations for Sectoral Wages

$$\begin{aligned} LOG(WAGR) =\ & 0.77^* LOG(GVAAGR/ETAGR) \\ & + 2.20^* LOG(PGDPAGR) - 4.63 + ECT\_WAGR \end{aligned} \tag{7.285}$$

$$\begin{aligned} LOG(WCON) =\ & 0.81^* LOG(GVACON/ETCON) + 0.21^* LOG(PGDPCON) \\ & + 5.12 - 0.41^*DST0308 - 0.14^* DB0910 \\ & + 0.16^* DST9803 + ECT\_WCON \end{aligned} \tag{7.286}$$

$$\begin{aligned} LOG(WFIBU) =\ & 0.37^* LOG(GVAFIBU/ETFIBU) \\ & + 0.80^* LOG(PGDPFIBU) + 4.68 + ECT\_WFIBU \end{aligned} \tag{7.287}$$

$$\begin{aligned} LOG(WMAN) =\ & 0.95^* LOG(GVAMAN/ETMAN) \\ & + 0.50^* LOG(PGDPMANNO) + 2.95 + 0.58^*DP2011 \\ & + 0.40^* DP2012 + ECT\_WMAN \end{aligned} \tag{7.288}$$

$$\begin{aligned} LOG(WMIN) =\ & 0.17^* LOG(GVAMIN/ETMIN) + 0.17^* LOG(PGDPMIN) \\ & + 9.85 + 0.31^*DP2009 - 0.21^* DP2011 - 0.17^* DP2016 \\ & + ECT\_WMIN \end{aligned} \tag{7.289}$$

$$LOG(WTRACOM) = 0.14^* \, LOG(GVATRACOM/ETTRACOM)$$
$$+ 0.77^* \, LOG(PGDPTRACOM) + 6.36$$
$$- 0.32^* \, DSH2003 - 0.22^* \, DP2011 + ECT\_WTRACOM$$
$$(7.290)$$

$$LOG(WU) = 1.61^* \, LOG(GVAU/ETU) + 0.95^* \, LOG(PGDPU) + 1.09$$
$$- 0.05^* @TREND - 0.57 * \, DST1012 + ECT\_WU$$
$$(7.291)$$

7.6.2.1 Identities for Unit Labor Cost by Sector

$$ULCAGR = WAGR * ETAGR/GVAAGR \qquad (7.292)$$

$$ULCCON = WCON * ETCON/GVACON \qquad (7.293)$$

$$ULCDIS = WDIS * ETDIS/GVADIS \qquad (7.294)$$

$$ULCFIBU = WFIBU * ETFIBU/GVAFIBU \qquad (7.295)$$

$$ULCFIBUOTH = WFIBU * ETFIBU/GVAFIBUOTH \qquad (7.296)$$

$$ULCGOV = GWSA\_Z * ETGOV/GVAGOV \qquad (7.297)$$

$$ULCMANNO = WMAN * ETMANNO/GVAMANNO \qquad (7.298)$$

$$ULCOILREF = WMAN * ETOILREF/GVAOILREF \qquad (7.299)$$

$$ULCOTHS = W * ETOTHS/GVAOTHS \qquad (7.300)$$

$$ULCTRACOM = WTRACOM * ETTRACOM/GVATRACOM \qquad (7.301)$$

$$ULCU = WU * ETU/GVAU \qquad (7.302)$$

$$ULCSER = W\_OLD * ETSER/GVASER \qquad (7.303)$$

$$ULCSER = W\_OLD * ETNOIL/GVANOIL \qquad (7.304)$$

$$ULCOIL = W\_OLD * ETOIL/GVAOIL \qquad (7.305)$$

7.6.2.2   An Identity for Labor Compensation

$$
\begin{aligned}
\text{LABCOMP} = \Big(& \text{ETAGR}^* \text{ WAGR} + \text{ETCON}^* \text{ WCON} + \text{ETDIS}^* \text{ WDIS} \\
& + \text{ETFIBU}^* \text{ WFIBU} + \text{ETGOV}^* \\
& \quad \left((\text{GWSA\_Z}^* 10^6) / (\text{ETGOV}^* 10^3) \right) \\
& + \text{ETMANNO}^* \text{WMAN} + \text{ETPETCH}^* \text{ WPETCH} \\
& + \text{ETMINOTH}^* \text{ W\_CEIC} + \text{ETOTHS}^* \text{ W\_CEIC} \\
& + \text{ETTRACOM}^* \text{WTRACOM} + \text{ETU}^* \text{ WU} \\
& + \text{ETOILREF}^* \text{ W\_CEIC} + \text{ETOILMIN}^* \text{ W\_CEIC} \Big) / 1000 \\
& + \text{DIS\_LABCOMP}
\end{aligned}
$$

$$(7.306)$$

7.7   Energy Block Equations and Identities

7.7.1   *Energy Demand Equations*

7.7.1.1   Industry

$$
\begin{aligned}
\text{LOG (DCOIL\_IND)} = \; & 1.32^* \text{ LOG (GVAIND} - \text{GVAU)} \\
& - 0.65^* \text{ LOG (PCOIL\_IND/PGDPIND}^* \text{ 100)} \\
& + 1.76^* \text{ LOG (PDIS\_IND/PGDPIND}^* \text{ 100)} \\
& - 25.77 + \text{ECT\_DCOIL\_IND}
\end{aligned}
$$

$$(7.307)$$

$$
\begin{aligned}
\text{LOG(DDIS\_IND)} = \; & 0.21^* \text{ LOG(GVAMANNO)} \\
& - 0.13^* \text{ LOG(PDIS\_IND/PGDPMANNO}^* \text{ 100)} \\
& - 2.06 + 0.03^* \text{@TREND} \\
& - 0.17^* \text{ DBT2016} - 0.16^* \text{ DP1986} + \text{ECT\_DDIS\_IND}
\end{aligned}
$$

$$(7.308)$$

$$LOG(DELE\_IND) = 0.61^* LOG(GVAMANNO)$$
$$-0.31^* LOG(PELE\_IND^* 100/PGDPMANNO)$$
$$+0.94^* LOG(POP1564) - 13.12 + 0.61^* DSH9005$$
$$+0.41^* DP2006 + ECT\_DELE\_IND$$

(7.309)

$$LOG(DHFO\_IND) = 0.94^* LOG(GVAMANNO)$$
$$-0.13^* LOG(PHFO\_IND/PGDPIND^* 100)$$
$$+0.59^* LOG(PNGA\_IND/PGDPIND^* 100)$$
$$-11.22 - 0.42^* DP2009 + ECT\_DHFO\_IND \quad (7.310)$$

$$LOG(DNGA\_IND) = 0.44^* LOG(GVAMANNO)$$
$$-0.43^* LOG(PNGA\_IND/PGDPIND^* 100)$$
$$+0.08^* LOG(PHFO\_IND/PGDPIND^* 100)$$
$$+0.47^* LOG(NG\_PRO) - 3.34 + 0.17^* DP2015$$
$$-0.14^* DP1997 + ECT\_DNGA\_IND$$

(7.311)

$$LOG(DOTH\_IND) = 0.06^* LOG(GVAMANNO)$$
$$-0.09^* LOG(POTH\_IND/PGDPMANNO^* 100)$$
$$+1.14^* LOG(NGL) - 9.68 + ECT\_DOTH\_IND$$

(7.312)

7.7.1.2 Transport

$$LOG(DDIS\_TRA) = 0.81^* LOG(GVANOIL)$$
$$-0.22^* LOG(PDIS\_TRA/PGDPNOIL^* 100)$$
$$+0.08^* LOG(PGAS\_TRA/PGDPNOIL^* 100) - 7.56$$
$$+ECT\_DDIS\_TRA$$

(7.313)

$$LOG(DGAS\_TRA) = 0.20^* LOG(GVANOIL)$$
$$-0.21^* LOG(PGAS\_TRA/CPI^* 100)$$
$$+1.23^*LOG(POP) - 10.97 + ECT\_DGAS\_TRA$$

(7.314)

$$\text{LOG(DKER\_TRA)} = 0.31^* \text{ LOG(GVANOIL)}$$
$$-0.10^* \text{ LOG(PKER\_TRA/PGDPTRACOM}^* 100)$$
$$- 3.83 + \text{ECT\_DKER\_TRA}$$

$$(7.315)$$

7.7.1.3   Residential

$$\text{LOG(DELE\_RES/POP)} = 0.39^* \text{ LOG(DI/POP)}$$
$$- 0.32^* \text{ LOG(PELE\_RES\_CONS/CPI}^* 100)$$
$$+ 0.001^* \text{ CDD} - 8.79 - 0.26^* \text{ DST1998}$$
$$+ 0.25^* \text{ DP1997} + \text{ECT\_DELE\_RES}$$

$$(7.316)$$

$$\text{LOG(DKER\_RES/POP)} = 0.26^* \text{ LOG(DI/POP)}$$
$$- 0.25^* \text{ LOG(PKER\_RES/CPI}^* 100)$$
$$+ 0.29^* \text{ LOG(PELE\_RES\_INV/CPI}^* 100)$$
$$- 12.70 + 0.72^* \text{ DP1991} + \text{ECT\_DKER\_RES}$$

$$(7.317)$$

$$\text{LOG(DLPG\_RES)} = 0.28^* \text{ LOG(GDP)} - 0.13^* \text{ LOG(PLPG\_RES/PGDP}^* 100)$$
$$+ 0.28^* \text{LOG(PELE\_RES\_CONS/CPI}^* 100) - 4.95$$
$$+ 0.35^* \text{ DP2011} + \text{ECT\_DLPG\_RES}$$

$$(7.318)$$

7.7.2   *Commercial, Government and Agriculture*

$$\text{LOG(DELE\_COMM)} = 0.44^* \text{ LOG(GVADIS + GVATRACOM + GVAFIBU}$$
$$+ \text{GVAOTHS + GVACON)}$$
$$-0.15^* \text{ LOG(PELE\_COMM/CPI}^* 100)$$
$$- 0.17^* \text{ LOG(IFDIS + IFTRACOX + IFFIBU}$$
$$+ \text{IFOTHS + IFCON)} - 6.93 + 0.08^* \text{@TREND}$$
$$- 0.11^* \text{ DBT2017} + \text{ECT\_DELE\_COMM}$$

$$(7.319)$$

$$\text{LOG(DELE\_GOV)} = 0.57^* \text{ LOG(GVAGOV)}$$
$$-0.12^* \text{ LOG(PELE\_GOV/PGDPGOV}^* 100)$$
$$- 7.34 + 0.03^*\text{@TREND} + 0.169704273369^* \text{ DP2018}$$
$$+ \text{ECT\_DELE\_GOV}$$
$$(7.320)$$

$$\text{LOG(DELE\_AGR)} = 1.86^* \text{ LOG(GVAAGR)}$$
$$-0.25^* \text{ LOG(PELE\_AGR/PGDPAGR}^* 100)$$
$$- 0.09^* \text{ LOG(IFAGR)}$$
$$+ 0.34^* \text{ LOG(WAGR/PGDPAGR}^* 100)$$
$$- 22.01 + 0.29^* \text{ DP2009} + \text{ECT\_DELE\_AGR} \quad (7.321)$$

7.7.2.1 An Identify for Electricity Supply

$$\text{ELE\_STOT\_KSA} = (\text{DCOIL\_U} + \text{DDIS\_U} + \text{DHFO\_U}$$
$$+ \text{DNGA\_U})^* \text{ ELE\_EF} + \text{ELE\_SS}$$
$$+ \text{DIS\_ELE\_STOT\_KSA} \quad (7.322)$$

7.7.3 *Identities to Calculate Total Energy Demand in TOE for Customer Types and the Kingdom*

$$\text{DEN\_TOT\_IND} = \text{DCOIL\_IND} + \text{DDIS\_IND} + \text{DHFO\_IND}$$
$$+ \text{DOTH\_IND} + \text{DNGA\_IND} + \text{DELE\_IND} \quad (7.323)$$

$$\text{DEN\_TOT\_TRA} = \text{DGAS\_TRA} + \text{DDIS\_TRA} + \text{DKER\_TRA} \quad (7.324)$$

$$\text{DEOTH\_TRA} = \text{DDIS\_TRA} + \text{DKER\_TRA} \quad (7.325)$$

$$\text{DEN\_TOT\_RES} = \text{DELE\_RES} + \text{DLPG\_RES} + \text{DKER\_RES} \quad (7.326)$$

$$\text{DEN\_TOT\_CGA} = \text{DELE\_COMM} + \text{DELE\_GOV} + \text{DELE\_AGR} \quad (7.327)$$

$$DEN\_TOT\_KSA = DEN\_TOT\_IND + DEN\_TOT\_TRA$$
$$+ DEN\_TOT\_RES + DEN\_TOT\_CGA \quad (7.328)$$

$$DELE\_TOT\_KSA = DELE\_RES + DELE\_IND + DELE\_COMM \quad (7.329)$$
$$+ DELE\_GOV + DELE\_AGR + DELE\_OTH$$

7.7.4 Identities to Calculate Energy Demand in Million SAR by Customer Type

7.7.4.1 Industry

$$CCOIL\_IND = DCOIL\_IND^* PCOIL\_IND \quad (7.330)$$

$$CDIS\_IND = DDIS\_IND^* PDIS\_IND \quad (7.331)$$

$$CHFO\_IND = DHFO\_IND^* PHFO\_IND \quad (7.332)$$

$$COTH\_IND = DOTH\_IND^* POTH\_IND \quad (7.333)$$

$$CNGA\_IND = DNGA\_IND^* PNGA\_IND \quad (7.334)$$

$$CELE\_IND = DELE\_IND^* PELE\_IND \quad (7.335)$$

$$CEN\_TOT\_IND = CCOIL\_IND + CDIS\_IND + CHFO\_IND$$
$$+ COTH\_IND + CNGA\_IND + CELE\_IND \quad (7.336)$$

7.7.4.2 Residential

$$CLPG\_RES = DLPG\_RES^* PLPG\_RES \quad (7.337)$$

$$CKER\_RES = DKER\_RES^* PKER\_RES \quad (7.338)$$

$$CELE\_RES = DELE\_RES^* PELE\_RES \quad (7.339)$$

$$CEN\_TOT\_RES = CLPG\_RES + CKER\_RES + CELE\_RES \quad (7.340)$$

7.7.4.3 Transport

$$CGAS\_TRA = DGAS\_TRA^* PGAS\_TRA \qquad (7.341)$$

$$CDIS\_TRA = DDIS\_TRA^* PDIS\_TRA \qquad (7.342)$$

$$CKER\_TRA = DKER\_TRA^* PKER\_TRA \qquad (7.343)$$

$$CEN\_TOT\_TRA = CGAS\_TRA + CDIS\_TRA + CKER\_TRA \qquad (7.344)$$

7.7.5   Commercial and Public Services and Agriculture and Forestry

$$CELE\_COMM = DELE\_COMM^* PELE\_COMM \qquad (7.345)$$

$$CELE\_GOV = DELE\_GOV^* PELE\_GOV \qquad (7.346)$$

$$CELE\_AGR = DELE\_AGR^* PELE\_AGR \qquad (7.347)$$

$$CEN\_TOT\_CGA = CELE\_COMM + CELE\_GOV + CELE\_AGR \qquad (7.348)$$

7.7.6   Identity to Calculate Energy Demand in Million SAR for the Kingdom

$$DNGA\_TOT = DNGA\_IND + DNGA\_U + DNGA\_IND\_NEU \\ + DNGA\_EOU \qquad (7.349)$$

$$CNGA\_TOT = DNGA\_TOT^* PNGA\_IND \qquad (7.350)$$

$$CEN\_TOT\_KSA = CEN\_TOT\_IND + CEN\_TOT\_RES \\ + CEN\_TOT\_TRA + CEN\_TOT\_CGA \qquad (7.351)$$

$$OILUSE = (DEN\_TOT\_KSA - DNGA\_TOT)/(365^* \, 0.1486) \\ + DIS\_OILUSE \qquad (7.352)$$

7.8 CO$_2$ Emissions Block Equations and Identities

7.8.1 Industry

$$CO_2\_COIL\_IND = \left(DCOIL\_IND^* 10^{6^*} 7.33\right) * 0.43 \qquad (7.353)$$

$$CO_2\_DIS\_IND = \left(DDIS\_IND^* 10^{6^*} 0.99^* 7.5^* 42\right) * 0.01 \qquad (7.354)$$

$$CO_2\_HFO\_IND = \left(DHFO\_IND^* 10^{6^*} 6.7\right) * 0.43 \qquad (7.355)$$

$$CO_2\_NGA\_IND = \left(DNGA\_IND^* 10^{6^*} 39.2\right) * 0.05 \qquad (7.356)$$

$$CO_2\_ELE\_IND = \left(DELE\_IND^* 10^{6^*} 11.63\right) * 0.65 \qquad (7.357)$$

7.8.2 Transport

$$CO_2\_DIS\_TRA = \left(DDIS\_TRA^* 10^{6^*} 0.99^* 7.5^* 42\right) * 0.01 \qquad (7.358)$$

$$CO_2\_GAS\_TRA = \left(DGAS\_TRA^* 10^{6^*} 0.95^* 8.5^* 42\right) * 0.01 \qquad (7.359)$$

$$CO_2\_KER\_TRA = \left(DKER\_TRA^* 10^{6^*} 0.95^* 7.8^* 42\right) * 0.01 \qquad (7.360)$$

7.8.3 Residential

$$CO_2\_ELE\_RES = \left(DELE\_RES^* 10^{6^*} 11.63\right) * 0.645 \qquad (7.361)$$

$$CO_2\_KER\_RES = \left(DKER\_RES^* 10^{6^*} 0.95^* 7.8^* 42\right) * 0.01 \qquad (7.362)$$

$$CO_2\_LPG\_RES = \left(DLPG\_RES^* 10^{6^*} 0.89^* 11.6^* 42\right) * 0.24 \qquad (7.363)$$

7.8.4 CO_2 from Commercial, Government, Agriculture, and Other Electricity Use

$$CO_2\_ELE\_COMM = \left(DELE\_COMM^* 10^{6^*} 11.63\right) * 0.65 \tag{7.364}$$

$$CO_2\_ELE\_GOV = \left(DELE\_GOV^* 10^{6^*} 11.63\right) * 0.65 \tag{7.365}$$

$$CO_2\_ELE\_AGR = \left(DELE\_AGR^* 10^{6^*} 11.63\right) * 0.65 \tag{7.366}$$

$$CO_2\_ELE\_OTH = \left(DELE\_OTH^* 10^{6^*} 11.63\right) * 0.65 \tag{7.367}$$

7.8.5 CO_2 from Total Electricity Generated and Based on the Fuel Mix Components

$$CO_2\_ELE\_STOT\_KSA = \left(ELE\_STOT\_KSA^* 10^{6^*} 11.63\right) * 0.65 \tag{7.368}$$

$$CO_2\_COIL\_U = \left(DCOIL\_U^* 7.33^* 10^6\right) * 0.43 \tag{7.369}$$

$$CO_2\_DIS\_U = \left(DDIS\_U^* 10^{6^*} 0.99^* 7.5^* 42\right) * 0.01 \tag{7.370}$$

$$CO_2\_HFO\_U = \left(DHFO\_U^* 10^{6^*} 1.04^* 6.7\right) * 0.43 \tag{7.371}$$

$$CO_2\_NGA\_U = \left(DNGA\_U^* 10^{6^*} 39.2\right) * 0.05 \tag{7.372}$$

$$
\begin{aligned}
CO_2\_ELE\_KSA\_PFM = &\ CO_2\_COIL\_U + CO_2\_DIS\_U \\
&+ CO_2\_HFO\_U + CO_2\_NGA\_U
\end{aligned}
\tag{7.373}
$$

7.8.6   Total CO_2 Emissions by Sector

$$
\begin{aligned}
CO_2\_EN\_TOT\_IND = &\ CO_2\_COIL\_IND + CO_2\_DIS\_IND \\
&+ CO_2\_HFO\_IND + CO_2\_NGA\_IND + CO_2\_ELE\_IND
\end{aligned}
\tag{7.374}
$$

$$CO_2\_EN\_TOT\_TRA = CO_2\_GAS\_TRA + CO_2\_DIS\_TRA + CO_2\_KER\_TRA \tag{7.375}$$

$$CO_2\_EN\_TOT\_RES = CO_2\_ELE\_RES + CO_2\_LPG\_RES + CO_2\_KER\_RES \tag{7.376}$$

$$CO_2\_EN\_TOT\_CGAO = CO_2\_ELE\_COMM + CO_2\_ELE\_GOV \tag{7.377}$$
$$+ CO_2\_ELE\_AGR + CO_2\_ELE\_OTH$$

7.8.7 Total CO_2 Emissions from Oil Use and for the Kingdom

$$CO_2\_OILUSE = \left(OILUSE^{*}365^{*}10^{6}\right) * 0.43 \tag{7.378}$$

$$CO_2\_EN\_TOT\_KSA = CO_2\_EN\_TOT\_IND + CO_2\_EN\_TOT\_TRA \tag{7.379}$$
$$+ CO_2\_EN\_TOT\_RES + CO_2\_EN\_TOT\_CGAO$$

7.9 Population and Age Cohorts Block Equations and Identities

7.9.1 Identities for Saudis and Non-Saudis

$$POPS = POPSM + POPSF \tag{7.380}$$
$$POPNS = (POP - POPS) + DIS\_POPNS \tag{7.381}$$

7.9.2 Identities for Age Cohorts

$$POP014 = POPM014 + POPF014 \tag{7.382}$$
$$POP1519 = POPM1519 + POPF1519 \tag{7.383}$$
$$POP2024 = POPM2024 + POPF2024 \tag{7.384}$$
$$POP2529 = POPM2529 + POPF2529 \tag{7.385}$$

$$POP3034 = POPM3034 + POPF3034 \qquad (7.386)$$

$$POP3539 = POPM3539 + POPF3539 \qquad (7.387)$$

$$POP4044 = POPM4044 + POPF4044 \qquad (7.388)$$

$$POP4549 = POPM4549 + POPF4549 \qquad (7.389)$$

$$POP5054 = POPM5054 + POPF5054 \qquad (7.390)$$

$$POP5559 = POPM5559 + POPF5559 \qquad (7.391)$$

$$POP6064 = POPM6064 + POPF6064 \qquad (7.392)$$

$$POP65A = POPM65A + POPF65A \qquad (7.393)$$

$$
\begin{aligned}
POP = {} & POP014 + POP1519 + POP2024 + POP2529 + POP3034 + POP3539 \\
& + POP4044 + POP4549 + POP5054 + POP5559 + POP6064 \\
& + POP65A + DIS\_POP
\end{aligned}
$$

$$(7.394)$$

7.9.3   Identities for Working Age Group

$$POPW = POPWF + POPWM \qquad (7.395)$$

$$
\begin{aligned}
POPWF = {} & POPF1519 + POPF2024 + POPF2529 + POPF3034 + POPF3539 + \\
& POPF4044 + POPF4549 + POPF5054 + POPF5559 + POPF6064
\end{aligned}
$$

$$(7.396)$$

$$
\begin{aligned}
POPWM = {} & POPM1519 + POPM2024 + POPM2529 + POPM3034 + \quad (7.397) \\
& POPM3539 + POPM4044 + POPM4549 + POPM5054 + \\
& POPM5559 + POPM6064
\end{aligned}
$$

Chapter 8
KGEMM Simulations

As mentioned earlier, MEMs are evaluated and validated using in-sample and out-of-sample simulations, and policy analysis, among other validation methods. In this section, we run KGEMM for in-sample forecasting and out-of-sample policy analysis to evaluate its predictive ability.[1] Hasanov and Joutz (2013) provide an overview of the literature that covers in-sample and out-of-sample forecasts and other methods for evaluating the predictive ability of MEMs. This includes Calzolari and Corsi (1977), Beenstock et al. (1986), Klein et al. (1999), Fair (1984, 1994, 2004), Bardsen and Nymoen (2008).

MEMs can be run using either the *static simulation* method, in which the model takes historical lagged values, or the *dynamic simulation* method, in which the model takes predicted lagged values. The predicted lagged values are the combination of historical lagged values and any errors in the model's predictions. The smaller the prediction errors of the model, the better the model can perform/approximate in simulations. Therefore, it would be advisable to run the model with dynamic simulation to see how significant or insignificant its prediction errors are in simulating the in-sample or out-of-sample values of the endogenous variables. Static, dynamic, deterministic, and stochastic MEM simulation methods have been comprehensively discussed in Klein et al. (1999) and Fair (1984, 1994, 2004), among others. This section employs the *dynamic simulation method*.

---

[1] The literature discusses using both long- and short-run equations/models for forecasting and projections purposes: Hara et al. (2009) and Yoshida (1990), among others, note that ECM-based MEMs provide realistic projections. Engle et al. (1989) compare forecasts from short-, long, and ECM models. Hendry et al. (2019) discuss that both level- and difference-based models should be considered in forecasting/projections. Fanchon and Wendel (1992) finds VAR in level outperforming VEC in first difference. Engle and Yoo (1987) finds the same for the short-horizon forecasting. We use the long-run version of KGEMM because our out-of-sample simulations span 9 years and because of the discussion in Appendix A.5.1. Note that Weyerstrass et al. (2018); Khan and ud Din (2011); Weyerstrass and Neck (2007), Musila (2002), Fair (1979, 1993), among others also used long-run version of their macroeconometric models in their policy analyses and simulations.

© The Author(s) 2023
F. J. Hasanov et al., *A Macroeconometric Model for Saudi Arabia*,
SpringerBriefs in Economics, https://doi.org/10.1007/978-3-031-12275-0_8

8.1   In-Sample Simulation

As mentioned previously, an in-sample simulation exercise is an evaluation/valida-
tion method to check how well a model can approximate historical data. We run
KGEMM for the period 1999–2019 to check its in-sample predictive ability of
approximating the Saudi Arabian historical data.[2]

The results of the in-sample simulations are plotted in Appendix D. Figures D.1,
D.2, D.3, D.4, D.5, and D.6 in the appendix illustrate selected key endogenous
variables from each block. Interested readers can refer to the details of the in-sample
forecasting for each variable in Appendix D. The figures show that the model closely
approximates the historical time path of the endogenous variables under consideration. It performs especially well in capturing the historical turning points and
sudden changes in data.

It can be concluded that KGEMM's in-sample predictive ability for the historical
values of the endogenous variables is quite high. The literature suggests that if a
model successfully approximates historical time paths of the variables, then there is a
high probability that the model will also perform well in out-of-sample simulations
or policy analyses.

8.2   Out-of-Sample Simulations

This sub-section simulates KGEMM to evaluate the economic, energy, and environmental effects of domestic and global changes. It should first be stated that these
simulations aim to illustrate the model's ability in addressing domestic and global
changes through the linkages across its blocks. Two things have to be noted in this
regard: (i) for economic, energy and CO_2 emissions variables, input values are just
the authors' calculations and output values are the results of the KGEMM simulations
both based on many assumptions (which might not be adequate representations of
the real life). Therefore, either input or output values in the simulations do not represent any official and or policy views at all. (ii) The simulations conducted here do
not aim to evaluate any policy options. SV2030 provides a number of targets and
initiatives to consider, related to fiscal stance, energy transitions (e.g., domestic
consumption of fossil fuels and renewable deployments), competitiveness, investments, non-oil export expansion, and diversification among others. Hasanov et al.
(2020) simulated KGEMM to assess the effects of domestic energy price reform (and
also fiscal reform at some extent). Also, Hasanov et al. (2022c) simulated KGEMM
to assess the non-oil exports effects of the expansions in the non-oil tradable and
non-tradable sectors. Moreover, Hasanov and Razek (2022) assessed the positive
impacts of the Public Investment Fund's new investment strategy for 2021–2025 on
the Saudi competitiveness by using KGEMM. Furthermore, Elshurafa et al. (2022)

---

[2]The reason for starting in 1999 is that data for some variables in the model are only available from
that year.

used KGEMM to quantify the macroeconomic and sectoral effects of diesel displacement from the agriculture sector. Lastly, Hasanov et al. (2022a) couple KGEMM with power generation models to evaluate economic, energy, and environmental effects of renewable deployments at the distributed generation and utility farm scales.

Given the above-mentioned KGEMM simulations done already, we do not want to repeat the same or very similar exercises here. Rather to provide readers with new insights here, we simulate KGEMM to assess the effects of the following scenarios: changes in (i) global oil prices, (ii) foreign direct investments to Saudi Arabia, and (iii) renewable penetration in the electricity generation. The scenario analyses cover the period 2022–2030. We simulate two scenarios in each out-of-sample exercise— business as usual (BaU) scenario and one of the three scenarios (denoted by S1, S2, and S3) mentioned above. The simulations end in 2030 to be in line with the time span of the SV2030 although the model can be solved till 2035. In the BaU, it is assumed that the Saudi Arabian economy moves forward as it did in 2021. Precisely, the BaU scenario includes the fiscal reform items (in particular, the implementations of expat levy in 2017, and 5% and 15% VAT rates in 2018 and 2020, respectively)[3] and domestic energy price increases in 2016 and 2018, and does not include the goal of having 50% of renewable and 50% of natural gas in power generation by 2030 because we simulate this here as a scenario (S3) in 8.2.3. Thus, the differences between the BaU scenario and given scenario will be stemmed only from the inputs in a given scenario. As an output of each exercise, we consider not only economic indicators but also energy and environmental indicators. The idea is to assess the effects of given changes from the sustainable development perspectives by considering economic-energy-environmental dimensions. To this end, we consider non-oil value added (GVANOIL), non-oil exports (XGNOIL), non-oil government budget revenues (GREVNOIL), households' disposable income (DI), total energy consumption (DEN_TOT_KSA), and total CO_2 emissions from energy consumption in the kingdom (CO2_EN_TOT_KSA). The rationale behind this selection would be as follows: the first three indicators show developments in the non-oil sector, its exports and revenue collection, which are the main economic streamlines in the SV2030 and its realization programs. A wellbeing of the nation and hence increasing disposable income of the households is the end goal of any economic policies. Lastly, energy consumption and associated emissions are considered from the United Nations sustainable development goals standpoint. The description of each variable is given in Appendix B.[4] We discuss policy background, inputs, and outputs of each scenario in the next sub-sections. We keep our discussions very brief, since we have three scenarios to examine and since out-of-sample simulations are not the entire objective of this book.

---

[3] BaU scenario also accounts for other fiscal implementations in 2017 such as Umrah and Hajj visa fees and other visa fees.

[4] As Appendix B documents, GVANOIL, XGNOIL, GREVNOIL, DI, DEN_TOT_KSA are measured in million scale while CO_2_EN_TOT_KSA is measured in metric ton. For readers' convenience, we scaled up these measures to billions in the graphical illustrations.

8.2.1   The Effects of Global Oil Price Changes

As in any oil-exporting country, oil prices and related revenues play an important role in economic activities including non-oil sector in Saudi Arabia. Oil constitutes large shares in total exports, budget revenues, and total economy in the Saudi economy as mentioned earlier in this book. There is a consensus in the literature that oil-related revenues are important for the development of the non-oil sector mainly through fiscal spending. Given this, we simulate KGEMM to examine effects of the international price of Arabian light crude oil (WPO_AL) on economic, energy, and environmental relationships of the Kingdom. As an input, the international price of Arab light crude oil in Scenario 1 (S1) is increased by 25% in each year of the 2022–2030 period compared to the values in the BaU scenario, as shown in Fig. 8.1.[5]

Figure 8.2 documents the effect of this increase on the selected indicators.

The graphs in the figure demonstrate increases in the selected indicators in S1 compared to BaU when the Arabian light crude oil international price increases. This is pretty much expected given the nature of the Saudi economy as discussed above. High oil price increases oil income, which is channeled into the rest economy through increased oil sector's demand and increased government demand for other

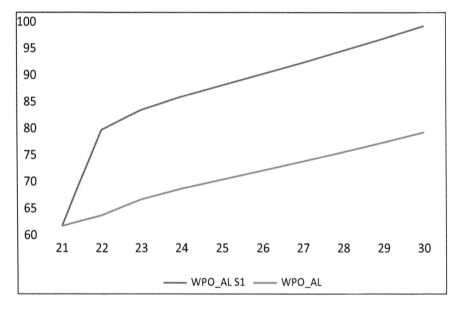

Fig. 8.1 Arabian light crude oil international price, US$ per barrel

---

[5]The reason we considered 25% is because under this setup, Arabian light price reaches up to US
$100 per barrel in 2030.

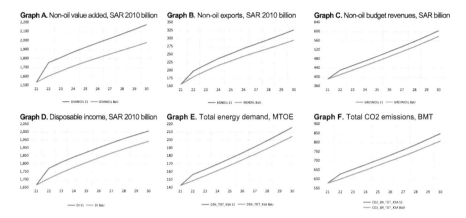

Fig. 8.2 Projections of the selected indicators in S1 and BaU scenarios, 2021–2030

sectors' goods and services as Eqs. (7.1)–(7.26) describe. This increases total demand and sectoral economic activities (see Eqs. (7.27)–(7.39) and (7.61)–(7.76)). This is the first round and demand-side effect, and it translates into the supply-side effect over time mainly through investment-capital accumulation as the Eqs. (7.43)–(7.51) and (7.114)–(7.138) explains. XGNOIL increases because domestic production measured by GVANOIL increases (see Eq. (7.193). An expansion in economic activities leads to more employment and wages and resultantly, the disposable income of the household's raises (see Eqs. (7.264)–(7.274) and (7.285)–(7.291), and (7.306) and (7.109)). Expanded economic activities demand more energy (see Eqs. (7.61)–(7.76) and (7.307)–(7.321)) in S1 compared to BaU. Numerically, calculated implied elasticities for the average of 2022–2030 show that a 1% increase in the international price of Arabian light crude oil leads to a 0.4%, 0.4%, 0.2%, and 0.14% increase in GVANOIL, XGNOIL, GREVNOIL, and DI, respectively, while DEN_TOT_KSA and CO_2_EN_TOT_KSA only increase by 0.2% each.[6]

---

[6]Following the macroeconometric modeling literature, period average implied elasticity (e) is calculated as the ratio of mean percentage change deviation of an output variable to the mean percentage change deviation of an input variable. Precisely, $e = (\frac{1}{T} * \sum_{t}^{T} \frac{OV\_S_t}{OV\_BaU_t} * 100 - 100)/(\frac{1}{T} * \sum_{t}^{T} \frac{IV\_S_t}{IV\_BaU_t} * 100 - 100)$. Where, OV_S_t and OV_BaU_t are the values of the output variable (say GVANOIL) in a given scenario (say S1) and in the BaU scenario, respectively; IV_S_t and IV_BaU_t are the values of the input variable (say WPO_AL) in a given scenario (say S1) and in the BaU scenario, respectively; t denotes time, that is year; T indicates the total number of years. In our case, t changes from 2022 to 2030 and $T = 9$.

8.2.2 The Effects of Foreign Direct Investments Inflow to Saudi Arabia

The National Investment Strategy (NIS) has been announced in October, 2021. The strategy highlights a significant increases in foreign direct investments (FDI) inflow and domestic investments in the coming years. Precisely, the cumulative total (FDI inflow+Domestic) investment of 12.4 SAR trillion in KSA during 2021–2030 (Jadwa Investment 2021). 388 SAR billion of FDIs inflow and 1.65 SAR trillion of domestic investment and hence the total of 2 SAR trillion in 2030 have been indicated.[7] Table 8.1 records the shares of the sources in the total investment by 2030.

The strategy targets to raise FDI inflow from SAR 17 billion in 2019 to SAR 388 billion in 2030—this is about 23 times increase in 10 years. Likewise, it is targeted to increase domestic investments and overall investments by 2.6 times and 3.1 times, respectively, during 2019–2030.

Obviously, the NIS and associated domestic and foreign investment targets have large policy implications regarding their impacts on the development of Saudi economy. They also have implications for energy and environmental dimensions of the Kingdom. It was also discussed that accomplishing the above-mentioned targets necessitates well-designed development measures determined by the NIS and this is based on four main milestones, namely, enhancing investment opportunities, targeting different investor types, diversifying financing options, and improving competitiveness.[8] We do not discuss more policy implications of the NIS here to save space, but vividly this deserves a scenario analysis to quantify its impact on the Kingdom. To do so, we focused on the FDI inflow aspect of the NIS. This is because FDI inflow is exogenous to the Saudi economy, and it is considered so in the KGEMM framework. Thus, it is more realistic to simulate the impact of FDI inflow, as a global factor, on Saudi Arabia. As the input for scenario 2 (S2), we obtained nominal values of FDI inflow for 2022–2030 in SAR billion from the online media

Table 8.1 Breakdown of the total investment by stakeholder by 2030

Stakeholders	Share in total of 12.4 SAR trillion, %	Investment, SAR trillion
Shareek program	40	4.96
PIF investment	24	2.98
Local investment	21	2.60
FDI	15	1.86
Total	**100**	**12.40**

Source: Modified from Jadwa Investment 2021

---

[7]https://www.spa.gov.sa/viewfullstory.php?lang=en&newsid=2294440#2294440, https://www.spa.gov.sa/viewfullstory.php?lang=en&newsid=2295200

[8]See https://www.spa.gov.sa/viewfullstory.php?lang=en&newsid=2295200

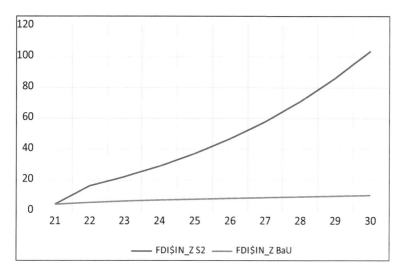

Fig. 8.3 Projected values of FDIs inflow in the S2 and BaU scenarios, US$ billions

source of https://www.argaam.com/en/article/articledetail/id/1503922 and then converted them to US$ billions using the exchange rate.[9] Figure 8.3 illustrates the FDI inflow values in the S2 scenario (FDI$IN_Z S2) and those in the BaU scenario (FDI$IN_Z BaU) over the simulation period.

The figure shows that values for the FDIs inflow are significantly large in S2 scenario compared to the values in the BaU scenario. The difference between the FDIs inflow values in two scenarios increases from about 3 times in 2022 to 10 times in 2030; these are large numbers and should have sizeable growth effects. Figure 8.4 reports the results for the selected indicators.

The graphs in the figure convey heterogeneous information. In other words, for GVANOIL, XGNOIL, DEN_TOT_KSA, and CO_2_EN_TOT_KSA, the deviations of the S2 scenario values from the BaU scenario values are considerable, whereas that for the GREVNOIL and DI are not. Numerically, in 2030, the percentage change deviations of the S2 values from the BaU values for GVANOIL, XGNOIL, DEN_TOT_KSA, and CO_2_EN_TOT_KSA are 23%, 25%, 14%, and 14%, respectively. While the deviations for GREVNOIL and DI are 4% and 1%, respectively. At the first glance, small deviations in the case of latter variables might be seen puzzling as the increases in FDIs inflow in the S2 scenario are quite large compared to that of the BaU scenario. However, a closer look reveals out a few points that are worth considering. First, historically, the size of FDIs inflow in total domestic investments

---

[9]Alternatively, we can calculate FDI inflow values for each year of the simulation period using the announced value of SAR 388 billion in 2030 and the historical value of SAR 17 billion in 2019, and extrapolate different development paths. However, we chose to use the values already calculated by www.argaam.com because we believe this media source has more information content for its calculations.

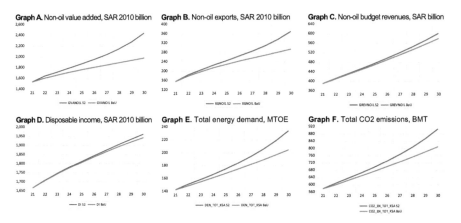

Fig. 8.4 Projections of the selected indicators in S2 and BaU scenarios, 2021–2030

and thus its role in the economy was quite limited and even diminishing over time. In terms of numbers, the size rose from 19% in 2005 to a peak of 33% in 2008 and has been steadily declining since then, falling to just below 3% in 2019. A simple cointegration analysis shows that the magnitude of the impact of the FDIs inflow on the non-oil activities was very small compared to that of the domestic invest-ments.[10] Second, if we calculate the implied elasticities of the most largely impacted variables, i.e., XGNOIL and GVANOIL, with respect to FDIs inflow, they would be as small as 0.0216 and 0.0197, respectively, for 2022–2030, pointing to minor growth effects of FDIs inflow for the non-oil activities. Third, another reason why GREVNOIL and FDI are less affected by the increase in FDIs inflows may be due to outflow remittances. Eq. (7.109) illustrates that net national disposable income declines when outflow remittances (REMOF) increase. In this regard, in 2030, percentage deviation of REMOF value in S2 from the value in BaU is 25%, indicating a quite large amount of leakage. Fourth, the growth in the other compo-nent of the net national disposable income, namely, labor compensation (LABCOMP), which positively affects it, is very small. Numerically, the percentage deviation of LABCOMP value in S2 from the value in BaU is as small as 0.2% in 2022 and it grows to 1.5% only in 2030. This is not surprising because of the two reasons: the expansion in the economic activity in this scenario is investment-driven and the labor elasticity of output is smaller than that of capital elasticity for a number of the non-oil activity sectors, namely, manufacturing less petrochemical; transpor-tation and communication; petrochemical; agriculture; utility; retail, wholesale, hotels, and catering (see identities for the estimated potential output equations by economic activity sector in Sect. 7.1). Both reasons indicate a limited role of employment in non-oil economic activities in this scenario. In addition, the increase

---

[10]A long-term, cointegrated, regression for the period 2007–2019 was estimated as LOG (GVANOIL) = 0.036*LOG(FDI\$IN_Z*RXD/PIF*100) + 0.281*LOG((IFNOIL)-(FDI \$IN_Z*RXD/PIF*100)) + 7.857 + 0.034*@TREND.

in non-oil sector employment (ETNOIL) in the S2 scenario compared to the BaU scenario is 0.6% in 2022 and 4.8% in 2030. As a result, limited role of employment coupled with its limited increase makes LABCOMP to increase with a minor magnitude in the S2 scenario. Moreover, the third component of DI, namely, government transfers to households (GCGPE) does not increase in the S2 scenario compared to the BaU scenario and even gets slightly small due to the decrease in government oil revenues (GREVOIL) as explained below. Fifth, low growth in employment and wages and thus in net national disposable income and household consumption makes GREVNOIL to grow less too as the VAT collections is one of its main components. Sixth, another reason for a small increase in GREVNOIL would be none to negative growth rates of government expenditure (GEXP). Numerically, its growth in S2 compared to BaU is on average −0.4%. The main reason for it is that an expansion in economic activity demands more energy to be consumed domestically (see changes in DEN_TOT_KSA), and this results in less amount of oil being available for export (XOILC) since the oil production (OILMBD) in KGEMM is treated as exogenous due to the global oil market conditions such as OPEC+ agreements (see Eq. (7.199)). Consequently, government oil revenues (GREVOIL) in S2 decrease by an average of 2.5% over 2022–2030 compared to BaU. Since the share of GREVOIL in total government revenues (GREV) is considerably large (the average of 1969–2019 was almost 80%), the latter declines slightly in S2 compared to BaU although GREVNOIL increases in S2 as figure above shows. As a result, GEXP declines and it is one of the key drivers of economic growth including non-oil economic activity, which is the base for GREVNOIL collections.

In the conclusion of the scenario 2 exercise, some insights can be derived from the simulation. The FDIs inflow has a positive impact on the economy, but historical structure and business environment in the economy should be changed to make the magnitude of this impact larger. The simulation results here support the four main milestones (enhancing investment opportunities, targeting different investor types, diversifying financing options, and improving competitiveness) that are already considered in the NIS framework as the main policy measures to make FDIs inflow more impactful in the economy. Second, the authorities may wish to think about measures to further increase the labor contribution to output in some non-oil economic activity sectors. Investments in research and development, education, trainings, and other human capital enhancing activities might be fostered in this regard. Third, the authorities also may wish to think about measures to reduce leakages, such as outflow remittances, which would further increase aggregate demand and domestic economic activities. Increasing the expat levy rate does not seem a best measure in this regard because it might encourage foreign workers to consider another Gulf countries for work. One measure, which seems reasonable, is to further facilitate business and investment opportunities, as well as ownership and property rights for foreigners. In this regard, it is acknowledged that the government successfully implemented reforms, measures, and initiatives in line with Saudi Vision 2030 recently.[11] This would encourage foreign workers to invest, establish, or expand their business and own properties in Saudi Arabia. The other measure might be further development of service sectors including entertainment, such as cinema, sport games, so that foreigners spend their money domestically, which would boost economic activities through spillover effects. Fourth, none to very small growth in GEXP in the S2 scenario brings up two policy insights: (i) the share of renewable in total domestic energy consumption (DEN_TOT_KSA) should be increased. The point here is that increased economic activity will demand more energy, resulting in less oil to export. Increasing the share of renewable to meet domestic energy demand will displace more oil from domestic use. The government has already announced its strategy of completely displacing liquid fuels in the electricity generation and making it based on renewable and natural gas only with the shares of 50% and 50% by 2030. This would allow to save more oil that can be either exported as a crude or refined domestically for export purpose, which would bring more foreign exchange reserves, which can be used for covering the government debt or put in human capital, research and development, innovation, and other long-run drivers of productivity. Renewable deployments also will reduce CO_2 emissions, which would help to achieve environmental targets. (ii) weaken the role of government spending in the development of the non-oil sector activities and putting more emphasis on the private sector. Note that this is one of the key targets of SV2030—to increase the private sector's contribution to GDP from 40% to 65% by 2030.

8.2.3 The Effects of Raising the Share of Renewables in Power Generation Mix to 50% by 2030

Saudi Arabian government has very comprehensive strategies aiming at increasing the share of renewables in energy consumption. *Energy and Sustainability strategy* is one of the important streamlines of SV2030, a roadmap for the development of the Kingdom. *The National Renewable Energy Program* (*NREP*) is an important initiative under this strategy with the purpose of increasing the share of renewable energy production, achieve a balance in the mix of local energy sources, and fulfill Saudi Arabia's obligations toward reducing CO_2 emissions.[12] One of the key targets of *NREP* is achieving optimum energy mix to produce electricity.[13] It targets removing liquid fuel from the mix to make it comprised of renewables and gas, each with a share of 50% by 2030.[14] Obviously, the targeted figures make it important to assess

---

[11] https://www.argaam.com/en/article/articledetail/id/1467828

[12] Energy & Sustainability – Vision 2030. https://www.vision2030.gov.sa/thekingdom/explore/energy/?msclkid=0d24312cb65211ecb7e408e39a812fec

[13] https://www.moenergy.gov.sa/en/OurPrograms/Pages/default.aspx

[14] https://www.moenergy.gov.sa/en/OurPrograms/EnergyMix/Pages/default.aspx

their potential economic, energy, and environmental implications. Such a green energy transition brings two main benefits at least: reducing environmental pollution and gaining extra revenues from exporting displaced fossil fuels.

Given that the share of natural gas in the power mix was almost 50% in 2019 (see source in footnote 19), the target of the optimum energy mix is to increase the share of renewable to 50% by 2030. Put differently, the use of crude oil, diesel, and HFO in the electricity generation mix will be replaced by natural gas over time, so that the shares of these liquid fuels in the mix will be zero by 2030. This opens a great avenue to export this replaced liquid fuels to make more foreign exchange reserves or use them domestically (for example, crude can be used to produce refined products). These are the two options to deal with the displaced liquid fuels from the power mix, but the first option might be seen more attractive.

Obviously, increasing the share of renewables to 50% by 2030 requires a large amount of investments among other efforts. Although we have not came across any announced investment figures for this purpose, some media resources mention investing 380 billion SAR by 2030.[15]

In this scenario (S3), we simulate KGEMM to assess economic, energy, and environmental effects of the above given renewable initiative. First, we calculated the needed amount of renewable energy for the power mix. We considered solar given the fact that it is the main renewable energy source in Saudi Arabia so far, as discussed earlier in this book. Solar energy was 0.063 MTOE and 0.075 MTOE in 2019 and 2020, respectively, the Kingdom according to IEA (2021). We forecasted it to be 0.09 MTOE in 2021 assuming the same growth rate of 2020. We also forecasted total electricity production to be 37.74 MTOE in 2030 using different factors including efficiency of fossil fuels and contribution of renewable, i.e., solar energy. Given that it is targeted the half of the total generation will be solar (and the other half will be generated from natural gas) and considering solar energy forecasted for 2021, we extrapolated solar energy between 2022 and 2030 in S3 scenario. Next, we calculated crude oil equivalent of the projected solar energy using the power generation efficiency factor of crude oil in Saudi Arabia from the electricity-related agencies for S3 scenario.[16] Finally, we extrapolated the announced investment figure for renewable energy and deflated the resulted values by investment deflator for 2022–2030. In scenario S3, we assume that domestic oil use (OILUSE) will be decreased by the crude oil values to be displaced and utility investment will be increased by the calculated real investment values. These two are the inputs that differentiates S3 from BaU. Note that we included these two inputs in the S3 as add factors (named OILUSE_ADD and IFU_ADD) rather treating OILUSE and IFU

---

[15] https://www.reuters.com/world/middle-east/saudi-arabia-plans-100-bln-renewables-investment-says-minister-2021-12-13/. https://www.zawya.com/en/projects/saudi-arabia-plans-100bln-renewables-investment-says-minister-ex3w7c6i

[16] The resulted crude oil values, to be displaced, in MTOE, were converted to million barrel per day using the conversion factor of (0.1486*365). This is because we will reduce domestic oil use (OILUSE) by the calculated crude oil values, which will be displaced, and OILUSE in the model is measured in million barrel per day.

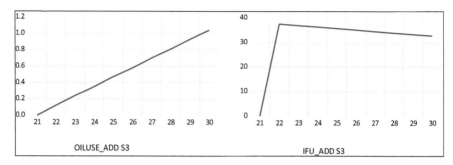

Fig. 8.5 Projected OILUSE_ADD in million barrel per day and IFU_ADD in SAR 2010 billion in S3 scenario, 2021–2030

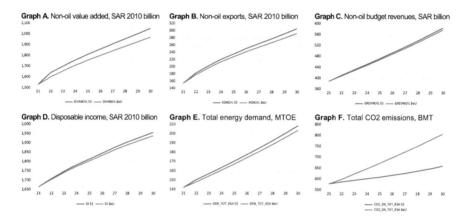

Fig. 8.6 Projections of the selected indicators in S3 and BaU scenarios, 2021–2030

exogenous. This is because both variables are the endogenous variables and hence should change in line with economic activity performance in S3 scenario, but treating them exogenous would ignore this reality. Figure 8.5 illustrates calculated crude oil to be displaced and subtracted from domestic crude oil use, and renewable investment to be added into the utility sector investment.

The figure demonstrates that both variables are zero in 2021. This is to show that our scenario simulation starts in 2022 and this does not mean that either OILUSE or IFU are zero in 2021. The displaced crude oil in S3 (OILUSE_ADD S3) is on average 15% of OILUSE in BaU in 2022–2030. In the same token, additional utility sector investment due to the renewable projects in S3 is on average 112% of IFU in BaU in the same period. These mean that there will be increases in the crude oil export revenues (associated with the displaced crude oil) and increases in utility sector investments in S3 compared BaU. We expect that they will create positive changes in the economy and environment in the S3 scenario. The results of the simulations for the selected variables are illustrated in Fig. 8.6.

We would like to point out some observations from the graphs briefly. First, all the indicators demonstrate growth, whereas CO_2 emissions declines in the S3 scenario compared to the BaU scenario. Second, macroeconomic indicators increase with different paces. Numerically, on average in 2022–2030, GVANOIL S3 and XGNOIL S3 increase by 3.3% and 3.6%, respectively, while GREVNOIL S3 and DI S3 rise by 1.0% and 0.6%, respectively. GVANOIL S3 increases due to the aggregate demand increases in the short-run and due to the supply-side expansions (mainly capital stock but non-oil employment also increased albeit slight) in the long run both caused by injecting displaced crude oil revenues and renewable investments into the economy. GREVNOIL S3 rises because GVANOIL S3, i.e., non-oil economic activities increase. Increases in DI S3 are mainly caused by increases in LABCOMP S3, which grows by 1.0% on average in 2022–2030 compared to LABCOMP BaU. Third, DEN_TOT_KSA S3 increases on average by 2.0% compared to BaU. The increase is caused by the increasing aggregate demand and economic activities. Last, but not least, CO_2_EN_TOT_KSA declines in a growing pace in the S3 scenario compared to the BaU scenario. Numerically, the drop is 1.8% in 2022 and reaches to 18.2% in 2030. Apparently, the declining CO_2 effect of the renewable deployments, which removes crude oil use, outpaces the increasing effect of additional fossil fuel energy consumption due to the expanded economic activities in the S3 scenario.

Acknowledgments The authors are thankful to the former KGEMM team members, Nayef Al-Musehel, Ziyad Alfawzan, Shahad Al-Arenan, Noha Abdel Razek, Waheed Olagunju, Hanadi Al Sunaid and current members, Abdulelah Darandary, Ryan Al Yamani for their contributions to the project. We also thank the participants of the EcoMod 2019 Economic Modeling and Data Science conference, in particular Jean Louis Brillet and Geoffrey Hewings, for their comments. We are also grateful to Amro Elshurafa, Andrea Carlo Bollino, Anwar Gasim, Axel Pierru, John Qualls, Fatih Karanfil, Lester Hunt, and Walid Matar for their expertise on the relationships in the energy block. We are indebted to Abdulaziz Dahlawi for his great help in data processing. Our thanks also go to Chay Allen for editing discussion paper version of this book and Evelyn Simpson for supporting library resources. The authors accept sole responsibility for any errors and omissions. The views expressed in this book are the authors' and do not necessarily represent the views of their affiliated institutions.

Appendixes

Appendix A: KGEMM Methodological Framework and Philosophy

Energy, financial, macroeconomic, econometric, forecasting, and policy models need to perform well in a complex environment with numerous interrelated actions and decisions occurring simultaneously by heterogeneous agents. Modern economies are evolving; there are both gradual and sudden structural changes and shifts due to institutional, technological, financial, international competitiveness, political, social and legal changes. The philosophy underlying the econometric methodology for the development and use of KGEMM is derived from the principles espoused by Haavelmo (1943a, b, 1944) on the theory of reduction, followed by the general-to-specific or LSE tradition developed by many including Hendry and Johansen (2015). Empirical (policy and forecasting) models are supposed to capture these factors in an environment where the data are non-stationary; the degree of misspecification is unknown for the data generation process (DGP), but it is no doubt large. The data available may be inaccurate, a proxy for theoretical constructs and an agent's decision-making criteria, produced with a lag, and subject to revision. The methodology for KGEMM begins with a focus on understanding and replicating the Saudi Arabian macroeconomy and energy.

Model building is an attempt to characterize the properties of observed energy-economic data using simple parametric relationships, which remain reasonably constant over time, account for the findings of previous models, and are interpretable in an energy-economic sense. There are three key aspects in applied empirical model building: *data properties*, including integration and cointegration; *dynamic specification*, including the use of equilibrium correction models; and *model evaluation and model design*.

This Appendix is divided into four sections. The first section lays out the typology of macroeconomic modeling techniques and how their methodologies relate to one another. The second section discusses the econometric philosophy

© The Author(s) 2023
F. J. Hasanov et al., *A Macroeconometric Model for Saudi Arabia*,
SpringerBriefs in Economics, https://doi.org/10.1007/978-3-031-12275-0

underlying KGEMM's methodology. The third section explains the econometric methodology that the KGEMM team uses to develop the behavioral equations of the model. The fourth section details other issues of the model's development and how it can be used for policy analysis.

A Typology of the Macroeconomic Modeling Techniques

Pagan (2003a, b) lays out a useful structure for understanding the empirical modeling frontier and the strategic trade-offs faced by researchers. The frontier defines the tension between building models that are consistent or coherent theoretically and empirically. Below are two quotes from his paper and a slight modification of his frontier diagram.

> Macroeconomic model building has always faced the challenge of how one trades off theoretical and empirical coherence. If one thinks of a curve which summarizes this trade-off, where we locate on it ultimately depends on preferences. But how does one get to this point? Broadly two strategies have been employed. One is to start with statistical models that closely fit the data, and then try to impose a theoretical structure upon them – what we will term the 'bottoms-up' approach. The other is to embellish the framework laid out by some miniature theoretical model – what we will call the 'top-down' approach. The first generation of macro models tended to follow the first strategy, although in many ways the vision of the Cowles Commission was the latter. Recently there has been a return to the original vision, particularly in central banks that have attained independence and have an inflation target.

> I want to start the lecture with a graph. Over the years I have found it useful to think about the activities engaged in by econometric researchers with this representation. It shows the frontier curve that connects up the degree to which our current modelling methods aim to exhibit coherence with the ideas of economic theories and the degree to which they attempt to cohere with the data. At each end of the frontier the coherence is perfect for one of these characteristics and zero for the other. Crudely speaking, we might say that economics has primacy for those modelling strategies located at the top left hand corner while statistics is dominant at the bottom right hand end. For this reason, I will refer to the models at the top end as 'economic' and those at the bottom as 'statistical.' Those along the frontier are hybrid models. Another way of expressing this is to say that, at the bottom we have models that simply summarize the data, and at the top we have models that aim to interpret the data. Along the curve we have work that attempts to trade off the two objectives. When we are inside the frontier it is possible to improve modelling on either one or both dimensions.

Pagan's original diagram has been augmented to illustrate where the computable general equilibrium (CGE) models and mixed complementarity (MCP) models fit on the frontier. They are located in the upper-left corner because their specifications are based solely on theoretical and technological specifications. The data requirements of these models are typically very large and depend on social accounting matrices and input-output tables obtained from 5 year and/or infrequent censuses. Thus, they are a snapshot for a single year. Arbitrary bridge equations have been used when two or more censuses are linked (Fig. A.1).

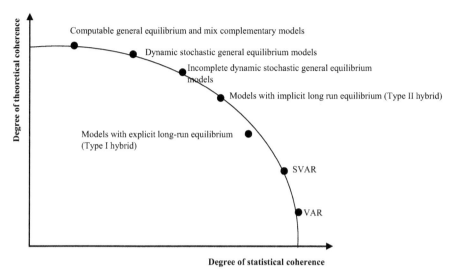

Source: Adapted from Pagan (2003a).

Fig. A.1 Adrian Pagan's "empirical" modeling frontier and research strategy trade-offs. (Source: Adapted from Pagan (2003a))

Pagan notes that "economic" models are popular in academia and are most relevant for "storytelling," while "statistical" models are mostly relevant to approximate data, and hence are widely used in predictions/forecasting. Pagan further states that models involved in policy decision making need to bring together a degree of theoretical and empirical coherence. In other words, the models used for policy purposes should be neither economic nor statistical; they should be hybrid models based on equilibrium correction models (ECMs). Other studies also discuss the relevance of the hybrid models for policy decision making (see, e.g., Hara et al. 2009 inter alia).

Econometric Philosophy Underlying KGEMM

Haavelmo (1943a, b, 1944) provides the first rigorous treatment of causality. His fundamental contributions to understanding the formulation and identification of causal models linked economic theory and econometrics. Yet their reception and interpretation within the econometrics community is still debated along the trade-offs of theoretical coherence and empirical coherence suggested by Pagan (2003a). Table A.1 illustrates the different approaches between economists and statisticians. The current dominant orthodoxy can be summarized as economic analysis that formulates the correct (theoretical) model and econometrics, which merely has the task of estimating the parameters of interest from the best available data. This

Table A.1 Approaches and/or methodology for research

Economists	Statisticians
Formulate an economically well-specified model as the empirical model.	Formulate a statistically well-specified model for the data based on the DGP.
Apply statistical techniques to estimate the parameters.	Analyze the statistical model to answer the economic questions of interest.
Methodology for research	
Use statistics passively as a tool to obtain derived results.	The statistical model is taken seriously and used actively as a means of analyzing the underlying DGP of the economic phenomenon.

approach is wrong on several fronts. There is frequently no one correct theory, alternative theories can be observationally equivalent, theoretical models treat dynamics in an ad hoc manner, and the available data may not be the same as the theoretical constructs.

Haavelmo recommended applying the general principles of analyzing statistical models instead of the economists' methods. The applied econometrician must use a probability approach to their craft. He suggested they should start by assuming a probability structure to the data. This is effectively conjecturing the existence of a *DGP* and taking the data properties issue seriously. A critical feature of the DGP's components is that it can include competing theories. Thus, in the end the researcher discovers if one theory dominates the other(s) or different aspects seem relevant, leading to theoretical and empirical discoveries.

In reality, the DGP is unknown. The general principles suggest an iterative approach or progressive research strategy.

- Conjecture the DGP.
- Develop the associated probability theory.
- Use theory for modeling the empirical evidence.
- Revise the starting point when the results do not match consistently.

The approach to deriving a model, or the context of model discovery, is based on the theory of reduction. This explains the origin of empirical models based on reduction steps or operations, which are conducted on the DGP. Ideally, this implies the application of statistical models instead of the researcher imposing theoretical models based on systems of equations.

A second area Haavelmo cautioned empirical modelers about was that measured or available data from official sources are often far from the definitions of the true variables. Moreover, even if they were close, this would not necessarily mean that they correspond to the variables from economic theory. For example, when modeling private consumption what is the relevant period for making decisions regarding expenditures on services, non-durables, and durables? Is that consistent with how the data are collected?

Data from official sources depend on

- The measurement system.
- Frequency of collection or data intervals.
- Discrepancy with decision-making intervals.
- Sample length.
- Survey of samples versus population.
- Data revisions—accuracy of preliminary estimates.
- Seasonality adjustments.
- Timeliness.
- Level of aggregation.
- Protection of confidential personal and industry information.

In 1989, Haavelmo stated:

> The basis of econometrics, the economic theories that we have been led to believe in by our forefathers, were perhaps not good enough. It is quite obvious that if the theories we build to simulate actual economic life are not sufficiently realistic, that is, if the data we get to work on in practice are not produced in a way theory suggests, then it is rather meaningless to confront actual observations with relations that describe something else.

The purpose of empirical investigations is to test a theory. A prerequisite for valid inferences about the theory is that there must be a close correspondence between measured variables and the true variables. In the words of Haavelmo:

> It is then natural to adopt the convention that a theory is called true or false according as the hypotheses implied are true or false, when tested against the data chosen as the 'true' variables. Then we may speak interchangeably about testing hypotheses or testing theories.

Data issues will persist but are likely to improve as statistical agencies build up their capacity, processes, and delivery of data. Despite the problems in collecting and measuring macroeconomic data, the information is valuable. It can help in decision-making by governments, firms, individuals regarding commerce, and public finance. Theoretical arguments are needed to understand the relationships among variables regardless of the weak to poor correspondences that exist between the theoretical variables and the measured data. The cautions about realism in the data and the value of empirical data are serious but may be framed in terms of the signal-to-noise ratio in the data.

Hendry (2018) emphasizes that the debate can be addressed by nesting the theory-driven and data-driven approaches. This enables the researcher to retain insights from theory while exploring the empirical interactions when evaluating the theoretical and data evidence. Moreover, the combination of a clearly mapped out scientific method with advances in computing power and statistical programs, *Autometrics,* in particular provide econometricians the ability to distinguish between correlation and causation in developing empirical models. *Autometrics* is written to follow the theory of reduction through the general-to-specific approach of model testing and evaluation.

Models are designed to satisfy selection criteria through hypothesis tests. These can be from explicit theory and/or "long-run ratios." The reduction from a general model to a specific one relates to no loss of relevant information. Starting from a specific model and then branching out to address econometric issues like serial correlation and dynamics produces path-dependent models. The fundamental concepts from econometrics are natural vehicles for the theory of reduction and correspond to no loss of relevant information.

Consider:

1. Parameters of interest.
2. Innovation.
3. Autocorrelation.
4. Exogeneity.
5. Invariance.
6. Identification.
7. Granger non-causality.
8. Common factors.
9. Cointegration.

All of these concepts are related to the evaluation of information and the formation of null hypotheses for diagnostic testing, for model evaluation and design criteria for model selection. The reduction process is inherently iterative: Many reduction paths could be considered, which may lead to different terminal specifications. Retain those models which survive. If multiple models survive "testimation," then a new general model is formed. In that case, conduct encompassing tests between these (possibly non-nested) specifications. If no single specific model is chosen, selection can be done by information criterion and sub-sample reliability.

The reduction approach is based on *explicit model design criteria*. This is based on an approximation of the local data generating process (LDGP). The LDGP is a reduction of the DGP that should include all possible relevant variables. Hypothesis tests examine the information losses from testing reductions. These can include tests for autocorrelation, heteroscedasticity, omitted variables, multicollinearity, and non-constancy. The objective is to find a congruent model.

This is superior to "symptomatology" approach in traditional econometrics where the theoretical model is directly imposed on data. The approach is invalid: there is no unique alternative to any null. Often, following adjustments of the linear model assumptions, the outcome is path dependent.

The *reductions* can be organized into 11 stages:

1. Data transformation and aggregation.
2. Parameters of interest—are introduced by the transformations and identifiable.
3. Data partition is probably the most fundamental determinant of empirical modeling's success or not.
4. Marginalization without loss of information.
5. Sequential factorization for creating the innovation process.
6. Mapping to I(0) or stationary space for valid inference.
7. Conditional factorization into "endogenous" and "exogenous" or non-modelled variables.

8. Constancy of parameters and models.
9. Lag truncation.
10. Functional form or how can the DGP be approximated through model design criteria.
11. Derive the local data generating process (LDGP) as a reduction of the DGP or nested within it. The properties of the LDGP are given or explained by the reduction process.

Congruency
We often read a model is (non) congruent. This is an important concept in our econometric philosophy and methodology.

Empirical models are at best approximations of the true data-generating process. The econometric model should exhibit certain desirable properties that render it a valid representation of the true DGP. Hendry (1995) and Mizon (1995) suggest the following six criteria according to the LSE methodology:

1. There are identifiable structures in the empirical model that are interpretable in light of economic theory.
2. The residuals must be white noise for the model to be a valid simplification of the DGP.
3. The empirical model must be admissible on accurate observations. For example, nominal interest rates and prices cannot be negative.
4. The conditioning variables are at least weakly exogenous for the parameters of interest in the model. Forecasting models require strong exogeneity, while policy models require super exogeneity.
5. The parameters of interest must be constant over time and remain invariant to certain classes of interventions. This relates to the purpose of the model in the previous criteria.
6. The model must be able to explain the results from rival models; it is able to encompass them.

The Econometric Methodology KGEMM Uses

The theory of reduction is operationalized through the general-to-specific approach advocated by Campos et al. (2005), and Hendry (1993, 1995, 2000). The approach begins with a general hypothesis about the relevant explanatory variables and dynamic process (i.e., the lag structure of the model). The general hypothesis is considered acceptable to all schools of thought. This is referred to as the general unrestricted model or GUM. The autoregressive distributed lag (ADL) model begins with a regression of the variable of interest, y_t, on lagged values of itself and current and lagged values of the explanatory variables, z_t.

$$y_t = a_0 + \sum_{i=1}^{p} a_i y_{t-i} + \sum_{j=0}^{m} b_j z_{t-j} + \varepsilon_t$$

The error term is assumed to be white noise. In this case, the model is referred to as an ADL (p, m) because it contains p lagged dependent variables and m lagged explanatory variables. In the single equation, we are implicitly assuming a conditional model where the z variables are assumed to be weakly exogenous. The intercept can be expanded to include other deterministic variables like seasonal dummy variables, trend, shift dummy variables, and one-off effects. This single equation representation can be generalized to a vector autoregression.

The model is then narrowed by testing for simplifications to/or restrictions on the general model. The final or conditional model attempts to characterize the properties of the sample data in simple parametric relationships, which remain reasonably constant over time. It also accounts for the findings of previous models and is interpretable economically and financially. Rather than using *econometrics* to illustrate theory, the goal is to "discover" which alternative theoretical views are tenable and test them scientifically.

At this point, we have not made any assumptions on the order of integration for the y and z variables. The later assumptions can be evaluated in specifications of the model in order to avoid the problems of nonsense and spurious regressions.

Before estimating a GUM of an ADL or vector autoregressive regression (VAR) system, the first step involves examining the time series properties of the individual data series. We look at patterns and trends in the data and test for stationarity and the order of integration. Second, we form the GUM of the ADL equation or VAR. This step involves testing for the appropriate lag length of the system, including residual diagnostic tests and tests for model/system stability. Third, we examine the equation or system for potential cointegration relationship(s). Data series which are integrated of the same order may be combined to form economically meaningful series which are integrated of lower order. The cointegrating relations are tested for interpretation as an equilibrium correction mechanism. In the case of a system, we test for weak exogeneity. Based on these results, a conditional ECM of the endogenous variables may be specified and further reduction tests are performed and economic hypotheses tested.

There are two types of testing. The first is model evaluation, which is somewhat "mechanistic." These tests are performed in the context of testing for model congruency with respect to the data and economic theory. Criteria represent the null hypotheses and the associated test statistics are used to test the hypotheses. Model evaluation tests should be interpreted as destructive activity on the model. They are necessary (not sufficient) conditions for inference testing, forecasting, and policy analysis. An example would include the appropriate lag length to use in capturing the dynamics of the relationships between the variables.

The second type of testing is referred to as model design. After a statistical model has been estimated, these tests are source of value added or "art" conducted by the econometrician. Examples include hypotheses for unit elasticities, relative price elasticities, and symmetric responses are part of the toolkit or pallet.

Autometrics Doornik (2009) implements the general-to-specific modeling algorithm following on the program by Hendry (2001). There are five basic steps:

1. Specification of the GUM by the empirical modeler.
2. Tests for misspecification usually through residual diagnostics.
3. Begin model reduction process. Investigation of possible paths for variable selection. Elimination of "irrelevant" variables.
4. Test terminal models or paths for congruency.
5. Evaluate terminal models for the final model(s) through encompassing tests.

Table A.2 organizes the arguments against data mining by class on the left and refutations on the right.

There have been four generations in the evolution of this argument:

1. The general-to-specific approach performed manually. LSE or Hendry prior to 1999.
2. The algorithmic approach of Hoover and Perez (1999) was an attempt to systematize the LSE approach. This was based on a mixed empirical Monte Carlo framework.
3. Hendry and Krolzig (1999) PcGets.
4. Doornik (2009) *Autometrics*.

These mechanistic models appear to be immune to the standard criticisms. However, they do require that the initial general model GUM is appropriate. Also, they, PcGets and Autometrics, do not recognize the possible data transformations. These are model design issues where the applied econometrician provides value added before and/or after the reduction program, *Autometrics* is run.

Table A.2 Data mining: Four pejorative senses and four refutations

Class or sense of data mining	Counter evidence
1. *Repeated testing* Select spurious regressors to maximize t-ratios. $\Rightarrow t - ratios \downarrow, \sigma \uparrow as\ T\uparrow$	*Recursive estimation and additional data* We can use larger critical values $\Rightarrow t - ratios \uparrow, \sigma\ remains\ constant\ as\ T\uparrow$
2. *Data independence* $y = f(x)$ *and corr*(x, z) $\neq 0 \Rightarrow y$ *and z are correlated*	*Super exogeneity and encompassing* Models are empirically constant The parameters relating to models are empirically constant The parameters relating y to z, even if the $corr(x, z)$ *is changing* Thus we can include x and z in our models
1. *Corroboration* z's are chosen for "sensible" coefficient estimates. There could be omitted variables?	*Gets and autometrics: encompassing* General-to-specific modeling
2. *Overparameterization* Overfitting and degrees of freedom issues	*High information content of data* *Autometrics* and *gets* can detect this

The model's econometric specification, especially ECMs, are estimated using the principles outlined above employing the *Autometrics* program in *Gets* module of *OxMetrics*. The software is designed to mimic the principles of general-to-specific in testing. Final equations will be transferred/coded into EViews to use in model building. The program will cut the equation development and testing time to a fraction of what it otherwise would be. The software is designed to follow the scientific method underlying the theory of reduction, taking advantage of advances in computing power and econometric techniques.

Other Issues of Model Development and Application for Policy Analysis

Endogeneity

As it is discussed in the econometric literature, although the OLS estimation of the long-run parameters is super consistent, it may suffer from bias issue and inferences based on them are invalid since the limiting distribution of the estimation is dependent on nuisance parameters (see, e.g., Phillips and Loretan 1991; Pesaran and Shin 1999). The bias issue, especially the simultaneity bias, caused by endogeneity between dependent variable and explanatory variable as they can be jointly determined is widely concerned in economics. Fortunately, the methods mentioned fourth section that we employ to estimate long-run relationships account for this issue and hence, render the endogeneity issue being less important (e.g., see discussion in Pesaran and Shin 1999; Stock 1987; Phillips and Durlauf 1986). In this regard, it appears that one may prefer to build and simulate a macroeconometric model based on long-run equations, i.e., cointegrated relationships, as it effectively rules out the endogeneity issue (for such approach, see Weyerstrass et al. 2018; Khan and ud Din 2011; Weyerstrass and Neck 2007; Musila 2002).

As for the endogeneity issue in the short-run estimations, one can consider instrumental variable (IV) estimations such as Two-stage OLS (TSLS). However, the literature on econometric modeling discusses that the gain from IV estimations is very little compared to those from OLS on many occasions (e.g., see Johansen and Magnussen 1996; Fair 1994, 2004; Lin 1994; Christ 1951). Additionally, as Bradley et al. (1995) discuss among other studies, the gain from IV estimations may be very limited when sample span is small. Moreover, it is a well-known issue that it is quite difficult to find the right instruments. In earlier KGEMM versions, we estimated the short-run equations using different IV methods (such as TSLS, Generalized Method of Moments, Limited Information Maximum Likelihood, and K-class). We have noticed that the difference between the coefficients estimated from IV methods and those from the OLS were very small in many cases as it is discussed in the literature (e.g., see Johansen and Magnussen 1996 for the Saudi case). Therefore, we did not use IV methods in estimating the short-run relationships in this fifth version of KGEMM, but it may be considered in future version.

Invariance and the Lucas Critique

The 'Lucas critique' is a criticism of econometric policy evaluation procedures that fail to recognize that optimal decision rules of economic agents vary systematically with changes in policy. In particular, it criticizes using estimated statistical relationships from past data to forecast the effects of adopting a new policy, because the estimated regression coefficients are not invariant and will change along with agents' decision rules in response to a new policy. A classic example of this fallacy was the erroneous inference that a regression of inflation on unemployment (the Phillips curve) represented a structural trade-off for policy to exploit (Ljungqvist 2008).

This brief note describes what the Lucas critique implies and testing for it. The fundamental point and Lucas himself agrees with is that the Lucas critique is a possibility theorem; it is not a truism. The lack of invariance in the parameters of a conditional model can arise from multiple sources.

The basis for the Lucas critique can be illustrated with a simple relationship. In the example below, consider the x variable as a policy variable and y as the variable that policy is trying to influence.

$$y_t = \beta_0 \, x_t + u_t$$

Assume this is estimated by OLS. The properties of the disturbance term depend on the data generating process (DGP). The simple relationship is a special case of a more general model. For example, it could have come from a first order Gaussian VAR for the two time series.

$$\begin{pmatrix} y_t \\ x_t \end{pmatrix} = \begin{pmatrix} \pi_{10} \\ \pi_{20} \end{pmatrix} + \begin{pmatrix} \pi_{11} & \pi_{12} \\ \pi_{21} & \pi_{22} \end{pmatrix} \begin{pmatrix} y_{t-1} \\ x_{t-1} \end{pmatrix} + \begin{pmatrix} \varepsilon_{yt} \\ \varepsilon_{xt} \end{pmatrix}$$

The joint distribution for error terms is white noise with a mean of zero and possible non-zero variance-covariance matrix. This means there is no autocorrelation.

$$\begin{pmatrix} \varepsilon_{yt} \\ \varepsilon_{xt} \end{pmatrix} \sim N \left(\mathbf{0}, \begin{pmatrix} \sigma_y^2 & \sigma_{xy} \\ \sigma_{xy} & \sigma_x^2 \end{pmatrix} \mid y_{t-1}, x_{t-1} \right)$$

The simple relationship above given the Gaussian distribution and the assumption that the conditional distribution for y_t conditional on x_t is given by

$$y_t = \beta_0^* \, E[x_t \mid I_{t-1}] + \varepsilon_t$$

$$x_t = \pi_{22} x_{t-1} + \varepsilon_{xt}$$

Here the original unrestricted VAR model has been transformed into a conditional model in the first equation and a marginal model in the second equation. This is just an application of Bayes' theorem. The series x is stationary implying that

$-1 < \pi_{22} < 1$. Recall the terms ε_t and ε_{xt} are independent white noise processes. The term $\mathcal{I}_{t-1}$ denotes the information set available to form rational expectations. In this example, the notation can be rewritten as $E[x_t | I_{t-1}] = E[x_t | x_{t-1}]$. The conditional expectation for the disturbance given current x_t is zero, $E[\varepsilon_t | x_t] = 0$. Then y_t is a normal variable with a mean:

$$E[y_t | x_{t-1}] = \pi_{22} \beta_0^* x_{t-1}.$$

Moreover x_t is a normal variable with mean.

$$E[x_t | x_{t-1}] = \pi_{22} x_{t-1}.$$

Then the conditional mean of y_t given x_t is given by

$$E[y_t | x_t] \equiv \mu_{Y|X} = \beta_0^* x_t + E[u_t | x_t]$$

The last term is not equal to zero, because x_t must be correlated with u_t due to

$$u_t = \varepsilon_t - \beta_0^* \varepsilon_{xt}$$

And the two equations from the conditional distribution above. The expectation for u_t given x_t can be written as

$$E[u_t | x_t] = -\beta_0^* \, E[\varepsilon_{xt} | x_t] \; since \; E[\varepsilon_t | x_t] = 0 \; by \; assumption \; from \; the \; DGP.$$

Given the assumption of normality, there is a regression function:

$$E[\varepsilon_{xt} | x_t] = \delta x_t \; where \; \delta = \frac{E[\varepsilon_{xt} x_t]}{Var[x_t]} = \frac{\sigma_{ext}^2}{Var[x_t]}$$

The numerator in the last term is the variance of ε_{xt}. The stationarity condition implies the variance of x is defined.

$$Var[x_t] = \frac{\sigma_{ext}^2}{1 - \pi_{22}^2}$$

Therefore the regression coefficient is just $\delta = (1 - \pi_{22}^2)$.

The conditional expectation for y_t when the DGP is characterized by rational expectations becomes

$$\mu_{Y|X} = \beta_0^* x_t - \beta_0^* (1 - \pi_{22}^2) x_t = \beta_0^* \pi_{22}^2 x_t$$

When regressing y_t on x_t by OLS the estimated coefficient $\widehat{\beta}_0$ is always consistent. However, in this case we see that the coefficient in this example is not a single parameter, but $\beta_0^* \pi_{22}^2$. Thus we obtain

$$plim\left(\widehat{\beta}_0\right) = \beta_0^* \pi_{22}^2 < \beta_0^*, because - 1 < \pi_{22} < 1.$$

The essence of the Lucas critique is that any change in the formation of expectation, represented here by π_{22}, is predicted to lead to a change in the $plim\left(\widehat{\beta}_0\right).\beta_0^* is$ *often referred to as a deep structural parameter. This implies that the estimator for* β_0^* *will not yield the correct conclusions about how a policy change in* x_t *affects* y_t.

This implies that the initial OLS parameter β_0 is not invariant to changes in expectations, π_{22}. Therefore, x_t is not super-exogenous when the DGP is characterized by rational expectations in the Gaussian VAR above. However, this is not true, β_0^* is invariant to changes in x_t under the assumption of the conditional distribution for y_t conditional on x_t as written in the two-equation system.

As mentioned above, the important point is that the Lucas critique is a possibility theorem; it is not a truism. The lack of invariance in the parameters of a conditional model can arise from multiple sources. Pitfalls like omitted variables and misspecified dynamics can lead to the lack of invariance even when instrumental variables/generalized method of moments (IV/GMM) estimation techniques are employed. The critical point is the exact set of assumptions. Consider a rational expectations model for planned consumption.

Empirical Testing for the Lucas Critique

Engle and Hendry (1993) and Engle et al. (1983) developed tests for invariance and super exogeneity. Their approach checks whether the predicted invariance occurs in the conditional model following a significant structural break in the marginal part of the model.

In the conditional plus marginal model considered above, if there is a structural break in the marginal model for x_t, then it is likely that one (or more) parameters in the conditional model for y_t will change around the break. But this does not follow logically. A lack of change or invariance in the parameters for the specific break being tested could be as a result of a true structural break. Recursive tests for stability of the conditional and marginal models and parameters should have been conducted previously.

Formal testing can be performed by examining the stability of the marginal model. Structural breaks (impulses, shifts, and/or trends) can be estimated using *Autometrics*. Impulse and step dummies are introduced into the conditional model to test for super exogeneity. The null hypothesis of invariance is that these do not add explanatory power. An F-test or Wald test is used. If the null hypothesis is rejected, the Lucas critique is "confirmed." But, failure to reject the null does not imply that it is true. Expectations are still important except in this case, where the impact is not that strong. The specification of rational expectations in the model is too focused. It does not reveal or capture how expectations are formed and transmitted through the model.

Favero and David Hendry (1992) and Ericsson and Irons (1994, 1995) provide reviews of the literature on testing for the Lucas critique. Rudebusch (2005), among others, also shows the empirical unimportance of the Lucas critique to monetary policy. Moreover, Ericsson and Irons (1994, 1995) conclude that virtually no evidence exists that empirically substantiates the Lucas critique. They also empirically refute the critique using a super exogeneity test. The mnemonics and descriptions of the variables used in the fifth version of KGEMM are documented below in Appendix B.

Appendix B: KGEMM Variables

#	Mnemonic	Description and unit
1.	AGRLANDSH	Agricultural land, % of land area
2.	C_RATIO	Value Added Tax Collection Efficiency Ratio
3.	CAPAGR	Capital stock, non-energy private excluding private dwellings,agriculture, and forestry, real, Million SAR at 2010 prices
4.	CAPCON	Capital stock, non-energy private excluding private dwellings, construction, real, Million SAR at 2010 prices
5.	CAPDIS	Capital stock, non-energy private excluding private dwellings, retail, wholesale, hotels, and catering, real, Million SAR at 2010 prices
6.	CAPFIBU	Capital stock, non-energy private excluding private dwellings, financial and business services, real, Million SAR at 2010 prices
7.	CAPGOV	Capital stock, non-energy private excluding private dwellings, government, real, Million SAR at 2010 prices
8.	CAPMANNO	Capital stock, non-energy private excluding private dwellings, manufacturing excluding petroleum refining, real, Million SAR at 2010 prices
9.	CAPMANNOLPC	Capital stock, non-energy private excluding private dwellings, manufacturing excluding petroleum refining and petrochemicals, real, Million SAR at 2010 prices
10.	CAPNOIL	Capital stock, in non-oil sector, real, Million SAR at 2010 prices
11.	CAPOILREF	Capital stock, in Oil Refinery, real, Million SAR at 2010 prices
12.	CAPOTHS	Capital stock, non-energy private excluding private dwellings, other services, real, Million SAR at 2010 prices
13.	CAPPETCH	Capital stock for Petrochemical, real, Million SAR at 2010 prices
14.	CAPU	Capital stock, non-energy private excluding private dwellings, utilities, real, Million SAR at 2010 prices
15.	CCOIL_IND	Consumption of Crude Oil, Industry, Million SAR
16.	CDD	Cooling Degree Days

(continued)

(continued)

#	Mnemonic	Description and unit
17.	CDIS_IND	Consumption of Diesel, Industry, nominal, Million SAR
18.	CDIS_TRA	Consumption of Diesel, Transport, nominal, Million SAR
19.	CELE_AGR	Consumption of Electricity, Agriculture, nominal, Million SAR
20.	CELE_COMM	Consumption of Electricity, Commercial, nominal, Million SAR
21.	CELE_GOV	Consumption of Electricity, Government, nominal, Million SAR
22.	CELE_IND	Consumption of Electricity, Industry, nominal, Million SAR
23.	CELE_RES	Consumption of Electricity, Residential, nominal, Million SAR
24.	CEN_TOT_CGA	Consumption of Total Energy, Commercial, Government, Agriculture, nominal, Million SAR
25.	CEN_TOT_IND	Consumption of Total Energy, Industry, nominal, Million SAR
26.	CEN_TOT_KSA	Consumption of Total Energy, KSA, nominal, Million SAR
27.	CEN_TOT_RES	Consumption of Total Energy, Residential, nominal, Million SAR
28.	CEN_TOT_TRA	Consumption of Total Energy, Transport, nominal, Million SAR
29.	CGAS_TRA	Consumption of Gasoline, Transport, nominal, Million SAR
30.	CHFO_IND	Consumption of HFO, Industry, nominal, Million SAR
31.	CKER_RES	Consumption of Kerosene, Residential, nominal, Million SAR
32.	CKER_TRA	Consumption of Kerosene, Transport, nominal, Million SAR
33.	CLPG_RES	Consumption of LPG, Residential, nominal, Million SAR
34.	CNGA_IND	Consumption of Natural Gas, Industry, nominal, Million SAR
35.	CNGA_TOT	Consumption of Total Natural Gas, nominal, Million SAR
36.	CO2_COIL_IND	CO_2 Emissions from Crude Oil Consumption in Industry, Metric tons
37.	CO2_COIL_U	CO_2 Emissions, Crude Oil, Utility, Metric tons
38.	CO2_DIS_IND	CO_2 Emissions from Diesel Consumption in Industry, Metric tons
39.	CO2_DIS_TRA	CO_2 Emissions from Diesel Consumption in Transport, Metric tons
40.	CO2_DIS_U	CO_2 Emissions, Diesel, Utility, Metric tons
41.	CO2_ELE_AGR	CO_2 Emissions from Electricity Consumption in Agriculture Sector, Metric tons
42.	CO2_ELE_COMM	CO_2 Emissions from Electricity Consumption in Commercial Sector, Metric tons
43.	CO2_ELE_GOV	CO_2 Emissions from Electricity Consumption in Government Sector, Metric tons
44.	CO2_ELE_IND	CO_2 Emissions from Electricity Consumption in Industry, Metric tons
45.	CO2_ELE_KSA_PFM	CO_2 Emissions, Electricity Generation Fuel Mix, Utility, Metric tons

(continued)

(continued)

#	Mnemonic	Description and unit
46.	CO_2_ELE_OTH	CO_2 Emissions from Electricity Consumption in Other, Metric tons
47.	CO_2_ELE_RES	CO_2 Emissions from Electricity Consumption in Residential Sector, Metric tons
48.	CO_2_ELE_STOT_KSA	CO_2 Emissions from Electricity Supply, Total Kingdom, Metric tons
49.	CO_2_EN_TOT_CGAO	CO_2 Emissions from Total Energy Use in Commercial, Government, Agriculture, and Other, Metric tons
50.	CO_2_EN_TOT_IND	CO_2 Emissions from Total Energy Use in Industry, Metric tons
51.	CO_2_EN_TOT_KSA	CO_2 Emissions from Total Energy Use, KSA, Metric tons
52.	CO_2_EN_TOT_RES	CO_2 Emissions from Total Energy Use, Residential, Metric tons
53.	CO_2_EN_TOT_TRA	CO_2 Emissions from Total Energy Use in Transport, Metric tons
54.	CO_2_GAS_TRA	CO_2 Emissions from Gasoline Consumption in Transport, Metric tons
55.	CO_2_HFO_IND	CO_2 Emissions from HFO Consumption in Industry, Metric tons
56.	CO_2_HFO_U	CO_2 Emissions from HFO Consumption in Utility, Metric tons
57.	CO_2_KER_RES	CO_2 Emissions from Kerosene type Jet Fuel Consumption in Residential Sector, Metric tons
58.	CO_2_KER_TRA	CO_2 Emissions from Kerosene type Jet Fuel Consumption in Transport, Metric tons
59.	CO_2_LPG_RES	CO_2 Emissions from LPG Consumption in Residential Sector, Metric tons
60.	CO_2_NGA_IND	CO_2 Emissions from Natural Gas Consumption in Industry, Metric tons
61.	CO_2_NGA_U	CO_2 Emissions from Natural Gas Consumption in Utility, Metric tons
62.	CO_2_OILUSE	CO_2 Emissions from Domestic Oil Use, Metric tons
63.	CONS	Consumption, private, real, Million SAR at 2010 prices
64.	CONS_Z	Consumption, private, nominal, Million SAR
65.	COTH_IND	Consumption of Other Energy in Industry, nominal, Million SAR
66.	CPI	Consumer price index, Index 2010 = 100
67.	CPI_USA	United States - Consumer price index, Index, 2010 = 100 (rebased from 1982/84 = 10)
68.	CPIART	Consumer price index, recreation & culture, Index 2010 = 100
69.	CPIART_W	Weight for CPIART. It takes 0.035 for 1970-2012 and 0.034 for 2013-2020 as reported by GaStat
70.	CPICLOTH	Consumer price index, clothing, Index 2010 = 100
71.	CPICLOTH_W	Weight for CPICLOTH. It takes 0.084 for 1970–2012 and 0.062 for 2013–2020 as reported by GaStat

(continued)

(continued)

#	Mnemonic	Description and unit
72.	CPICOMM	Consumer price index, communication, Index 2010 = 100
73.	CPICOMM_W	Weight for CPICOMM. It takes 0.081 for 1970-2012 and 0.085 for 2013–2020 as reported by GaStat
74.	CPIEDU	Consumer price index, education, Index 2010 = 100
75.	CPIEDU_W	Weight for CPIEDU. It takes 0.027 for 1970–2012 and 0.042 for 2013–2020 as reported by GaStat
76.	CPIFOOD	Consumer price index, food & beverages, Index 2010 = 100
77.	CPIFOOD_W	Weight for CPIFOOD. It takes 0.217 for 1970-2012 and 0.188 for 2013–2020 as reported by GaStat
78.	CPIHEAL	Consumer price index, health, Index 2010 = 100
79.	CPIHEAL_W	Weight for CPIHEAL. It takes 0.026 for 1970-2012 and 0.023 for 2013–2020 as reported by GaStat
80.	CPIHH	Consumer price index, household items, Index 2010 = 100
81.	CPIHH_W	Weight for CPIHH. It takes 0.091 for 1970–2012 and 0.085 for 2013–2020 as reported by GaStat
82.	CPIHTL	Consumer price index, hotels & restaurants, Index 2010 = 100
83.	CPIHTL_W	Weight for CPIHTL. It takes 0.056 for 1970–2012 and 0.065 for 2013–2020 as reported by GaStat
84.	CPIMISC	Consumer price index, other, Index 2010 = 100
85.	CPIMISC_W	Weight for CPIMISC. It takes 0.069 for 1970–2012 and 0.057 for 2013–2020 as reported by GaStat
86.	CPITOBC	Consumer price index, tobacco, Index 2010 = 100
87.	CPITOBC_W	Weight for CPITOBC. It takes 0.005 for 1970–2012 and 0.007 for 2013–2020 as reported by GaStat
88.	CPITRA	Consumer price index, transport, Index 2010 = 100
89.	CPITRA_W	Weight for CPITRA. It takes 0.104 for 1970–2012 and 0.100 for 2013–2020 as reported by GaStat
90.	CPIU	Consumer price index, Housing, Water, Electricity, Gas and Other Fuels, 2010 = 100
91.	CPIU_W	Weight for CPIU. It takes 0.205 for 1970–2012 and 0.253 for 2013–2020 as reported by GaStat
92.	DB0910	Blip dummy variable, positive unity value in 2009 and negative unity value in 2010, zero value otherwise
93.	DB1617	Blip dummy variable, positive unity value in 2016 and negative unity value in 2017, zero value otherwise
94.	DBT2010	Dummy variable, take 1, 2, . . . , 10 for 2010, 2011, . . ., 2019 and zero value otherwise
95.	DBT2015	Dummy variable, take 1,2,.., 5 for 2015, 2016, . . ., 2019 and zero value otherwise
96.	DBT2016	Dummy variable, take 1,2,..,4 for 2016, 2017, . . ., 2019 and zero value otherwise
97.	DBT2017	Dummy variable, take 1,2,3 for 2017, 2018, 2019 and zero value otherwise
98.	DBT2018	Dummy variable, take 1,2, for 2018 and 2019 and zero value otherwise

(continued)

(continued)

#	Mnemonic	Description and unit
99.	DCOIL_IND	Demand for Crude Oil in Industry, MTOE
100.	DCOIL_U	Demand for Crude Oil in Utility, MTOE
101.	DD	Demand Deposits, nominal, Million SAR
102.	DDIS_IND	Demand for Diesel in Industry, MTOE
103.	DDIS_TRA	Demand for Diesel in Transport Sector, MTOE
104.	DDIS_U	Demand for Diesel in Utility, MTOE
105.	DEBT_GOV	General Government Debt, nominal, Million SAR
106.	DEBTG_GOV	General Government Gross Debt, nominal, Million SAR
107.	DELE_AGR	Demand for electricity in Agricultural sector, MTOE
108.	DELE_COMM	Demand for electricity in Commercial services, MTOE
109.	DELE_EOU	Electricity Energy Industry Own Use, MTOE
110.	DELE_GOV	Demand for electricity in Public (government) services, MTOE
111.	DELE_IND	Demand for electricity in Industrial sector, MTOE
112.	DELE_OTH	Demand for electricity, Other, MTOE
113.	DELE_RES	Demand for electricity in Residential sector, MTOE
114.	DELE_TOT_KSA	Demand for Electricity, Total, Kingdom, MTOE
115.	DEN_TOT_CGA	Demand for Electricity, Total, Commercial, Public and Agriculture, MTOE
116.	DEN_TOT_IND	Demand for Energy, Total, Industry, MTOE
117.	DEN_TOT_KSA	Demand for Energy, Total, Kingdom, MTOE
118.	DEN_TOT_RES	Demand for Energy, Total, Residential, MTOE
119.	DEN_TOT_TRA	Demand for Energy, Total, Transport, MTOE
120.	DEOTH_TRA	Other energy demand in transportation, MTOE
121.	DETH_IND_NEU	Demand for Ethane in Industry Sector, Non-Energy Use, MTOE
122.	DGAS_TRA	Demand for Motor Gasoline excl. biofuels in Transport, MTOE
123.	DHFO_IND	Demand for HFO in Industry Sector, MTOE
124.	DHFO_U	Demand for HFO in Utility, MTOE
125.	DI	Disposable Income, real, Millions SAR at 2010 prices
126.	DI_T_Z	Total Disposable Income, nominal, Million SAR
127.	DI_Z	Private Disposable Income, Millions SAR
128.	DIS_CAPAGR	Discrepancy term for the identity of CAPAGR
129.	DIS_CAPCON	Discrepancy term for the identity of CAPCON
130.	DIS_CAPDIS	Discrepancy term for the identity of CAPDIS
131.	DIS_CAPFIBU	Discrepancy term for the identity of CAPFIBU
132.	DIS_CAPGOV	Discrepancy term for the identity of CAPGOV
133.	DIS_CAPMANNOLPC	Discrepancy term for the identity of CAPMANNOLPC
134.	DIS_CAPNOIL	Discrepancy term for the identity of CAPNOIL
135.	DIS_CAPOILREF	Discrepancy term for the identity of CAPOILREF
136.	DIS_CAPOTHS	Discrepancy term for the identity of CAPOTHS
137.	DIS_CAPPETCH	Discrepancy term for the identity of CAPPETCH
138.	DIS_CAPU	Discrepancy term for the identity of CAPU

(continued)

(continued)

#	Mnemonic	Description and unit
139.	DIS_CPI	Discrepancy term for the identity of CPI
140.	DIS_DI_Z	Discrepancy term for the identity of DI_Z
141.	DIS_ELE_STOT_KSA	Discrepancy term for the identity of DIS_ELE_STOT_KSA
142.	DIS_ET	Discrepancy term for the identity of ET
143.	DIS_ETNOIL	Discrepancy term for the identity of ETNOIL
144.	DIS_EXPL	Discrepancy term for the identity of EXPL
145.	DIS_FDAGR	Discrepancy term for the identity of FDAGR
146.	DIS_FDCON	Discrepancy term for the identity of FDCON
147.	DIS_FDDIS	Discrepancy term for the identity of FDDIS
148.	DIS_FDFIBU	Discrepancy term for the identity of FDFIBU
149.	DIS_FDGOV	Discrepancy term for the identity of FDGOV
150.	DIS_FDI$	Discrepancy term for the identity of FDI$
151.	DIS_FDI$OUT	Discrepancy term for the identity of FDI$OUT
152.	DIS_FDMANNOLPC	Discrepancy term for the identity of FDMANNOLPC
153.	DIS_FDOTHS	Discrepancy term for the identity of FDOTHS
154.	DIS_FDPETCH	Discrepancy term for the identity of FDPETCH
155.	DIS_FDTRACOM	Discrepancy term for the identity of FDTRACOM
156.	DIS_FDU	Discrepancy term for the identity of FDU
157.	DIS_GI	Discrepancy term for the identity of GI
158.	DIS_GREVNOIL	Discrepancy term for the identity of GREVNOIL
159.	DIS_GREVOIL	Discrepancy term for the identity of GREVOIL
160.	DIS_GVANIT_Z	Discrepancy term for the identity of GVANIT_Z
161.	DIS_GVANOIL	Discrepancy term for the identity of GVANOIL
162.	DIS_GVANOIL_Z	Discrepancy term for the identity of GVANOIL_Z
163.	DIS_GVAOIL	Discrepancy term for the identity of GVAOIL
164.	DIS_GVAOIL_Z	Discrepancy term for the identity of GVAOIL_Z
165.	DIS_HUVF	Discrepancy term for the identity of HUVF
166.	DIS_IDAGR	Discrepancy term for the identity of IDAGR
167.	DIS_IDCON	Discrepancy term for the identity of IDCON
168.	DIS_IDDIS	Discrepancy term for the identity of IDDIS
169.	DIS_IDFIBU	Discrepancy term for the identity of IDFIBU
170.	DIS_IDGOV	Discrepancy term for the identity of IDGOV
171.	DIS_IDMANNOLPC	Discrepancy term for the identity of IDMANNOLPC
172.	DIS_IDMINOTH	Discrepancy term for the identity of IDMINOTH
173.	DIS_IDOIL	Discrepancy term for the identity of IDOIL
174.	DIS_IDOTHS	Discrepancy term for the identity of IDOTHS
175.	DIS_IDPETCH	Discrepancy term for the identity of IDPETCH
176.	DIS_IDTRACOM	Discrepancy term for the identity of IDTRACOM
177.	DIS_IDU	Discrepancy term for the identity of IDU
178.	DIS_IF	Discrepancy term for the identity of IF
179.	DIS_IFDOM	Discrepancy term for the identity of IFDOM
180.	DIS_IFNOILP	Discrepancy term for the identity of IFNOILP
181.	DIS_KOILREF	Discrepancy term for the identity of KOILREF

(continued)

(continued)

#	Mnemonic	Description and unit
182.	DIS_LABCOMP	Discrepancy term for the identity of LABCOMP
183.	DIS_LF	Discrepancy term for the identity of LF
184.	DIS_LIABP	Discrepancy term for the identity of LIABP
185.	DIS_M	Discrepancy term for the identity of M
186.	DIS_MG	Discrepancy term for the identity of MG
187.	DIS_MG_Z	Discrepancy term for the identity of MG_Z
188.	DIS_MOILREF	Discrepancy term for the identity of MOILREF
189.	DIS_OILUSE	Discrepancy term for the identity of OILUSE
190.	DIS_OVF	Discrepancy term for the identity of OVF
191.	DIS_PGDP	Discrepancy term for the identity of PGDP
192.	DIS_PGDPNOIL	Discrepancy term for the identity of PGDPNOIL
193.	DIS_POP	Discrepancy in Population, Thousand
194.	DIS_POPNS	Discrepancy in Non-Saudi Population, Thousand
195.	DIS_PSCAPE	Discrepancy term for the identity of PSCAPE
196.	DIS_REER	Discrepancy term for the identity of REER
197.	DIS_RLG	Discrepancy term for the identity of RLG
198.	DIS_TOIPC	Discrepancy term for the identity of TOIPC
199.	DIS_TOIT	Discrepancy term for the identity of TOIT
200.	DIS_U	Discrepancy term for the identity of U
201.	DIS_VAT_REV	Discrepancy term for the identity of VAT_REV
202.	DIS_WPO_AL_R	Discrepancy term for the identity of WPO_AL_R
203.	DIS_WTOUR	Discrepancy term for the identity of WTOUR
204.	DIS_X	Discrepancy term for the identity of X
205.	DIS_XGOIL$_Z	Discrepancy term for the identity of XGOIL$_Z
206.	DKER_RES	Demand for Kerosene type jet fuel excl. biofuels in Residential Sector, MTOE
207.	DKER_TRA	Demand for Kerosene type jet fuel excl. biofuels in Transportation Sector, MTOE
208.	DLPG_IND_NEU	Demand for Liquefied Petroleum Gases in Industry, Non-Energy Use, MTOE
209.	DLPG_RES	Demand for Liquefied Petroleum Gases in Residential sector, MTOE
210.	DNAP_IND_NEU	Demand for Naphtha in Industry Sector, Non-Energy Use, MTOE
211.	DNGA_EOU	Demand for Natural Gas in Energy industry own use, MTOE
212.	DNGA_IND	Final Demand for Natural Gas in Industry Sector, MTOE
213.	DNGA_IND_NEU	Demand for Natural Gas (Methane) for Non-Energy Use, MTOE
214.	DNGA_TOT	Demand for Natural Gas, Total, MTOE
215.	DNGA_U	Demand for Natural Gas in Utility, MTOE
216.	DOILREF_ARGENTIN	Refined oil, total demand, Argentina, MTOE
217.	DOILREF_AUSTRALI	Refined oil, total demand, Australia, MTOE
218.	DOILREF_AUSTRIA	Refined oil, total demand, Austria, MTOE
219.	DOILREF_BELGIUM	Refined oil, total demand, Belgium, MTOE

(continued)

(continued)

#	Mnemonic	Description and unit
220.	DOILREF_BRAZIL	Refined oil, total demand, Brazil, MTOE
221.	DOILREF_BULGARIA	Refined oil, total demand, Bulgaria, MTOE
222.	DOILREF_CANADA	Refined oil, total demand, Canada, MTOE
223.	DOILREF_CHILE	Refined oil, total demand, Chile, MTOE
224.	DOILREF_CHINA	Refined oil, total demand, China, MTOE
225.	DOILREF_CROATIA	Refined oil, total demand, Croatia, MTOE
226.	DOILREF_CZECH	Refined oil, total demand, Czech, MTOE
227.	DOILREF_DENMARK	Refined oil, total demand, Denmark, MTOE
228.	DOILREF_FINLAND	Refined oil, total demand, Finland, MTOE
229.	DOILREF_FRANCE	Refined oil, total demand, France, MTOE
230.	DOILREF_GERMANY	Refined oil, total demand, Germany, MTOE
231.	DOILREF_GREECE	Refined oil, total demand, Greece, MTOE
232.	DOILREF_HK	Refined oil, total demand, Hong Kong, MTOE
233.	DOILREF_HUNGARY	Refined oil, total demand, Hungary, MTOE
234.	DOILREF_INDIA	Refined oil, total demand, India, MTOE
235.	DOILREF_INDONESI	Refined oil, total demand, Indonesia, MTOE
236.	DOILREF_IRELAND	Refined oil, total demand, Ireland, MTOE
237.	DOILREF_ITALY	Refined oil, total demand, Italy, MTOE
238.	DOILREF_JAPAN	Refined oil, total demand, Japan, MTOE
239.	DOILREF_KOREA	Refined oil, total demand, Korea, MTOE
240.	DOILREF_MALAYSIA	Refined oil, total demand, Malaysia, MTOE
241.	DOILREF_MEXICO	Refined oil, total demand, Mexico, MTOE
242.	DOILREF_NETH	Refined oil, total demand, Netherlands, MTOE
243.	DOILREF_NORWAY	Refined oil, total demand, Norway, MTOE
244.	DOILREF_PHILIPPI	Refined oil, total demand, Philippines, MTOE
245.	DOILREF_POLAND	Refined oil, total demand, Poland, MTOE
246.	DOILREF_PORTUGAL	Refined oil, total demand, Portugal, MTOE
247.	DOILREF_ROMANIA	Refined oil, total demand, Romania, MTOE
248.	DOILREF_RUSSIA	Refined oil, total demand, Russia, MTOE
249.	DOILREF_SAFRICA	Refined oil, total demand, South Africa, MTOE
250.	DOILREF_SINGPORE	Refined oil, total demand, Singapore, MTOE
251.	DOILREF_SLOVAKIA	Refined oil, total demand, Slovakia, MTOE
252.	DOILREF_SPAIN	Refined oil, total demand, Spain, MTOE
253.	DOILREF_SWEDEN	Refined oil, total demand, Sweden, MTOE
254.	DOILREF_SWITZ	Refined oil, total demand, Switzerland, MTOE
255.	DOILREF_T	Refined oil demand, total, MTOE
256.	DOILREF_TAIWAN	Refined oil, total demand, Taiwan, MTOE
257.	DOILREF_THAILAND	Refined oil, total demand, Thailand, MTOE
258.	DOILREF_TURKEY	Refined oil, total demand, Turkey, MTOE
259.	DOILREF_UAEMOD	Refined oil, total demand, UAE, MTOE
260.	DOILREF_UK	Refined oil, total demand, United Kingdom, MTOE
261.	DOILREF_US	Refined oil, total demand, United States, MTOE
262.	DOMD	Domestic Demand, total, Million SAR at 2010 prices

(continued)

(continued)

#	Mnemonic	Description and unit
263.	DOMD_Z	Domestic Demand, total, Million SAR
264.	DOTH_IND	Demand for other refined oil products in Industry, MTOE
265.	DP1986	Dummy variable, taking unity in 1986 and zero otherwise
266.	DP1991	Dummy variable, taking unity in 1991 and zero otherwise
267.	DP1997	Dummy variable, taking unity in 1997 and zero otherwise
268.	DP2001	Dummy variable, taking unity in 2001 and zero otherwise
269.	DP2003	Dummy variable, taking unity in 2003 and zero otherwise
270.	DP2006	Dummy variable, taking unity in 2006 and zero otherwise
271.	DP200708	Dummy variable, taking unity in 2007 and 2008 and zero otherwise
272.	DP2008	Dummy variable, taking unity in 2008 and zero otherwise
273.	DP2009	Dummy variable, taking unity in 2009 and zero otherwise
274.	DP2010	Dummy variable, taking unity in 2010 and zero otherwise
275.	DP2011	Dummy variable, taking unity in 2011 and zero otherwise
276.	DP2012	Dummy variable, taking unity in 2012 and zero otherwise
277.	DP2013	Dummy variable, taking unity in 2013 and zero otherwise
278.	DP201314	Dummy variable, taking unity in 2013 and 2014 and zero otherwise
279.	DP2014	Dummy variable, taking unity in 2014 and zero otherwise
280.	DP2015	Dummy variable, taking unity in 2015 and zero otherwise
281.	DP2016	Dummy variable, taking unity in 2016 and zero otherwise
282.	DP2017	Dummy variable, taking unity in 2017 and zero otherwise
283.	DP201718	Dummy variable, taking unity in 2017 and 2018 and zero otherwise
284.	DP2018	Dummy variable, taking unity in 2018 and zero otherwise
285.	DP2019	Dummy variable, taking unity in 2019 and zero otherwise
286.	DQM	Other Quasi-Money Deposits, nominal, million Riyals
287.	DSH000102	Dummy variable, taking unity in 2000, 2001 and 2002 and zero otherwise
288.	DSH1981	Dummy variable, taking unity from 1981 to 2019 and zero otherwise
289.	DSH2003	Dummy variable, taking unity from 2003 to 2019 and zero otherwise
290.	DSH2008	Dummy variable, taking unity from 2008 to 2019 and zero otherwise
291.	DSH2010	Dummy variable, taking unity from 2010 to 2019 and zero otherwise
292.	DSH9005	Dummy variable, taking unity from 1990 to 2005 and zero otherwise
293.	DST0308	Dummy variable, taking unity from 2003 to 2008 and zero otherwise
294.	DST0312	Dummy variable, taking unity from 2003 to 2012 and zero otherwise
295.	DST1012	Dummy variable, taking unity from 2010 to 2012 and zero otherwise

(continued)

(continued)

#	Mnemonic	Description and unit
296.	DST1998	Dummy variable, taking unity from 1970 to 1998 and zero otherwise (Created by Autometrics in OxMetrics)
297.	DST9803	Dummy variable, taking unity from 1998 to 2003 and zero otherwise
298.	DTB9501	Dummy variable, taking value from negative unity in 2001 to negative 7 in 1995 and zero otherwise (Created by Autometrics in OxMetrics)
299.	DTS	Time and Savings Deposits, nominal, Million SAR
300.	ECT_CONS	Equilibrium Correction Term from the Long-run Equation of CONS
301.	ECT_CPIART_ULC	Equilibrium Correction Term from the Long-run Equation of CPIART
302.	ECT_CPICLOTH_ULC	Equilibrium Correction Term from the Long-run Equation of CPICLOTH
303.	ECT_CPICOM_ULC	Equilibrium Correction Term from the Long-run Equation of CPICOM
304.	ECT_CPIEDU_ULC	Equilibrium Correction Term from the Long-run Equation of CPIEDU
305.	ECT_CPIFOOD_ULC	Equilibrium Correction Term from the Long-run Equation of CPIFOOD
306.	ECT_CPIHEAL_ULC	Equilibrium Correction Term from the Long-run Equation of CPIHEAL
307.	ECT_CPIHH_ULC	Equilibrium Correction Term from the Long-run Equation of CPIHH
308.	ECT_CPIHTL_ULC	Equilibrium Correction Term from the Long-run Equation of CPIHTL
309.	ECT_CPIMISC_ULC	Equilibrium Correction Term from the Long-run Equation of CPIMISC
310.	ECT_CPITOBC_ULC	Equilibrium Correction Term from the Long-run Equation of CPITOBC
311.	ECT_CPITRA_ULC	Equilibrium Correction Term from the Long-run Equation of CPITRA
312.	ECT_CPIU_ULC	Equilibrium Correction Term from the Long-run Equation of CPIU
313.	ECT_DCOIL_IND	Equilibrium Correction Term from the Long-run Equation of DCOIL_IND
314.	ECT_DDIS_IND	Equilibrium Correction Term from the Long-run Equation of DDIS_IND
315.	ECT_DDIS_TRA	Equilibrium Correction Term from the Long-run Equation of DDIS_TRA
316.	ECT_DEBT_GOV	Equilibrium Correction Term from the Long-run Equation of DEBT_GOV
317.	ECT_DELE_AGR	Equilibrium Correction Term from the Long-run Equation of DELE_AGR
318.	ECT_DELE_COMM	Equilibrium Correction Term from the Long-run Equation of DELE_COMM
319.	ECT_DELE_GOV	Equilibrium Correction Term from the Long-run Equation of DELE_GOV

(continued)

(continued)

#	Mnemonic	Description and unit
320.	ECT_DELE_IND	Equilibrium Correction Term from the Long-run Equation of DELE_IND
321.	ECT_DELE_RES	Equilibrium Correction Term from the Long-run Equation of DELE_RES
322.	ECT_DETH_IND_NEU	Equilibrium Correction Term from the Long-run Equation of DETH_IND_NEU
323.	ECT_DGAS_TRA	Equilibrium Correction Term from the Long-run Equation of DGAS_TRA
324.	ECT_DHFO_IND	Equilibrium Correction Term from the Long-run Equation of DHFO_IND
325.	ECT_DKER_RES	Equilibrium Correction Term from the Long-run Equation of DKER_RES
326.	ECT_DKER_TRA	Equilibrium Correction Term from the Long-run Equation of DKER_TRA
327.	ECT_DLPG_IND_NEU	Equilibrium Correction Term from the Long-run Equation of DLPG_IND_NEU
328.	ECT_DLPG_RES	Equilibrium Correction Term from the Long-run Equation of DLPG_RES
329.	ECT_DNAP_IND_NEU	Equilibrium Correction Term from the Long-run Equation of DNAP_IND_NEU
330.	ECT_DNGA_IND	Equilibrium Correction Term from the Long-run Equation of DNGA_IND
331.	ECT_DNGA_IND_NEU	Equilibrium Correction Term from the Long-run Equation of DNGA_IND_NEU
332.	ECT_DOTH_IND	Equilibrium Correction Term from the Long-run Equation of DOTH_IND
333.	ECT_ETAGR	Equilibrium Correction Term from the Long-run Equation of ETAGR
334.	ECT_ETCON	Equilibrium Correction Term from the Long-run Equation of ETCON
335.	ECT_ETDIS	Equilibrium Correction Term from the Long-run Equation of ETDIS
336.	ECT_ETFIBU	Equilibrium Correction Term from the Long-run Equation of ETFIBU
337.	ECT_ETGOV	Equilibrium Correction Term from the Long-run Equation of ETGO
338.	ECT_ETMANNO	Equilibrium Correction Term from the Long-run Equation of ETMANNO
339.	ECT_ETMINOTH	Equilibrium Correction Term from the Long-run Equation of ETMINOTH
340.	ECT_ETOTHS	Equilibrium Correction Term from the Long-run Equation of ETOTHS
341.	ECT_ETPETCH	Equilibrium Correction Term from the Long-run Equation of ETPETCH
342.	ECT_ETTRACOM	Equilibrium Correction Term from the Long-run Equation of ETTRACOM
343.	ECT_ETU	Equilibrium Correction Term from the Long-run Equation of ETU

(continued)

(continued)

#	Mnemonic	Description and unit
344.	ECT_GAE_Z	Equilibrium Correction Term from the Long-run Equation of GAE_Z
345.	ECT_GC_Z_OTH	Equilibrium Correction Term from the Long-run Equation of GC_Z_OTH
346.	ECT_GCGPE	Equilibrium Correction Term from the Long-run Equation of GCGPE
347.	ECT_GI_Z	Equilibrium Correction Term from the Long-run Equation of GI_Z
348.	ECT_GMO_Z	Equilibrium Correction Term from the Long-run Equation of GMO_Z
349.	ECT_GVAAGR	Equilibrium Correction Term from the Long-run Equation of GVAAGR
350.	ECT_GVACON	Equilibrium Correction Term from the Long-run Equation of GVACON
351.	ECT_GVADIS	Equilibrium Correction Term from the Long-run Equation of GVADIS
352.	ECT_GVAFIBU	Equilibrium Correction Term from the Long-run Equation of GVAFIBU
353.	ECT_GVAGOV	Equilibrium Correction Term from the Long-run Equation of GVAGOV
354.	ECT_GVAMANNOLPC	Equilibrium Correction Term from the Long-run Equation of GVAMANNOLPC
355.	ECT_GVAOILMIN	Equilibrium Correction Term from the Long-run Equation of GVAOILMIN
356.	ECT_GVAOILREF	Equilibrium Correction Term from the Long-run Equation of GVAOILREF
357.	ECT_GVAOTHS	Equilibrium Correction Term from the Long-run Equation of GVAOTHS
358.	ECT_GVAPETCH	Equilibrium Correction Term from the Long-run Equation of GVAPETCH
359.	ECT_GVATRACOM	Equilibrium Correction Term from the Long-run Equation of GVATRACOM
360.	ECT_GVAU	Equilibrium Correction Term from the Long-run Equation of GVAU
361.	ECT_GWSA_Z	Equilibrium Correction Term from the Long-run Equation of GWSA_Z
362.	ECT_IFAGR	Equilibrium Correction Term from the Long-run Equation of IFAGR
363.	ECT_IFCON	Equilibrium Correction Term from the Long-run Equation of IFCON
364.	ECT_IFDIS	Equilibrium Correction Term from the Long-run Equation of IFDIS
365.	ECT_IFFIBU	Equilibrium Correction Term from the Long-run Equation of IFFIBU
366.	ECT_IFMANNOLPC	Equilibrium Correction Term from the Long-run Equation of IFMANNOLPC

(continued)

(continued)

#	Mnemonic	Description and unit
367.	ECT_IFOTHS	Equilibrium Correction Term from the Long-run Equation of IFOTHS
368.	ECT_IFPETCH	Equilibrium Correction Term from the Long-run Equation of IFPETCH
369.	ECT_IFTRACOM	Equilibrium Correction Term from the Long-run Equation of IFTRACOM
370.	ECT_IFU	Equilibrium Correction Term from the Long-run Equation of IFU
371.	ECT_MD_UR	Equilibrium Correction Term from the Long-run Equation of M2 (In the case no restriction on the income and price coefficients)
372.	ECT_MGCAP	Equilibrium Correction Term from the Long-run Equation of MGCAP
373.	ECT_MGCONS	Equilibrium Correction Term from the Long-run Equation of MGCONS
374.	ECT_MGINTER	Equilibrium Correction Term from the Long-run Equation of MGINTER
375.	ECT_MS	Equilibrium Correction Term from the Long-run Equation of MS
376.	ECT_PGDPAGR	Equilibrium Correction Term from the Long-run Equation of PGDPAGR
377.	ECT_PGDPCON	Equilibrium Correction Term from the Long-run Equation of PGDPCON
378.	ECT_PGDPDIS	Equilibrium Correction Term from the Long-run Equation of PGDPDIS
379.	ECT_PGDPFIBU	Equilibrium Correction Term from the Long-run Equation of PGDPFIBU
380.	ECT_PGDPGOV	Equilibrium Correction Term from the Long-run Equation of PGDPGOV
381.	ECT_PGDPMANNO	Equilibrium Correction Term from the Long-run Equation of PGDPMANNO
382.	ECT_PGDPOILREF	Equilibrium Correction Term from the Long-run Equation of PGDPOILREF
383.	ECT_PGDPOTHS	Equilibrium Correction Term from the Long-run Equation of PGDPOTHS
384.	ECT_PGDPSER	Equilibrium Correction Term from the Long-run Equation of PGDPSER
385.	ECT_PGDPTRACOM	Equilibrium Correction Term from the Long-run Equation of PGDPTRACOM
386.	ECT_PGDPU	Equilibrium Correction Term from the Long-run Equation of PGDPU
387.	ECT_PSCE_OTH	Equilibrium Correction Term from the Long-run Equation of PSCE_OTH
388.	ECT_REMOF	Equilibrium Correction Term from the Long-run Equation of REMOF
389.	ECT_WAGR	Equilibrium Correction Term from the Long-run Equation of WAGR

(continued)

(continued)

#	Mnemonic	Description and unit
390.	ECT_WCON	Equilibrium Correction Term from the Long-run Equation of WCON
391.	ECT_WFIBU	Equilibrium Correction Term from the Long-run Equation of WFIBU
392.	ECT_WMAN	Equilibrium Correction Term from the Long-run Equation of WMAN
393.	ECT_WMIN	Equilibrium Correction Term from the Long-run Equation of WMIN
394.	ECT_WTRACOM	Equilibrium Correction Term from the Long-run Equation of WTRACOM
395.	ECT_WU	Equilibrium Correction Term from the Long-run Equation of WU
396.	ECT_XGNOIL	Equilibrium Correction Term from the Long-run Equation of XGNOI
397.	ECT_XOILREF	Equilibrium Correction Term from the Long-run Equation of XOILREF
398.	ELE_EF	Electricity generation efficiency of fossil fuels
399.	ELE_SS	Solar electricity production, MTOE
400.	ELE_STOT_KSA	Electricity Supply, Total Kingdom, MTOE
401.	ET	Total Employment, Person Thousand
402.	ETAGR	Employment, Agriculture, Fishing, and Forestry, Person Thousand
403.	ETCON	Employment, Construction, Person Thousand
404.	ETDIS	Employment, Distribution, Person Thousand
405.	ETFIBU	Employment Financial, Insurance, Real Estate, and Business services, Person Thousand
406.	ETGOV	Employment in Government, Person Thousand
407.	ETGOV	Employment, Government Total, Person Thousand
408.	ETMAN	Employment, Manufacturing, Person Thousand
409.	ETMANNO	Employment, Manufacturing: Non-Oil, Person Thousand
410.	ETMIN	Employment in Mining sector, Thousand
411.	ETMINOTH	Employment, Mining, and Quarrying: Non-Oil, Person Thousand
412.	ETNOIL	Employment in Non-Oil activities, Thousand
413.	ETNS	Total Employment Expatriate, Person Thousand
414.	ETOIL	Employment in Oil Sector, Thousand
415.	ETOILMIN	Employment, Oil and gas extraction, total, Persons Thousand
416.	ETOILREF	Employment in Oil Refinery, Thousand
417.	ETOTHS	Employment in Other Services, Person Thousand
418.	ETP	Total Employment, Private, Person Thousand
419.	ETPETCH	Employment in petrochemicals, Person Thousand
420.	ETPNS	Employment, Private, Expatriate, person Thousand
421.	ETPS	Employment, Private, Saudi, person Thousand
422.	ETSER	Total employment in service sector, Person Thousand

(continued)

(continued)

#	Mnemonic	Description and unit
423.	ETTRACOM	Employment, Transport and Communication, Person Thousand
424.	ETU	Employment, Utilities, Person Thousand
425.	EXPL	Expat Levies, nominal, Million SAR
426.	FDAGR	Final Demand in Agriculture, real, Million SAR at 2010 prices
427.	FDCON	Final Demand in Construction, real, Million SAR at 2010 prices
428.	FDDIS	Final Demand in retail, wholesale, hotels, and catering, real, Million SAR at 2010 prices
429.	FDFIBU	Final Demand in Utility, real, Million SAR at 2010 prices
430.	FDGOV	Final Demand for public administration, real, Million SAR at 2010 prices
431.	FDI$	Total foreign direct investment, Million USD
432.	FDI$IN_Z	Foreign Direct Investment Inflow Net, nominal, Million USD
433.	FDI$OUT_Z	Foreign Direct Investment Outflow, nominal, Million USD
434.	FDMANNOLPC	Final Demand in Non-oil Manufacturing, real, Million SAR at 2010 prices
435.	FDMINOTH	Final Demand in Non-oil Mining, real, Million SAR at 2010 prices
436.	FDOIL	Final Demand in Oil sector, real, Million SAR at 2010 prices
437.	FDOILREF	Final Demand in Oil Refinery, real, Million SAR at 2010 prices
438.	FDOTHS	Final Demand in Other services, real, Million SAR at 2010 prices
439.	FDPETCH	Final Demand in Petro-Chemical, real, Million SAR at 2010 prices
440.	FDTRACOM	Final Demand in Transport and Communication, real, Million SAR at 2010 prices
441.	FDU	Final Demand in Utilities, real, Million SAR at 2010 prices
442.	FI$IN_Z	Foreign Investment Inflow Net, nominal, Million USD
443.	FOI$IN_Z	Foreign Other Investment Net incurrence of liabilities, nominal, Million USD
444.	FPI$IN_Z	Foreign Portfolio Investment Net incurrence of liabilities, nominal, Million USD
445.	GAE_Z	Government Administrative Expenses, nominal, Million SAR
446.	GAP_GVAAGR	Gap from production function of GVAAGR
447.	GAP_GVACON	Gap from production function of GVACON
448.	GAP_GVADIS	Gap from production function of GVADIS
449.	GAP_GVAFIBU	Gap from production function of GVAFIBU
450.	GAP_GVAGOV	Gap from production function of GVAGOV
451.	GAP_GVAMANNO	Gap from production function of GVAMANNO
452.	GAP_GVAMANNOLPC	Gap from production function of GVAMANNOLPC
453.	GAP_GVANOIL	Gap from production function of GVANOIL
454.	GAP_GVAOILREF	Gap from production function of GVAOILREF

(continued)

(continued)

#	Mnemonic	Description and unit
455.	GAP_GVAOTHS	Gap from production function of GVAOTHS
456.	GAP_GVAPETCH	Gap from production function of GVAPETCH
457.	GAP_GVATRACOM	Gap from production function of GVATRACOM
458.	GAP_GVAU	Gap from production function of GVAU
459.	GB	Government balance, nominal, Million SAR
460.	GBNOIL	Non-oil government financial balance, nominal, Million SAR
461.	GC	Consumption, government, real, Million SAR at 2010 prices
462.	GC_Z	Consumption, government, nominal, Million SAR
463.	GC_Z_OTH	Government other consumption, nominal, Million SAR
464.	GCGPE	Personal sector transfers from central government, nominal, Million SAR
465.	GDP	GDP, real, Million SAR at 2010 prices
466.	GDP$_Z	GDP, nominal, Million USD
467.	GDP_MNA	GDP of Middle East & North Africa, Million USD at 2010 prices
468.	GDP_Z	GDP, nominal, Million SAR
469.	GDPPC_WLD	GDP per capita, real, Million USD at 2010 prices
470.	GEXP	Government expenditure, total, nominal, Million SAR
471.	GI	Investment, government, real, Million SAR at 2010 prices
472.	GI_Z	Investment, government, nominal, Million SAR
473.	GMO_Z	Government Maintenance and Operation, nominal, Millions SAR
474.	GREV	Government revenue, Total, nominal, Million SAR
475.	GREVNOIL	Government revenue, non-oil, nominal, Million SAR
476.	GREVOIL	Government revenue, oil, nominal, Million SAR
477.	GVAAGR	Gross value added in agriculture and forestry, real, Million SAR at 2010 prices
478.	GVAAGR_Z	Gross value added in agriculture and forestry, nominal, Million SAR
479.	GVACON	Gross value added, construction, real, Million SAR at 2010 prices
480.	GVACON_Z	Gross value added in construction, nominal, Million SAR
481.	GVADIS	Gross value added in retail, wholesale, hotels, and catering, real, Million SAR at 2010 prices
482.	GVADIS_Z	Gross value added in retail, wholesale, hotels, and catering, nominal, Million SAR
483.	GVAFIBU	Gross value added in financial and business services, real, Million SAR at 2010 prices
484.	GVAFIBU_Z	Gross value added in financial and business services, nominal, Million SAR
485.	GVAFIBUOTH	Gross value added in other financial and business services, real, Million SAR at 2010 prices
486.	GVAFIBUOTH_Z	Gross value added in other financial and business services, nominal, Million SAR

(continued)

(continued)

#	Mnemonic	Description and unit
487.	GVAFISIM	GDP, financial intermediaries, real, Million SAR at 2010 prices
488.	GVAFISIM_Z	GDP, financial intermediaries, nominal, Million SAR
489.	GVAGOV	Gross value added in public administration, real, Million SAR at 2010 prices
490.	GVAGOV_Z	Gross value added in public administration, nominal, Million SAR
491.	GVAIND	Gross value added in industry, real, Million SAR at 2010 prices
492.	GVAIND_Z	Gross value added in industry, real, Million SAR at 2010 prices
493.	GVAMAN	Gross value added in manufacturing, real, Million SAR at 2010 prices
494.	GVAMAN_Z	Gross value added in manufacturing, nominal, Million SAR
495.	GVAMANNO	Gross value added in non-oil manufacturing, real, Million SAR at 2010 prices
496.	GVAMANNO_Z	Gross value added in manufacturing, nominal, Million SAR
497.	GVAMANNOLPC	Gross value added in non-oil manufacturing excluding Petro-chemical, real, Million SAR at 2010 prices
498.	GVAMIN	Gross value added in mining and quarrying real, Million SAR at 2010 prices
499.	GVAMIN_Z	Gross value added in mining and quarrying real, nominal, Million SAR
500.	GVAMINOTH	Gross value added in non-oil extraction, real, Million SAR at 2010 prices
501.	GVAMINOTH_Z	Gross value added in extraction, nominal, Million SAR
502.	GVANIT	Gross value added, import taxes, real, Million SAR at 2010 prices
503.	GVANIT_Z	Gross value added, import taxes, nominal, Million SAR
504.	GVANOIL	Gross value added, non-oil sector, real, Million SAR at 2010 prices
505.	GVANOIL_Z	Gross value added, non-oil, nominal, Million SAR
506.	GVAOIL	Gross value added, oil sector, real, Million SAR at 2010 prices
507.	GVAOIL_Z	Gross value added, oil, nominal, Million SAR
508.	GVAOILMIN	Gross value added, oil mining, real, Million SAR at 2010 prices
509.	GVAOILMIN_Z	Gross value added, oil mining, nominal, Million SAR
510.	GVAOILREF	Gross value added, oil refining, real, Million SAR at 2010 prices
511.	GVAOILREF_Z	Gross value added, oil refining, nominal, Million SAR
512.	GVAOTHS	Gross value added in other services, excluding arts, entertainment, and recreation, real, Million SAR at 2010 prices
513.	GVAOTHS_Z	Gross value added in other services, excluding arts, entertainment and recreation, nominal, Million SAR

(continued)

(continued)

#	Mnemonic	Description and unit
514.	GVAPETCH	Gross value added in petrochemicals, real, Million SAR at 2010 prices
515.	GVAREAL	Gross value added, imputed rents, real, Million SAR at 2010 prices
516.	GVAREAL_Z	Gross value added, imputed rents, nominal, Million SAR
517.	GVASER	Gross value added in services, real, Million SAR at 2010 prices
518.	GVASER_Z	Gross value added in services, nominal, Million SAR
519.	GVATRACOM	Gross value added in transport and communication, real, Million SAR at 2010 prices
520.	GVATRACOM_Z	Gross value added in transport and communication, nominal, Millions SAR
521.	GVATRAPIPE	Gross value added in pipeline transportation hydrocarbon, real, Million SAR at 2010 prices
522.	GVAU	Gross value added, utilities, real, Million SAR at 2010 prices
523.	GVAU_Z	Gross value added in utilities, nominal, Million SAR
524.	GWSA_Z	Government Wages, Salaries and Allowances, nominal, Million SAR
525.	HUVF	Hajj and Umrah Visa Fees Collection, nominal, Million SAR
526.	IDAGR	Intermediate demand for agriculture, real, Million SAR at 2010 prices
527.	IDCON	Intermediate demand for construction, real, Million SAR at 2010 prices
528.	IDDIS	Intermediate demand for retail, wholesale, hotels, and catering, real, Million SAR at 2010 prices
529.	IDFIBU	Intermediate demand for FIBU, real, Million SAR at 2010 prices
530.	IDGOV	Intermediate demand for public administration, real, Million SAR at 2010 prices
531.	IDMANNOLPC	Intermediate demand for non-oil manufacturing, real, Million SAR at 2010 prices
532.	IDMINOTH	Intermediate demand for non-oil mining, real, Million SAR at 2010 prices
533.	IDOIL	Intermediate demand for oil sector, real, Million SAR at 2010 prices
534.	IDOILREF	Intermediate demand for oil refinery, real, Million SAR at 2010 prices
535.	IDOTHS	Intermediate demand for other services, real, Million SAR at 2010 prices
536.	IDPETCH	Intermediate demand for Petro-Chemical, real, Million SAR at 2010 prices
537.	IDTRACOM	Intermediate demand for transport and communication, real, Million SAR at 2010 prices
538.	IDU	Intermediate demand for utilities, real, Million SAR at 2010 prices
539.	IF	Investment, total fixed investment, real, Million SAR at 2010 prices

(continued)

(continued)

#	Mnemonic	Description and unit
540.	IF_Z	Investment, total fixed investment, nominal, Million SAR
541.	IFAGR	Investment in Agriculture, real, Million SAR at 2010 prices
542.	IFCON	Investment in Construction, real, Million SAR at 2010 prices
543.	IFDIS	Investment in Distribution, real, Million SAR at 2010 prices
544.	IFDOMP	Investment, domestic, private, real, Million SAR at 2010 prices
545.	IFFIBU	Investment in FIBU Millions SAR real, Million SAR at 2010 prices
546.	IFMANNO	Investment in non-oil manufacturing excluding Petro-chemical, real, Million SAR at 2010 prices
547.	IFMANNOLPC	Investment in non-oil manufacturing excluding Petro-chemical, real, Million SAR at 2010 prices
548.	IFMINOTH	Investment in non-oil Mining, real, Million SAR at 2010 prices
549.	IFNOIL	Investment funds, non-oil, total, real, Million SAR at 2010 prices
550.	IFNOIL_Z	Investment funds, non-oil, nominal, Million SAR
551.	IFNOILP	Investments, non-oil, Private Sector, real, Million SAR at 2010 prices
552.	IFNOILP_Z	Investment non-Oil Private Sector nominal, Million SAR
553.	IFOIL	Investment, Oil sector, real, Million SAR at 2010 prices
554.	IFOTHS	Investment in Others, real, Million SAR at 2010 prices
555.	IFPETCH	Investment in Petro-chemical, real, Million SAR at 2010 prices
556.	IFREF	Investment in Refined oil, Million SAR/MTOE
557.	IFTRACOX	Investment in Transport and Communication, real, Million SAR at 2010 prices
558.	IFU	Investment in Utility, real, Million SAR at 2010 prices
559.	IRD	Interest Rate Differential (between Interest payments (% of revenue) in UK and Saudi Interbank Lending Rate), %
560.	IR_UK	Interest payments (% of revenue) in UK, %
561.	IS	Investment Stock building, real, Million SAR at 2010 prices
562.	IS_Z	Stock building, nominal, Million SAR
563.	ISP	Industrial Support Package, real, Million SAR at 2010 prices
564.	KOILREF	Refined oil, capital stock, nominal, Thousands USD
565.	LABCOMP	Labour compensation, nominal, Million SAR
566.	LF	Labour force, Person thousands
567.	LIABP	Bank claims on private sector, nominal, Million SAR
568.	M	Imports, goods & services, real, Million SAR at 2010 prices
569.	M0	Money supply, M0, Currency Outside Banks, nominal, Million SAR
570.	M1	Money supply, M1, nominal, Million SAR
571.	M2	Money supply, M2, nominal, Million SAR
572.	M3	Money supply, M3, nominal, Million SAR
573.	M_Z	Imports, goods & services, nominal, Million SAR

(continued)

(continued)

#	Mnemonic	Description and unit
574.	MG	Import of Goods, real, Million SAR at 2010 prices
575.	MG_Z	Import of Goods, nominal, Million SAR
576.	MGCAP	Import of Goods, Capital Goods, real, Million SAR at 2010 prices
577.	MGCAP_Z	Import of Goods, Capital Goods, SAR Million
578.	MGCONS	Import of Goods, Consumer Goods, real, Million SAR at 2010 prices
579.	MGCONS_Z	Import of Goods, Consumer Goods, nominal, Million SAR
580.	MGINTER	Import of Goods, Intermediate Goods, real, Million SAR at 2010 prices
581.	MGINTER_Z	Import of Goods, Intermediate Goods, nominal, Million SAR
582.	MOILREF	Imports of oil refined goods, MTOE
583.	MS	Imports, services, real, Million SAR at 2010 prices
584.	MS$_CAN	Canada – Imports, services, constant prices and exchange rate, Million USD at 2010 prices
585.	MS$_DEU	Germany – Imports, services, constant prices and exchange rate, Million USD at 2010 prices
586.	MS$_FRA	France – Imports, services, constant prices and exchange rate, Million USD at 2010 prices
587.	MS$_GBR	United Kingdom – Imports, services, constant prices and exchange rate, Million USD at 2010 prices
588.	MS$_ITA	Italy – Imports, services, constant prices and exchange rate, Million USD at 2010 prices
589.	MS$_JPN	Japan – Imports, services, constant prices and exchange rate, Million USD at 2010 prices
590.	MS$_MEX	Mexico – Imports, services, constant prices and exchange rate, Million USD at 2010 prices
591.	MS$_TUR	Turkey – Imports, services, constant prices and exchange rate, Million USD at 2010 prices
592.	MS$_USA	United States – Imports, services, constant prices and exchange rate, Million USD at 2010 prices
593.	MS$_ZAF	South Africa – Imports, services, constant prices and exchange rate, Million USD at 2010 prices
594.	NEER	Nominal Effective Exchange Rate, units of MTP currency basket for a unit of SAR, 2010 = 100
595.	NFA	Net foreign assets, nominal, Million SAR
596.	NG_PRO	Production Of Natural Gas Liquids, Million Barrels
597.	NGL	Natural gas liquids, KTOE
598.	NNSA_Z	Net National Saving, Adjusted, nominal, Million SAR
599.	OILMBD	Oil production, Barrels per Day Millions
600.	OILUSE	Oil, domestic use, Barrels per Day Millions
601.	OVF	Other Visa Fees Collection, nominal, Million SAR
602.	PART	Labour Force Participation Rate for Population ages 15 and above, %
603.	PCOIL_IND	Price of Arab light in Industry, SAR/TOE
604.	PCONS	Consumption, private deflator, Index 2010 = 100

(continued)

(continued)

#	Mnemonic	Description and unit
605.	PDIS_IND	Price of Diesel in Industry Sector, SAR/TOE
606.	PDIS_TRA	Price of Diesel in Transport Sector, SAR/TOE
607.	PE_AGR	Price of energy in Agriculture, weighted average, SAR/TOE
608.	PE_CON	Price of energy in Construction, weighted average, SAR/TOE
609.	PE_DIS	Price of energy in Distribution, weighted average, SAR/TOE
610.	PE_FIBU	Price of energy in FIBU, weighted average, SAR/TOE
611.	PE_GOV	Price of energy in public administration, weighted average, SAR/TOE
612.	PE_MANNO	Price of energy in non-oil manufacturing, weighted average, SAR/TOE
613.	PE_OILREF	Price of energy in oil refining, weighted average, SAR/TOE
614.	PE_OTHS	Price of energy in other service sectors, weighted average, SAR/TOE
615.	PE_RES	Price of energy, weighted average, Residential, SAR/TOE
616.	PE_TRACOM	Price of energy in transport and communication, weighted average, SAR/TOE
617.	PE_U	Price of energy in utility, weighted average, SAR/TOE
618.	PELE_AGR	Electricity Price for Agriculture/forestry Sector, SAR/TOE
619.	PELE_COMM	Electricity Price for Commercial Sector, SAR/TOE
620.	PELE_GOV	Electricity Price for Government Sector, SAR/TOE
621.	PELE_IND	Electricity Price for Industry Sector, SAR/TOE
622.	PELE_RES	Electricity Price for Residential Sector, SAR/TOE
623.	PELE_RES_CONS	Electricity Price for Residential Sector, SAR/TOE
624.	PELE_RES_INV	Electricity Price for Residential Sector, SAR/TOE
625.	PETH_IND_NEU	Ethane Price in Saudi Arabia, SAR /TOE
626.	PGAS_TRA	Price of Gasoline in Transport Sector, SAR/TOE
627.	PGC	Consumption, government deflator, Index 2010 = 100
628.	PGDP	GDP deflator, Index 2010 = 100
629.	PGDP_US	US GDP deflator (base year 2010)
630.	PGDPAGR	GDP deflator, agriculture and fishing, Index 2010=100
631.	PGDPCON	GDP deflator, construction, Index 2010 = 100
632.	PGDPDIS	GDP deflator, distribution, Index 2010 = 100
633.	PGDPFIBU	GDP deflator, financial & business services, Index 2010 = 100
634.	PGDPFIBUOTH	GDP deflator, other financial & business services, Index 2010 = 100
635.	PGDPFISIM	GDP deflator, imputed financial services, Index 2010 = 100
636.	PGDPGOV	GDP deflator, government services, Index 2010 = 100
637.	PGDPIND	GDP deflator, industry, Index 2010 = 100
638.	PGDPMAN	GDP deflator, manufacturing, Index 2010 = 100
639.	PGDPMANNO	GDP deflator, non-oil manufacturing, Index 2010 = 100
640.	PGDPMIN	GDP deflator, quarrying and mining, Index 2010 = 100
641.	PGDPMINOTH	GDP deflator, non-oil quarrying and mining, Index 2010 = 100

(continued)

(continued)

#	Mnemonic	Description and unit
642.	PGDPNIT	GDP deflator, import taxes, Index 2010 = 100
643.	PGDPNOIL	GDP deflator, non-oil sector, Index 2010 = 100
644.	PGDPOIL	GDP deflator, oil sector, Index 2010 = 100
645.	PGDPOILMIN	Oil extraction GDP deflator, Index 2010 = 100
646.	PGDPOILREF	Oil refining GDP deflator, Index 2010 = 100
647.	PGDPOTHS	Other services (excluding arts, entertainment, and recreation) GDP deflator, Index 2010 = 100
648.	PGDPPETCH	GDP Deflator, Petrochemicals, 2010 = 100
649.	PGDPREAL	Imputed rent GDP deflator, Index 2010 = 100
650.	PGDPSER	GDP deflator, services, Index 2010 = 100
651.	PGDPTRACOM	GDP deflator, transport, storage & communication, Index 2010 = 100
652.	PGDPU	GDP deflator, electricity, gas, and water, Index 2010 = 100
653.	PHFO_IND	Price of HFO in Industry, SAR/TOE
654.	PIF	Investment deflator, Index 2010 = 100
655.	PIFI	Public Investment Fund Investments, real, Million SAR at 2010 prices
656.	PKER_RES	Price of Kerosene in Residential Sector, SAR/TOE
657.	PKER_TRA	Price of Kerosene in Transport Sector, SAR/TOE
658.	PLPG_IND_NEU	LPG price SAR /TOE
659.	PLPG_RES	Price of LPG in Residential Sector, SAR/TOE
660.	PM	Import deflator, total, Index 2010 = 100
661.	PMG	Import deflator, goods, Index 2010 = 100
662.	PMS	Import deflator, services, Index 2010 = 100
663.	PNAP_IND_NEU	Naphtha price SAR/TOE
664.	PNGA_IND	Price of Natural Gas, SAR/TOE
665.	PNGA_IND_NEU	Methane price in Saudi Arabia SAR/TOE
666.	POP	Population total, Person Thousands
667.	POP014	Domestic population age group between 0 and 14, Person Thousand
668.	POP1519	Domestic population age group between 15 and19, Person Thousand
669.	POP1564	Domestic population age group between 15 and 64, Person Thousand
670.	POP2024	Domestic population age group between 20 and 24, Person Thousand
671.	POP2529	Domestic population age group between 25 and 29, Person Thousand
672.	POP3034	Domestic population age group between 30 and 34, Person Thousand
673.	POP3539	Domestic population age group between 35 and 39, Person Thousand
674.	POP4044	Domestic population age group between 40 and 44, Person Thousand

(continued)

(continued)

#	Mnemonic	Description and unit
675.	POP4549	Domestic population age group between 45 and 49, Person Thousand
676.	POP5054	Domestic population age group between 50 and 54, Person Thousand
677.	POP5559	Domestic population age group between 55 and 59, Person Thousand
678.	POP6064	Domestic population age group between 60 and 64, Person Thousand
679.	POP65A	Domestic population age group between 65 and above, Person Thousand
680.	POPF014	Population 0–14, Females, person Thousand
681.	POPF1519	Population 1519, Females, person Thousand
682.	POPF2024	Population 20–24, Females, person Thousand
683.	POPF2529	Population 25–29, Females, person Thousand
684.	POPF3034	Population 30–34, Females, person Thousand
685.	POPF3539	Population 35–39, Females, person Thousand
686.	POPF4044	Population 40–44, Females, person Thousand
687.	POPF4549	Population 45–49, Females, person Thousand
688.	POPF5054	Population 50–54, Females, person Thousand
689.	POPF5559	Population 55–59, Females, person Thousand
690.	POPF6064	Population 60–64, Females, person Thousand
691.	POPF65A	Population 65 and above, Females, person Thousand
692.	POPM014	Population 0–14, Males, person Thousand
693.	POPM1519	Population 15–19, Males, person Thousand
694.	POPM2024	Population 20–24, Males, person Thousand
695.	POPM2529	Population 25–29, Males, person Thousand
696.	POPM3034	Population 30–34, Males, person Thousand
697.	POPM3539	Population 35–39, Males, person Thousand
698.	POPM4044	Population 40–44, Males, person Thousand
699.	POPM4549	Population 45–49, Males, person Thousand
700.	POPM5054	Population 50–54, Males, person Thousand
701.	POPM5559	Population 55–59, Males, person Thousand
702.	POPM6064	Population 60–64, Males, person Thousand
703.	POPM65A	Population 65 and Above, Males, person Thousand
704.	POPNS	Population, Non-Saudis, Thousand
705.	POPS	Population, Saudis, Thousand
706.	POPSF	Population, Saudis Female, Thousand
707.	POPSM	Population, Saudis Male, Thousand
708.	POPW	Working age population, Thousand
709.	POPWF	Working age population, Female, Thousand
710.	POPWM	Working age population, Male, Thousand
711.	POT_GVAAGR	Potential output in Agriculture and forestry, real, Million SAR at 2010 prices

(continued)

#	Mnemonic	Description and unit
712.	POT_GVACON	Potential output in Construction, real, Million SAR at 2010 prices
713.	POT_GVADIS	Potential output in Retail, Wholesale, Hotels, and Catering, real, Million SAR at 2010 prices
714.	POT_GVAFIBU	Potential output in Financial and Business services, real, Million SAR at 2010 prices
715.	POT_GVAGOV	Potential output in Public Administration, real, Million SAR at 2010 prices
716.	POT_GVAMANNO	Potential output in Non-oil Manufacturing, real, Million SAR at 2010 prices
717.	POT_GVAMANNOLPC	Potential output in Non-oil Manufacturing less Petro-chemicals, real, Million SAR at 2010 prices
718.	POT_GVANOIL	Potential output in Non-oil Sector, real, Million SAR at 2010 prices
719.	POT_GVAOILREF	Potential output in Oil Refinery, real, Million SAR at 2010 prices
720.	POT_GVAOTHS	Potential output in Other Services, real, Million SAR at 2010 prices
721.	POT_GVAPETCH	Potential output in Petrochemicals, real, Million SAR at 2010 prices
722.	POT_GVATRACOM	Potential output in Transport and Communication, real, Million SAR at 2010 prices
723.	POT_GVAU	Potential output in Utilities, real, Million SAR at 2010 prices
724.	POTH_IND	Price of other refined oil products used in Industry, weighted average, SAR/TOE
725.	PRODDN	Productivity Differential, Non-Oil Sector
726.	PRODDO	Productivity Differential, Oil Sector
727.	PSCAPE	Public capital expenditures, nominal, Million SAR
728.	PSCE	Public Sector Current Expenditures, nominal, Million SAR
729.	PSCE_OTH	Public Sector Other Current Expenditures, nominal, Million SAR
730.	PX	Export deflator, total, Index 2010=100
731.	QOILREF	Refined oil, supply, MTOE
732.	RCB	Interest rate, central bank policy, %, nominal 3 months
733.	RDEBT	Effective interest rate on external debt, %, nominal
734.	REER	Real Effective Exchange Rate, CPI based, units of MTP currency basket for a unit of SAR, 2010 = 100
735.	REERE	Real Effective Exchange Rate, Equilibrium
736.	REMOF	Personal remittances outflow, paid, Million USD
737.	RER	Real Exchange Rate of SAR against per USD
738.	RLEND	Interest rate, lending, %, nominal
739.	RLG	Interest rate, 10-year government bonds, %, nominal
740.	RRLEND	Real interest rate, %. Lending rate adjusted for CPI inflation
741.	RRLEND1	Real interest rate, %. Lending rate adjusted for PGDP inflation
742.	RRXD	Real exchange rate, SAR price of per USD, Index 2010 = 100

(continued)

(continued)

#	Mnemonic	Description and unit
743.	RSH	Interest rate, short-term, %, Nominal
744.	RXD	EOP exchange rate, SAR/USD nominal, nominal
745.	S12001	Dummy variable, taking unity from 1970 to 2001 and zero otherwise (Created by Autometrics in OxMetrics)
746.	TB	Trade Balance, real, Million SAR at 2010 prices
747.	TBNOIL	Trade Balance, Non-oil, real, Million SAR at 2010 prices
748.	TDAGR	Total demand for agriculture, real, Million SAR at 2010 prices
749.	TDCON	Total demand for construction, real, Million SAR at 2010 prices
750.	TDDIS	Total demand for retail, wholesale, hotels, and catering, real, Million SAR at 2010 prices
751.	TDFIBU	Total demand for FIBU, real, Million SAR at 2010 prices
752.	TDGOV	Total demand for public administration, real, Million SAR at 2010 prices
753.	TDMANNOLPC	Total demand for non-oil manufacturing, real, Million SAR at 2010 prices
754.	TDMINOTH	Total demand for other services, real, Million SAR at 2010 prices
755.	TDOIL	Total demand for oil sector, real, Million SAR at 2010 prices
756.	TDOILREF	Total demand for oil refinery, real, Million SAR at 2010 prices
757.	TDOTHS	Total demand for other services, real, Million SAR at 2010 prices
758.	TDPETCH	Total demand for Petro-Chemical, real, Million SAR at 2010 prices
759.	TDTRACOM	Total demand for transport and communication, real, Million SAR at 2010 prices
760.	TDU	Total demand for utilities, real, Million SAR at 2010 prices
761.	TFE	Total final expenditure, real, Million SAR at 2010 prices
762.	TI2009	Dummy variable, taking value from negative 1 in 2009 to negative 20 in 1990 and zero otherwise (Created by Autometrics in OxMetrics)
763.	TOIPC	Taxes on Income, Profits, and Capital Gains, nominal, Million SAR
764.	TOITT	Tax on International Trade and Transactions, nominal, Million SAR
765.	U	Unemployment, Person Thousands
766.	ULCAGR	Unit labor Cost in agriculture
767.	ULCCON	Unit labor Cost in construction
768.	ULCDIS	Unit labor cost in retail, wholesale, hotels, and catering
769.	ULCFIBU	Unit labor cost in financial and business services
770.	ULCFIBUOTH	Unit labor cost in other financial and business services
771.	ULCGOV	Unit labor cost in public administration
772.	ULCMANNO	Unit labor cost in non-oil manufacturing
773.	ULCNOIL	Unit labor cost in non-oil sector

(continued)

(continued)

#	Mnemonic	Description and unit
774.	ULCOIL	Unit labor cost in oil sector
775.	ULCOILREF	Unit labor cost in oil refining
776.	ULCOTHS	Unit labor cost in other services
777.	ULCSER	Unit labor cost in service sector
778.	ULCTRACOM	Unit labor cost in transport and communication
779.	ULCU	Unit labor cost in utilities
780.	UR	Unemployment Rate, %
781.	UR_C	Cyclical Component of Unemployment Rate, %
782.	UR_N	Non-accelerating Inflation Rate of Unemployment
783.	VAT_RATE	Rate of Value Added Tax, %
784.	VAT_REV	VAT Revenues
785.	VAT_REV_DUMMY	Dummy variable for VAT
786.	W_CEIC	Wage, Average annual, Riyal, calculated based on CEIC employment and Earnings data
787.	W_OLD	Wage, Average annual, SAR
788.	WAGR	Wage in Agriculture, SAR
789.	WCON	Wage in Construction, SAR
790.	WDIS	Wage in Distribution, SAR
791.	WEALTH	Wealth, Private Sector, real, Million SAR at 2010 prices
792.	WFIBU	Wage in Financial and Business services, SAR
793.	WMAN	Wage in Manufacturing, SAR
794.	WMIN	Wage in Mining, SAR
795.	WPETCH	Wage rate in Petro-chemical, SAR
796.	WPMF$_WLD	World non-fuel exports price, Index, 2005 = 100
797.	WPO_AL	World Crude Oil Spot Price: Arabian Light, US$ per barrel, nominal
798.	WPO_AL_R	World Crude Oil Spot Price: Arabian Light, US$ per barrel, Real, 2005 = 100
799.	WSER	Wage in services, nominal, SAR
800.	WTOUR	KSA Tourism demand indicator, Index 2010 = 100,
801.	WTRACOM	Wage in Transport and Communication, SAR
802.	WTREF	World trade index, refined oil
803.	WU	Wage in Utilities, nominal, SAR
804.	X	Exports, goods & services, real, Million SAR at 2010 prices
805.	X$_Z	Exports, goods & services, nominal, Million USD
806.	X_Z	Exports, goods & services, nominal, Million SAR
807.	XG	Real Exports of Goods, real, Million SAR at 2010 prices
808.	XG$_Z	Exports of goods, USD Millions, Nominal
809.	XGNOIL	Exports of goods, non-oil, real, Million SAR at 2010 prices
810.	XGNOIL$_Z	Exports of goods, non-oil, nominal Million USD
811.	XGNOIL_Z	Exports of goods, non-oil, nominal, Million SAR
812.	XGOIL	Real Exports goods, Oil, real, Million SAR at 2010 prices
813.	XGOIL$_Z	Exports of goods, oil, nominal, Million USD
814.	XGOIL_Z	Exports, oil, nominal, Million SAR

(continued)

(continued)

#	Mnemonic	Description and unit
815.	XOILC	Crude Oil for Export, Million Barrels per Day
816.	XOILREF	Saudi Exports of Refined Oil Products, Including LPG and Natural gasoline, Million Barrels
817.	XS	Exports, services, real, Million SAR at 2010 prices
818.	XS$_Z	Exports of services, nominal, Million USD
819.	XS_Z	Exports, services, nominal, Million SAR
820.	XSCOM_Z	Exports, communication services, nominal, Million SAR
821.	XSFIN_Z	Exports, financial services, nominal, Million SAR
822.	XSGOV_Z	Exports, government, nominal, Million SAR
823.	XSII_Z	Exports, investment income, nominal, Million SAR
824.	XSIP_Z	Exports, insurance and pension services, nominal, Million SAR
825.	XSOBS_Z	Exports, other business services, nominal, Million SAR
826.	XSOIL_Z	Exports, oil Services, nominal, Million SAR
827.	XSTRAN_Z	Exports, transportation service, nominal, Million SAR
828.	XSTRAV_Z	Exports, travel service, nominal, Million SAR

Appendix C: Estimated Final ECM Specifications

This appendix records in Sects. A.3.1, A.3.2, A.3.3, A.3.4, and A.3.5 the estimated final ECM specifications associated with the long-run equations reported in Sect. 7. We obtained final ECM specifications from general unrestricted ECM specifications using *Autometrics*, a machine learning econometric modeling methodology in the *Gets* module of OxMetrics, as discussed in Sect. 4 and Appendix A.3. The lag orders of two and one are considered in the formulation of general unrestricted ECMs depending on sample spans being available for estimations. Estimated initial and congruent general unrestricted ECM specifications are not reported here to save space, but they are available from the authors on request.

For the readers convenience, we describe one of the ECM equations below and the rest of the equations follow the same logic. As an example, we select the first appeared ECM equation, i.e., Eq. (1).

$$\text{DLOG(IFDIS)} = -0.06 - 0.25^* \text{ ECT\_IFDIS}(-1) + 2.65^* \text{ DLOG(GVADIS)} - 0.01^* \text{ D(RRLEND1)} - 1.26^* \text{ DI2014}$$

Where, D denotes the first difference. LOG indicates the natural logarithmic transformation. IFDIS, GVADIS, and RRLEND1 are the variables (see Appendix B for the definitions and notations of the variables). DI2014 is a dummy variable taking unity in 2014 and zero otherwise. ECT_IFDIS is the residuals of the long-run equation of private investment in the retail, wholesale, hotels, and catering sector, i.e., equilibrium correction term. In general, ECT_X denotes equilibrium correction term for the variable X. (−n) attached to a given variable indicates n years of lagged series of a given variable. For example, ECT_IFDIS(−1) indicates one year lagged ECT_IFDIS.

This final ECM specification above indicates that the growth rates of private investment in the retail, wholesale, hotels, and catering sector increases by 2.7% if the growth rate of the sector's output increases by 1% while a 1 percentage point rise in the changes of real lending rate causes 1% decrease in the sector's investment, holding other factors constant. Speed of adjustment (SoA), i.e., the coefficient of ECT_IFDIS lagged by one year shows that in 1 year, 25% of the disequilibrium corrects to the long-run relationship (that private investment in the retail, wholesale, hotels, and catering sector establishes with its output and the real lending rate) given in Eq. (44).

Final ECM Specifications for the Real Block

ECM Equations for Investments by Economic Activity Sector

$$
\begin{aligned}
\mathrm{DLOG(IFDIS)} = &-0.060 - 0.25^*\mathrm{ECT\_IFDIS}(-1) \\
&+ 2.65^*\mathrm{DLOG(GVADIS)} - 0.01^*\mathrm{D(RRLEND1)} \\
&- 1.26^*\mathrm{DI2014}
\end{aligned} \tag{1}
$$

$$
\begin{aligned}
\mathrm{DLOG(IFCON)} = &-0.06 - 0.71^*\mathrm{ECT\_IFCON}(-1) - 0.01^*\mathrm{D(RRLEND1)} \\
&- 0.47^*\mathrm{DI2014} - 0.64^*\mathrm{TI2004} + 0.83^*\mathrm{TI2005} \\
&- 0.20^*\mathrm{TI2008}
\end{aligned} \tag{2}
$$

$$
\begin{aligned}
\mathrm{DLOG(IFFIBU)} = &-0.03 - 0.97^*\mathrm{ECT\_IFFIBU}(-1) + 2.88^*\mathrm{DLOG(GVAFIBU)} \\
&+0.34^*\mathrm{DLOG(IFFIBU}(-1)) - 0.86^*\mathrm{DP2010}
\end{aligned} \tag{3}
$$

$$
\begin{aligned}
\mathrm{DLOG(IFMANNO)} = &-0.03 - 0.69^*\mathrm{ECT\_IFMANNO}(-1) \\
&+1.41^*\mathrm{DLOG(GVAMANNO)} \\
&-0.01^*\mathrm{D(RRLEND1)} + 1.54^*\mathrm{DLOG(RER)} \\
&+0.39^*\mathrm{DP2014} - 0.33^*\mathrm{DP1995}
\end{aligned} \tag{4}
$$

$$
\begin{aligned}
\mathrm{DLOG(IFOTHS)} = &-0.46 - 0.57^*\mathrm{ECT\_IFOTHS}(-1) \\
&- 0.08^*\mathrm{D(RRLEND1)} + 6.98^*\mathrm{DLOG(RER)} \\
&+ 0.48^*\mathrm{TI2006} - 0.53^*\mathrm{TI2009} - 1.76^*\mathrm{SI2003}
\end{aligned} \tag{5}
$$

$$
\begin{aligned}
\mathrm{DLOG\,(IFPETCH)} = &\,0.03 + 3.71^*\mathrm{DLOG\,(GVAPETCH)} \\
&-2.36^*\mathrm{DLOG\,(GVAPETCH}(-1)) \\
&-0.06^*\mathrm{D\,(RRLEND1)} + 7.59^*\mathrm{DLOG\,(RER)} \\
&-0.49^*\mathrm{ECT\_IFPETCH}(-1) + 1.710^*\mathrm{DP2012} \\
&-0.73^*\mathrm{DP2003} + 0.54^*\mathrm{DP2015}
\end{aligned} \tag{6}
$$

$$DLOG(IFTRACOX) = 0.10 - 0.08^*ECT\_IFTRACOM(-1)$$
$$+1.97^*DLOG(GVATRACOM)$$
$$-1.83^*DLOG(GVATRACOM(-1)) - 0.57^*DP2006$$
$$-0.49^*DI2008 - 0.44^*DP2001$$

$$(7)$$

$$DLOG(IFU) = -0.001 - 0.76^*ECT\_IFU(-1) + 1.35^*DLOG(GVAU)$$
$$+5.63^*DLOG(RER(-1)) - 0.50^*DP1995 \qquad (8)$$
$$-0.56^*DP2009 - 0.28^*DP2012$$

$$DLOG(IFAGR) = -0.10 + 8.23^*DLOG(GVAAGR)$$
$$+ 4.31^*DLOG(REER) - 0.42^*ECT\_IFAGR(-1)$$
$$+ 1.83^*DI2010 + 1.78^*DI2011 + 1.63^*DI2012 \qquad (9)$$

ECM Equations for Sectoral Gross Value Added by Economic Activity Sector

$$DLOG\ (GVAAGR) = -0.00001 - 0.20^*ECT\_GVAAGR(-1)$$
$$+ 0.07^*DLOG\ (DELE\_AGR) - 0.06^*DP1994$$
$$- 0.06^*DI2009 \qquad (10)$$

$$DLOG(GVACON) = -0.01 - 0.36^*ECT\_GVACON(-1) + 0.04^*D(DP1998)$$
$$+ 0.23^*DLOG(TDCON) + 0.32^*DLOG(GVACON(-1))$$

$$(11)$$

$$DLOG(GVADIS) = -0.02 - 0.66^*ECT\_GVADIS(-1)$$
$$+ 0.58^*DLOG(GVADIS(-1)) + 0.31^*DLOG(GVADIS(-2))$$
$$+ 0.39^*DLOG(TDDIS) - 0.08^*DP2000 + 0.10^*DP2010$$

$$(12)$$

$$DLOG(GVAFIBU) = -0.01 + 0.30^*DLOG(GVAFIBU(-1))$$
$$+0.86^*DLOG(TDFIBU) \qquad (13)$$
$$-0.35^*ECT\_GVAFIBU(-1) - 0.03^*D(DP1998)$$

$$DLOG(GVAGOV) = -0.001 - 0.42^*ECT\_GVAGOV(-1)$$
$$+ 0.68^*DLOG(GVAGOV(-1)) + 0.16^*DLOG(TDGOV)$$
$$- 0.06^*DLOG(TDGOV(-1)) + 0.03^*DI1992$$
$$- 0.02^*DI1998 - 0.03^*DI2008 + 0.05^*DP1997$$

$$(14)$$

$$DLOG(GVAMANNO) = 0.04 - 0.40^*ECT\_GVAMANNO(-1)$$
$$+0.30^*DLOG(TDMANNO) + 0.09^*DLOG(DNGA\_IND)$$
$$+0.12^*DLOG(DHFO\_IND) + 0.02^*DLOG(DCOIL\_IND)$$
$$(15)$$

$$DLOG(GVAOILREF) = 0.01 - 0.89^*ECT\_GVAOILREF(-1)$$
$$+0.53^*DLOG(TDOIL) - 0.43^*DLOG(TDOIL(-1))$$
$$+0.58^*DLOG(OILUSE^*365^*0.1486 - DCOIL\_U)$$
$$-0.31^*DLOG$$
$$(DNGA\_IND + DNGA\_IND\_NEU + DNGA\_EOU)$$
$$-0.14^*DI2013 - 0.17^*SI2013 + 0.03^*SI2005$$
$$(16)$$

$$DLOG(GVAOTHS) = 0.01 - 0.92^*ECT\_GVAOTHS(-1)$$
$$+0.31^*DLOG(TDOTHS) + 0.08^*DLOG(DELE\_COMM)$$
$$+0.25^*DLOG(GVAOTHS(-1)) + 0.03^*DP2007$$
$$-0.02^*SI1991 - 0.03^*SI2001 + 0.02^*SI2005$$
$$(17)$$

$$DLOG\ (GVAPETCH) = 0.07 + 0.40^*DLOG\ (TDPETCH) - 0.30^*DLOG\ (TDPETCH(-1))$$
$$+0.14^*DLOG\ (DETH\_IND\_NEU + DLPG\_IND\_NEU$$
$$+DNAP\_IND\_NEU + DNGA\_IND\_NEU)$$
$$-0.51^*ECT\_GVAPETCH(-1) - 0.09^*D(DP2008)$$
$$+0.07^*DP2000 + 0.10^*DP2003 - 0.05^*SI2017$$
$$(18)$$

$$DLOG\ (DETHINDNEU) = -0.004 + 0.64^*\ DLOG\ (GVAPETCH)$$
$$-0.58^*\ ECTDETHINDNEU(-1)$$
$$+0.15^*\ TI2000 - 0.17^*\ TI1999$$
$$(19)$$

$$DLOG\ (DLPG\_IND\_NEU) = -0.10 - 0.67^*\ DLOG\ (PLPG\_IND\_NEU/PGDPPETCH^*100)$$
$$+1.47^*\ DLOG\ (GVAPETCH)$$
$$-1.35^*\ ECT\_DLPG\_IND\_NEU(-1)$$
$$-0.70^*\ DP2003 + 0.23^*\ SI2006 + 0.38^*\ DP2015$$
$$(20)$$

$$DLOG\ (DNAP\_IND\_NEU) = -0.17 - 0.29^*\ DLOG\ (PNAP\_IND\_NEU/PGDPPETCH^*100)$$
$$-0.15^*\ DLOG\ (PNAP\_IND\_NEU(-1)/PGDPPETCH(-1) * 100)$$
$$+1.78^*\ DLOG\ (GVAPETCH)$$
$$-0.65^*\ ECT\_DNAP\_IND\_NEU(-1)$$
$$+0.17^*SI2014 - 0.27^*\ DP2007$$
$$(21)$$

$$\begin{aligned}
\text{DLOG (DNGA\_IND\_NEU)} = & -0.01 + 0.55^* \text{ DLOG (DNGA\_IND\_NEU}(-1)) \\
& +0.37^* \text{ DLOG (GVAPETCH)} \\
& -1.22^* \text{ ECT\_DNGA\_IND\_NEU}(-1) \\
& +0.04^* \text{ SI2000}
\end{aligned}$$

(22)

$$\begin{aligned}
\text{DLOG(GVATRACOM)} = & -0.002 - 0.40^*\text{ECT\_GVATRACOM}(-1) \\
& +0.60^*\text{DLOG(TDTRACOM)} \\
& +0.44^*\text{DLOG(DDIS\_TRA)} \\
& +0.42^*\text{DLOG(TDTRACOM}(-1))+ \\
& 0.23^*\text{DLOG(GVATRACOM}(-1)) \\
& -0.10^*\text{D(DP1991)} - 0.15^*\text{DP2000}
\end{aligned}$$

(23)

$$\begin{aligned}
\text{DLOG(GVAU)} = & 0.03 + 0.22^*\text{DLOG(DNGA\_U)} + 0.11^*\text{DLOG(DCOIL\_U)} \\
& +0.23^*\text{DLOG(DDIS\_U + DHFO\_U)} \\
& -0.52^*\text{ECT\_GVAU}(-1) + 0.09^*\text{DP2010}
\end{aligned}$$

(24)

ECM Equation for Private Consumption

$$\begin{aligned}
\text{DLOG(CONS)} = & 0.03 - 0.23^*\text{ECT\_CONS}(-1) + 0.16^*\text{DLOG(DI)} \\
& -0.01^*\text{D(RCB} - @\text{PCH(CPI)} * 100) \\
& -0.06^*\text{DLOG(WEALTH)} - 0.05^*\text{DB1112}
\end{aligned}$$

(25)

Final ECM Specifications for the Fiscal, Monetary, and External Blocks

ECM Equations for Government Expenditure Items and Debt

$$\begin{aligned}
\text{DLOG (GWSA\_Z)} = & 0.05 - 0.18^*\text{ECT\_GWSA\_Z}(-1) \\
& + 0.07^*\text{DLOG (GREV)} - 0.13^*\text{DI1994} \\
& - 0.26^*\text{DI1995} - 0.34^*\text{DI1996} + 0.14^*\text{DP2009}
\end{aligned}$$

(26)

$$DLOG\ (GAE\_Z) = 0.03 - 0.29^*ECT\_GAE\_Z(-1)$$
$$+\ 0.12^*DLOG\ (GREV(-1)) + 0.25^*DI1979$$
$$+\ 0.39^*DI2009 \tag{27}$$

$$DLOG\ (GMO\_Z) = -0.01 - 0.16^*ECT\_GMO\_Z(-1)$$
$$+0.25^*DLOG\ (GMO\_Z(-1)) \tag{28}$$
$$+0.16^*DLOG\ (GREV(-1)) - 0.48^*D(DP1977)$$

$$DLOG\ (GCGPE) = 0.02 - 0.21^*ECT\_GCGPE(-1)$$
$$+\ 0.25^*DLOG\ (GREV) + 5.63^*DP1981$$
$$-\ 0.76^*DI1976 + 0.92^*DP1990 \tag{29}$$

$$DLOG\ (GC\_Z\_OTH) = 0.10 - 0.41^*ECT\_GC\_Z\_OTH(-1)$$
$$-0.14^*DLOG\ (GC\_Z\_OTH(-2)) + 0.62^*DLOG\ (GREV)$$
$$-0.35^*DLOG\ (GREV(-1)) + 1.05^*DP1991$$
$$-0.73^*DP1993 - 0.76^*DP1998 - 0.75^*DP2009$$
$$\tag{30}$$

$$DLOG\ (GI\_Z) = 0.004 - 0.17^*ECT\_GI\_Z(-1) + 0.39^*DLOG\ (GI\_Z(-2))$$
$$+\ 0.39^*DLOG\ (GREV) - 0.71^*DP1996 + 0.27^*DI1991 \tag{31}$$

$$D(DEBT\_GOV) = 7229.84 - 0.29^*ECT\_DEBT\_GOV(-1)$$
$$-0.18^*D(DEBT\_GOV(-1)) - 0.04^*D(GB(-2))$$
$$-229743.65^*DLOG\ (NFA) + 134151.48^*DLOG\ (NFA(-1))$$
$$+97073.73^*DP2008 - 51305.57^*D(DP2005)$$
$$\tag{32}$$

ECM Equation for M2 Money Balance

$$DLOG\ (M2/PGDP^*100) = -4.17 - 0.29^*DLOG\ (M2(-1)/PGDP(-1) * 100)$$
$$-0.32^*DLOG\ (M2(-2)/PGDP(-2) * 100)$$
$$-0.93^*ECT\_MD\_UR(-1) + 0.63^*DLOG\ (GDP)$$
$$-0.20^*DLOG(WPO\_AL\_R)$$
$$-0.31^*DLOG\ (WPO\_AL\_R(-1))$$
$$+0.62^*DLOG\ (REER) - 0.003^*D(IRD)$$
$$-0.20^*DLOG\ (WPO\_AL\_R(-2)) + 0.08^*DP2004$$
$$+0.06^*DP2009$$
$$\tag{33}$$

Exports Related ECM Equations

$$
\begin{aligned}
\text{DLOG(XGNOIL)} = &-0.62^*\text{ECT\_XGNOIL}(-1) + 0.19^*\text{DLOG(XGNOIL}(-1)) \\
&-1.73^*\text{DLOG(REER)} + 0.45^*\text{DLOG(REER}(-1)) \\
&-1.00^*\text{DLOG(REER}(-2)) - 0.66^*\text{DLOG(GDP\_MNA}^*\text{RXD)} \\
&-0.54^*\text{DLOG(GDP\_MNA}(-1) * \text{RXD}(-1)) \\
&+0.56^*\text{DLOG(GDP\_MNA}(-2) * \text{RXD}(-2)) \\
&+2.88^*\text{DLOG(GVANOIL)} - 1.81^*\text{DLOG(GVANOIL}(-2)) \\
&-0.32^*\text{DP1992} - 0.15^*\text{D(DP1994)}
\end{aligned}
$$

(34)

$$
\begin{aligned}
\text{DLOG(XOILREF)} = &- 0.05 + 1.69^*\text{DLOG(WTREF)} + 0.92^*\text{DLOG(GVAOILREF)} \\
&-0.18^*\text{DLOG(WPO\_AL\_R}(-2)) \\
&-0.64^*\text{ECT\_XOILREF}(-1) - 0.23^* \text{DP2000} \\
&-0.40^* \text{DP1987}
\end{aligned}
$$

(35)

Imports Related ECM Equations

$$
\begin{aligned}
\text{DLOG (MGCAP)} = &-0.04 + 1.31^*\text{DLOG (DOMD)} \\
&- 0.66^*\text{ECT\_MGCAP}(-1) + 0.18^*\text{D(DP2003)} \\
&+ 0.07^*\text{SI2008}
\end{aligned}
$$

(36)

$$
\begin{aligned}
\text{DLOG (MGCONS)} = &0.001 + 0.41^*\text{DLOG (MGCONS}(-1)) + 0.96^*\text{DLOG (DOMD)} \\
&-1.15^*\text{ECT\_MGCONS}(-1) + 0.09^*\text{D(DP1995)} \\
&+0.18^*\text{D(DP2003)} - 0.16^*\text{DP2018}
\end{aligned}
$$

(37)

$$
\begin{aligned}
\text{DLOG (MGINTER)} = &-0.03 + 2.25^*\text{DLOG (GVANOIL + GVAOIL)} \\
&- 0.38^*\text{DLOG (PGDP\_US/PGDP)} \\
&- 0.87^*\text{ECT\_MGINTER}(-1)
\end{aligned}
$$

(38)

$$
\begin{aligned}
\text{DLOG (MS)} = &0.03 - 0.53^*\text{ECT\_MS}(-1) + 2.67^*\text{DLOG (DOMD)} \\
&+1.74^*\text{DLOG (DOMD}(-1)) - 7.64^*\text{DLOG (RRXD)} \\
&-0.37^*\text{DP2015} - 0.46^*\text{DP1998} + 0.38^*\text{DP2006}
\end{aligned}
$$

(39)

ECM Equation for Outflow Remittances

$$
\begin{aligned}
\text{DLOG(REMOF*RXD/PGDP*100)} = {}& -0.0004 - 0.16\text{*ECT\_REMOF}(-1) \\
& + 0.31\text{*DLOG(REMOF}(-1) * \text{RXD}(-1)/ \\
& \text{PGDP}(-1) * 100) \\
& + 0.74\text{*DLOG(GDP)} \\
& + 0.26\text{*DLOG(ETNS}(-1)) \\
& - 1.36\text{*DLOG(PGDP)} \\
& - 0.03\text{*DLOG((EXPL/PGDP*100)} + 1) \\
& + 0.23\text{*D(DP1978)} \\
& - 0.16\text{*D(DP2016)} - 0.31\text{*DP1986}
\end{aligned}
$$

$$(40)$$

Final ECM Specifications for Domestic Prices Block

ECM Equations for Prices of the Household Consumption Basket Items

$$
\begin{aligned}
\text{DLOG(CPIU)} = {}& -0.05 + 0.26\text{*DLOG(CPIU}(-1)) + 0.56\text{*DLOG(PGDPREAL)} \\
& + 0.10\text{*DLOG(PE\_RES)} - 0.26\text{*ECT\_CPIU\_ULC}(-1) \\
& + 0.04\text{*S12011}
\end{aligned}
\qquad (41)
$$

$$
\begin{aligned}
\text{DLOG(CPIFOOD)} = {}& 0.01 + 0.75\text{*DLOG(PGDPAGR)} + 0.61\text{*DLOG(PGDPAGR}(-1)) \\
& + 0.28\text{*DLOG(PMG)} \\
& - 0.25\text{*ECT\_CPIFOOD\_ULC}(-1) + 0.001
\end{aligned}
$$

$$(42)$$

$$
\begin{aligned}
\text{DLOG(CPITRA)} = {}& 0.09 + 0.53\text{* DLOG(CPITRA}(-2)) + 0.15\text{* DLOG(PE\_TRACOM)} \\
& - 0.34\text{* ECT\_CPITRA\_ULC}(-1)
\end{aligned}
$$

$$(43)$$

$$
\begin{aligned}
\text{DLOG(CPIHH)} = {}& 0.02 + 0.03\text{*DLOG(WDIS)} + 0.09\text{*DLOG(PM)} \\
& - 0.30\text{*ECT\_CPIHH\_ULC}(-1) + 0.04\text{*S11984} \\
& - 0.08\text{*S12010} + 0.06\text{*S12011} - 0.08\text{*DP2017}
\end{aligned}
\qquad (44)
$$

$$
\begin{aligned}
\text{DLOG(CPICOMM)} = {}& -0.42 + 1.07\text{*DLOG(PGDPTRACOM)} \\
& - 0.33\text{*DLOG(PGDPTRACOM}(-1)) \\
& - 0.49\text{*ECT\_CPICOM\_ULC}(-1) \\
& - 0.02\text{*T11999} + 0.06\text{*D(DP2004)} \\
& - 0.10\text{*D(DP2000)} - 0.05\text{*S12015}
\end{aligned}
\qquad (45)
$$

DLOG (CPIHTL) $= -0.002 - 0.18^{*}\text{ECT\_CPIHTL\_ULC}(-1)$
$\qquad +0.59^{*}\text{DLOG (CPIHTL}(-1)) + 0.29^{*}\text{DLOG (PGDPDIS)}$
$\qquad +0.78^{*}\text{DLOG ((VAT\_RATE} + 100)/100)$
$\qquad +0.05^{*}\text{DP2011}$

$$(46)$$

DLOG (CPICLOTH) $= -0.01 + 0.37^{*}\text{DLOG (CPICLOTH}(-1))$
$\qquad +0.17^{*}\text{DLOG (PGDPMANNO)} + 0.05^{*}\text{DLOG (WDIS)}$
$\qquad -0.57^{*}\text{ECT\_CPICLOTH\_ULC}(-1)$
$\qquad +0.06^{*}\text{D(DP2016)}$

$$(47)$$

DLOG (CPIMISC) $= -0.001 + 0.31^{*}\text{DLOG (CPIMISC}(-1)) + 0.27^{*}\text{DLOG (PGDPSER)}$
$\qquad +0.12^{*}\text{DLOG (PMG)} - 0.32^{*}\text{ECT\_CPIMISC\_ULC}(-1)$
$\qquad +0.04^{*}\text{DP2007}$

$$(48)$$

DLOG (CPIEDU) $= 0.01 - 0.67^{*}\text{ECT\_CPIEDU\_ULC}(-1) + 0.00004$
$\qquad -06^{*}\text{GAP\_GVAGOV}(-1) + 0.04^{*}\text{DLOG (PGDPGOV)}$
$\qquad -0.30^{*}\text{DLOG (GVAGOV)} - 0.28^{*}\text{DLOG (GVAGOV}(-1))$
$\qquad -0.05^{*}\text{DP2007} + 0.05^{*}\text{SI2010} - 0.05^{*}\text{SI2007}$

$$(49)$$

DLOG (CPIART) $= -1.84 + 0.35^{*}\text{DLOG (CPIART}(-1)) + 1.02^{*}\text{DLOG (PGDPSER)}$
$\qquad +1.28^{*}\text{DLOG (PGDPSER}(-1)) + 0.10^{*}\text{DLOG (WSER)}$
$\qquad +0.34^{*}\text{DLOG (PM)} + 0.31^{*}\text{DLOG (PM}(-1))$
$\qquad +1.74^{*}\text{DLOG ((VAT\_RATE} + 100)/100)$
$\qquad -0.58^{*}\text{ECT\_CPIART\_ULC}(-1) + 0.09^{*}\text{DP2011}$

$$(50)$$

DLOG (CPIHEAL) $= -0.001 + 0.51^{*}\text{DLOG (CPIHEAL}(-1)) + 0.49^{*}\text{DLOG (CPIHEAL}(-2))$
$\qquad +0.14^{*}\text{DLOG (PGDPSER}(-2)) + 0.02^{*}\text{DLOG (PMS}(-2))$
$\qquad +0.60^{*}\text{DLOG ((VAT\_RATE} + 100)/100)$
$\qquad -0.24^{*}\text{ECT\_CPIHEAL\_ULC}(-1) - 0.12^{*}\text{DP2017}$

$$(51)$$

DLOG (CPITOBC) $= -3.73 - 0.33^{*}\text{ECT\_CPITOBC\_ULC}(-1)$
$\qquad +0.43^{*}\text{DLOG (CPITOBC}(-1)) + 0.55^{*}\text{DLOG (PGDPMANNO)}$
$\qquad +0.10^{*}\text{ DLOG(PELE\_COMM)} + 2.72^{*}\text{DLOG ((VAT\_RATE} + 100)/100)$
$\qquad -0.08^{*}\text{DP2015} + 0.07^{*}\text{DP1998}$

$$(52)$$

Note: ECT_PPP is the disequilibrium in the foreign market and estimated as log (cpi(−1)) − (−1.22*log(neer(−1)) + 0.35*log(wpc_wld(−1)) + 0.014*@trend (−1)).

ECM Equations for Sectoral Producer Prices

$$
\begin{aligned}
\text{DLOG(PGDPAGR)} = {}& 0.006 - 0.26^*\text{ECT\_PGDPAGR}(-1) \\
& + 0.06^*\text{DLOG(ULCAGR)} - 0.02^*\text{DI2003} \\
& - 0.02^*\text{DI2004} - 0.03^*\text{DP2000}
\end{aligned} \tag{53}
$$

$$
\begin{aligned}
\text{DLOG(PGDPCON)} = {}& 0.005 + 0.24^*\text{DLOG(PGDPNOIL)} \\
& + 0.30^*\text{DLOG(PGDPNOIL}(-1)) \\
& - 0.47^*\text{ECT\_PGDPCON}(-1) + 0.05^*\text{DP2014} \\
& + 0.04^*\text{DP2011} + 0.02^*\text{DI2008}
\end{aligned} \tag{54}
$$

$$
\begin{aligned}
\text{DLOG(PGDPDIS)} = {}& 0.001 + 0.26^*\text{DLOG(PGDPDIS}(-1)) \\
& + 0.40^*\text{DLOG(PGDPNOIL)} - 0.18^*\text{ECT\_PGDPDIS}(-1) \\
& + 0.06^*\text{DP1984} + 0.04^*\text{DP2008} + 0.05^*\text{DP2000}
\end{aligned} \tag{55}
$$

$$
\begin{aligned}
\text{DLOG(PGDPFIBU)} = {}& 0.002 + 0.75^*\text{DLOG(PGDPFIBU}(-1)) \\
& + 0.39^*\text{DLOG(PGDPNOIL)} \\
& - 0.39^*\text{DLOG(PGDPNOIL}(-1)) \\
& - 0.15^*\text{ECT\_PGDPFIBU}(-1) \\
& + 0.06^*\text{DP2012} - 0.06^*\text{DI2000}
\end{aligned} \tag{56}
$$

$$
\begin{aligned}
\text{DLOG(PGDPGOV)} = {}& -0.02 + 2.25^*\text{DLOG(PGDPNOIL)} \\
& + 0.08^*\text{DLOG(PELE\_GOV)} - 0.59^*\text{ECT\_PGDPGOV}(-1) \\
& + 0.03^*\text{SI1999} - 0.05^*\text{DP2014}
\end{aligned} \tag{57}
$$

$$
\begin{aligned}
\text{DLOG(PGDPMANNO)} = {}& -0.005 + 0.29^*\text{DLOG(PGDPMANNO}(-2)) \\
& + 0.76^*\text{DLOG(GVANOIL\_Z/GVANOIL}^*100) \\
& - 0.52^*\text{ECT\_PGDPMANNO}(-1) + 0.04^*\text{DI2008} \\
& + 0.07^*\text{DP2011}
\end{aligned} \tag{58}
$$

$$
\begin{aligned}
\text{DLOG(PGDPOILREF)} = {}& 0.02 + 0.44^*\text{DLOG(PGDPOIL)} \\
& - 0.64^*\text{ECT\_PGDPOILREF}(-1) \\
& + 0.20^*\text{DP2010}
\end{aligned} \tag{59}
$$

$$
\begin{aligned}
\text{DLOG(PGDPOTHS)} = {}& -0.001 + 0.36^*\text{DLOG(PGDPOTHS}(-1)) \\
& + 0.33^*\text{DLOG(PGDPNOIL)} - 0.55^*\text{ECT\_PGDPOTHS}(-1) \\
& + 0.07^*\text{DLOG(ULCOTHS)} - 0.01^*\text{DI2010} - 0.04^*\text{DP2007}
\end{aligned} \tag{60}
$$

$$DLOG(PGDPTRACOM) = 0.003 + 0.27^*DLOG(PGDPNOIL)$$
$$+0.04^*DLOG(ULCTRACOM)$$
$$-0.68^*ECT\_PGDPTRACOM(-1)$$
$$+0.10^*DP2000 + 0.01^*DI2009 - 0.02^*SI2008$$

$$(61)$$

$$DLOG(PGDPSER) = -0.32^*ECT\_PGDPSER(-1) + 0.02$$
$$+0.28^*DLOG(PM(-1)) + 0.15^*DLOG(PM(-2)) \quad (62)$$
$$+0.10^*DLOG(PELE\_COMM) + 0.03^*DP2018$$

$$DLOG(PGDPU) = -0.02 + 0.80^*DLOG(PGDPNOIL) + 0.12^*DLOG(PE\_U)$$
$$+0.15^*DLOG(PE\_U(-1)) - 0.43^*ECT\_PGDPU(-1)$$
$$-0.06^*DI2008 + 0.15^*DP2018$$

$$(63)$$

Final ECM Specifications for Labor and Wages Block

ECM Equations for Employment by Economic Activity Sector

$$DLOG(ETAGR) = 0.04 - 0.57^*ECT\_ETAGR(-1) + 1.98^*DLOG(GVAAGR)$$
$$-0.79^*DLOG(WAGR/PGDPAGR^*100)$$
$$-0.17^*DLOG(ETAGR(-1))$$

$$(64)$$

$$DLOG(ETCON) = -0.09 - 1.11^*ECT\_ETCON(-1)$$
$$-0.41^*DLOG(WCON/PGDPCON^*100)$$
$$-0.13^*DLOG(WCON(-1)/PGDPCON(-1) * 100) \quad (65)$$
$$+0.21^*SI2016 - 0.12^*TI2006 + 0.11^*TI2008$$

$$DLOG(ETDIS) = -0.48^*ECT\_ETDIS(-1) - 0.001 + 0.22^*DLOG(GVADIS)$$
$$-0.69^*DLOG(WDIS/PGDPDIS^*100) + 0.12^*D(DBT2016)$$
$$-0.07^*D(DP2003)$$

$$(66)$$

$$DLOG(ETFIBU) = 0.04 - 0.31^*ECT\_ETFIBU(-1)$$
$$- 0.38^*DLOG(WFIBU/PGDPFIBU^*100)$$
$$- 0.17^*D(DP201314) + 0.45^*DP2017 \quad (67)$$

$$DLOG(ETGOV) = 0.02 - 0.20^*ECT\_ETGOV(-1)$$
$$+ 0.59^*DLOG(GVAGOV) + 0.06^*DP2008$$
$$+ 0.08^*DP2013 - 0.07^*DP2018 \quad (68)$$

$$DLOG(ETMANNO) = 0.01 - 0.37^*ECT\_ETMANNO(-1)$$
$$+ 0.69^*DLOG(GVAMANNO) - 0.38^*DI2010$$
$$- 0.15^*DP2008 \tag{69}$$

$$DLOG(ETMINOTH) = 0.02 - 0.18^*ECT\_ETMINOTH(-1)$$
$$+0.18^*DLOG(ETMINOTH(-1)) + 0.13^*DP2002$$
$$-0.26^*DB0910 + 0.21^*DB1415$$
$$\tag{70}$$

$$DLOG(ETOTHS) = 0.006 - 1.35^*ECT\_ETOTHS(-1) + 0.59^*DLOG(GVANOIL)$$
$$-0.48^*DLOG(W\_CEIC/PGDPOTHS^*100)$$
$$+0.29^*DLOG(ETOTHS(-1)) + 0.12^*D(DP2014)$$
$$-0.09^*D(DP2009)$$
$$\tag{71}$$

$$DLOG(ETPETCH) = 1.04^*DLOG(GVAPETCH)$$
$$- 0.73^*ECT\_ETPETCH(-1) + 0.03$$
$$- 0.16^*DP2014 \tag{72}$$

$$DLOG(ETTRACOM) = 3.00 - 0.23^*ECT\_ETTRACOM(-1)$$
$$-0.12^*DLOG(WTRACOM/PGDPTRACOM^*100)$$
$$-0.13^*DP2012 + 0.10^*DP2007 - 0.08^*DB1314$$
$$\tag{73}$$

$$DLOG(ETU) = -0.01 - 0.81^*ECT\_ETU(-1) - 0.27^*DLOG(WU/PGDPU^*100)$$
$$+0.21^*DLOG(WU(-1)/PGDPU(-1) * 100)$$
$$+0.53^*DLOG(GVAU(-1)) - 0.24^*DP2012 - 0.09^*D(DP2008)$$
$$+0.28^*DP2014$$
$$\tag{74}$$

ECM Equations for Wages by Economic Activity Sector

$$DLOG(WAGR) = -1.04^*ECT\_WAGR(-1) - 5.29 + 0.31^*DLOG(WAGR(-1))$$
$$+1.27^*DLOG(GVAAGR/ETAGR)$$
$$+0.19^*DLOG(GVAAGR(-2)/ETAGR(-2))$$
$$+2.14^*DLOG(PGDPAGR) - 1.63^*DLOG(PGDPAGR(-1))$$
$$\tag{75}$$

$$DLOG(WCON) = -0.36^*ECT\_WCON(-1) + 0.001$$
$$+ 0.89^*DLOG(GVACON/ETCON) + 0.28^*DP2010$$
$$- 0.54^*DP2003 \tag{76}$$

$$DLOG(WFIBU) = -0.48^*ECT\_WFIBU(-1) + 0.01 - 0.31^*DLOG(WFIBU(-1))$$
$$+1.21^*DLOG(GVAFIBU/ETFIBU)$$
$$+0.34^*DLOG(GVAFIBU(-1)/ETFIBU(-1))$$
$$+0.72^*DLOG(PGDPFIBU) - 0.56^*DLOG(PGDPFIBU(-1))$$
$$-0.30^*DST0309$$

(77)

$$DLOG(WMAN) = -0.35^*ECT\_WMAN(-1) - 0.15$$
$$+1.16^*DLOG(GVAMAN/ETMAN)$$
$$+1.00^*DLOG(GVAMAN(-2)/ETMAN(-2))$$
$$+0.41^*DLOG(WMAN(-2))$$

(78)

$$DLOG(WMIN) = -0.65^*ECT\_WMIN(-1) - 0.01$$
$$+0.32^*DLOG(GVAMIN/ETMIN)$$
$$+0.18^*DLOG(PGDPMIN(-1)) - 0.18^*D(DP2011)$$

(79)

$$DLOG(WTRACOM) = -0.87^*ECT\_WTRACOM(-1) + 0.01$$
$$+0.42^*DLOG(GVATRACOM/ETTRACOM)$$
$$+0.86^*DLOG(PGDPTRACOM)$$
$$+0.27^*DLOG(WTRACOM(-1)) - 0.42^*DP2003$$
$$-0.26^*DP2011$$

(80)

$$DLOG(WU) = -0.52^*ECT\_WU(-1) - 0.02$$
$$+ 1.24^*DLOG(GVAU/ETU) - 0.63^*DP2010$$
$$+ 0.30^*DP2013$$

(81)

Final ECM Specifications for Energy Block

ECM Equations for Demand for Energy Products

Industry

$$DLOG (DCOIL\_IND) = 0.02 + 1.50^*DLOG (GVAIND - GVAU)$$
$$-0.64^*DLOG (PCOIL\_IND(-2)/PGDPIND(-2) * 100)$$
$$-0.32^*ECT\_DCOIL\_IND\_N(-1)$$
$$+0.75^*DLOG (PDIS\_IND/PGDPIND^*100)$$
$$+0.75^*DP1994 - 1.23^*DB1516 + 1.48^*DB8990$$
$$-1.54^*DP2012 - 0.71^*DB1314$$

(82)

$$\text{DLOG (DDIS\_IND)} = 0.04 + 0.10\text{*DLOG (DDIS\_IND}(-1))$$
$$-0.11\text{*DLOG (PDIS\_IND/PGDPMANNO*}100)$$
$$-1.19\text{*ECT\_DDIS\_IND\_N}(-1) - 0.12\text{*D(DBT2016)}$$
$$-0.16\text{*D(DP1986)}$$
$$-0.12\text{*DP2018} - 0.07\text{*DP2011}$$

$$(83)$$

$$\text{DLOG(DELE\_IND)} = -0.16 - 0.10\text{*DLOG(PELE\_IND/PGDPMANNO*}100)$$
$$-0.90\text{*ECT\_DELE\_IND}(-1) + 7.55\text{*DLOG(POPW)}$$
$$-0.29\text{*DSH050607} + 0.62\text{*DP1990} - 0.16\text{*DP2004}$$

$$(84)$$

$$\text{DLOG(DHFO\_IND)} = 0.03 + 0.15\text{*DLOG(PNGA\_IND/PGDPIND*}100)$$
$$-0.42\text{*ECT\_DHFO\_IND\_N}(-1) - 0.19\text{*D(DP2009)}$$
$$-0.25\text{*DP1997}$$

$$(85)$$

$$\text{DLOG(DNGA\_IND)} = 0.04 - 0.42\text{*ECT\_DNGA\_IND}(-1)$$
$$+0.77\text{*DLOG(GVAMANNO)} + 1.39\text{*DLOG(NG\_PRO)}$$
$$-0.88\text{*DLOG(NG\_PRO}(-1))$$
$$-0.21\text{*D(DP2001)} - 0.21\text{*DP2016} - 0.14\text{*DP2017}$$

$$(86)$$

$$\text{DLOG(DOTH\_IND)} = -0.004 + 0.16\text{*DLOG(DOTH\_IND}(-2))$$
$$+0.27\text{*DLOG(GVAMANNO)}$$
$$-0.06\text{*DLOG(POTH\_IND/PGDPMANNO*}100)$$
$$+0.78\text{*DLOG(NGL)} - 0.25\text{*DLOG(NGL}(-2))$$
$$-1.03\text{*ECT\_DOTH\_IND\_NEW}(-1) + 0.19\text{*DP1993}$$

$$(87)$$

Transport

$$\text{DLOG(DDIS\_TRA)} = 0.01 - 0.21\text{*DLOG(PDIS\_TRA/PGDPNOIL*}100)$$
$$-0.82\text{*ECT\_DDIS\_TRA\_N}(-1) + 0.11\text{*D(DP2016)}$$

$$(88)$$

$$\text{DLOG(DGAS\_TRA)} = -0.48\text{*ECT\_DGAS\_TRA\_N}(-1)$$
$$-0.11\text{*DLOG(PGAS\_TRA/PGDPNOIL*}100)$$
$$+0.06\text{*DB8990} - 0.05\text{*DBT88} + 0.02\text{*DBT90} + 0.04$$

$$(89)$$

$$DLOG(DKER\_RES/POP) = 0.01 - 0.24^*DLOG(PKER\_RES/CPI^*100)$$
$$-0.49^*ECT\_DKER\_RES\_N(-1)$$
$$+0.40^*DLOG(PELE\_RES\_CONS/CPI^*100)$$
$$-0.29 + 0.36^*DP1990 + 0.52^*D(DP1991)$$

(90)

Residential

$$DLOG(DELE\_RES/POP) = 0.03 - 0.31^*ECT\_DELE\_RES\_N(-1)$$
$$-0.11^*DLOG(PELE\_RES\_CONS^*100/CPI)$$
$$+0.31^*DLOG(DELE\_RES(-1)/POP(-1))$$
$$+0.39^*DLOG(CDD)$$
$$+0.08^*DB9899 - 0.07^*DP2011 - 0.09^*DP2018$$

(91)

$$DLOG(DKER\_RES/POP) = 0.01 - 0.24^*DLOG(PKER\_RES/CPI^*100)$$
$$-0.49^*ECT\_DKER\_RES\_N(-1)$$
$$+0.40^*DLOG(PELE\_RES\_CONS/CPI^*100)$$
$$-0.29^*DP1987 + 0.36^*DP1990 + 0.52^*D(DP1991)$$

(92)

$$DLOG(DLPG\_RES) = 0.20 - 0.21^*ECT\_DLPG\_N(-1) + 0.38^*DLOG(GDP)$$
$$+0.16^*DB1112 - 0.18^*DST2014 - 0.03^*DBT2011$$

(93)

Commercial, Government, and Agriculture

$$DLOG(DELE\_COMM) = -1.26^*ECT\_DELE\_COMM\_NEW(-1) + 0.07$$
$$+0.21^*DLOG(DELE\_COMM(-1))$$
$$+0.29^*DLOG(GVADIS + GVATRACOM$$
$$+GVAFIBU + GVAOTHS + GVACON)$$
$$-0.13^*DLOG(PELE\_COMM/CPI^*100)$$
$$-0.08^*DLOG(IFDIS + IFTRACOX + IFFIBU$$
$$+IFOTHS + IFCON) - 0.10^*D(DBT2017)$$
$$+0.13^*D(DP2012) - 0.08^*DB2002$$

(94)

$$\begin{aligned} \text{DLOG(DELE\_GOV)} = 0.05 - 0.08^*\text{DLOG(PELE\_GOV/PGDPGOV}^*100) \\ -0.76^*\text{ECT\_DELE\_GOV\_N}(-1) + 0.11^*\text{D(DP2017)} \\ +0.19^*\text{D(DP2018)} \end{aligned}$$

$$(95)$$

$$\begin{aligned} \text{DLOG(DELE\_AGR)} = 0.03 + 0.21^*\text{DLOG(DELE\_AGR}(-1)) \\ -0.05^*\text{DLOG(IFAGR)} + 0.04^*\text{DLOG(IFAGR}(-1)) \\ +0.27^*\text{DLOG(WAGR/PGDPAGR}^*100) \\ -1.02^*\text{ECT\_DELE\_AGR\_N\_N}(-1) \\ +0.32^*\text{D(DP2009)} \end{aligned}$$

$$(96)$$

Note

DPXXXX, where XXXX stands for a given year. DPXXXX takes a value of one for the year XXXX and a value of zero otherwise. For example, DP2014 is a dummy variable taking 1 in 2014, zero otherwise.

D(DPXXXX), where D and XXXX stand for difference operator and a given year. For example, D(DP2005) is a dummy variable taking 1 in 2005 and -1 in 2006, zero otherwise.

DBXXYY, where XX and YY stand for the last two digits of a given year and next year, respectively. For example, DB1314 is a dummy variable taking 1 in 2013 and -1 in 2014.

DIXXXX, where XXXX stands for a given year. For example, DI2014 is a dummy variable taking 1 in 2014 and -1 in 2015, zero otherwise.

SIXXXX, where XXXX stands for a given year. For example, SI2003 is a dummy variable, taking unity from 1970 to 2003 and zero otherwise.

TIXXXX, where XXXX stands for a given year. For example, TI2009 is a dummy variable taking -1 in 2009 through -20 in 1990, zero otherwise.

The last three types of dummy variables are created by Autometrics in Ox Metrics.

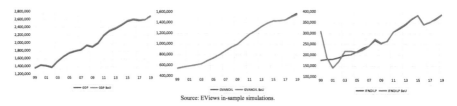

Source: EViews in-sample simulations.

Fig. D.1 The real block indicators: GDP, GVANOIL, and IFNOILP. (Source: EViews in-sample simulations)

Source: EViews in-sample simulations.

Fig. D.2 The fiscal block indicators: GEXP, GREVOIL, and GREVNOIL. (Source: EViews in-sample simulations)

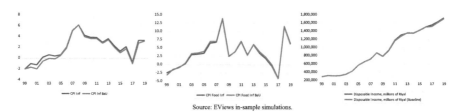

Source: EViews in-sample simulations.

Fig. D.3 The prices block indicators: CPI inflation, %, CPIFOOD inflation, % and DI_Z. (Source: EViews in-sample simulations)

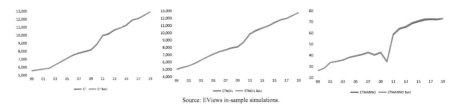

Source: EViews in-sample simulations.

Fig. D.4 The labor market block indicators: ET, ETNOIL, and ETMANNO. (Source: EViews in-sample simulations)

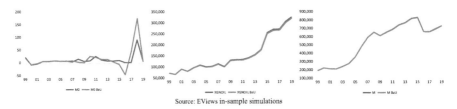

Source: EViews in-sample simulations

Fig. D.5 The monetary block and external block indicators: M0 growth, XGNOIL, M. (Source: EViews in-sample simulations)

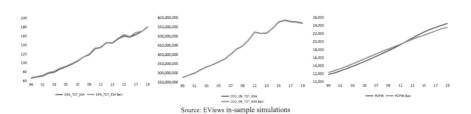

Source: EViews in-sample simulations

Fig. D.6 Energy block, CO_2 emissions block, and population and age cohort block indicators: DEN_TOT_KSA, CO2_EN_TOT_KSA, POPW. (Source: EViews in-sample simulations)

Table E.1 Consumer price indexes weights in Saudi Arabia. CPI is the weighted average of 12 components containing two values, old weights from 1970 to 2012 and new weights for 2013–2019 as documented the table below

Weights	CPIU_W	CPIFOOD_W	CPITRA_W	CPIHH_W	CPICOMM_W	CPIHTL_W
1970–2012	0.205	0.217	0.104	0.091	0.081	0.056
2013–2019	0.253	0.188	0.100	0.085	0.085	0.065
Weights	CPICLOTH_W	CPIMISC_W	CPIEDU_W	CPIART_W	CPIHEAL_W	CPITOBC_W
1970–2012	0.084	0.069	0.027	0.035	0.026	0.005
2013–2019	0.062	0.057	0.042	0.034	0.023	0.007

Appendix D: KGEMM in-Sample Simulations Results, 1999–2019

Appendix E. Consumer Price Indexes Weights and CO_2 Conversion Factors

CO_2 Conversion Factors and their Sources Used in the CO_2 Emissions Block
1 MTOE = 10^6 TOE.
https://en.wikipedia.org/wiki/Tonne_of_oil_equivalent#:~:text=6%20External%20
    links-Definitions,toe%20%3D%2041.868%20gigajoules%20(GJ)
1 TOE of Crude Oil = 7.33 Barrel of Crude Oil.
https://en.wikipedia.org/wiki/Tonne_of_oil_equivalent#:~:text=6%20External%20
    links-Definitions,toe%20%3D%2041.868%20gigajoules%20(GJ)
1 Barrel of Crude oil = 0.43 Metric Tons of CO_2
https://www.epa.gov/energy/greenhouse-gases-equivalencies-calculator-calcula
    tions-and-references
1 TOE of Diesel = 0.99 Ton of Diesel
https://en.wikipedia.org/wiki/Tonne_of_oil_equivalent#:~:text=6%20External%20
    links-Definitions,toe%20%3D%2041.868%20gigajoules%20(GJ)
1 Ton of Diesel = 7.5 Barrels of Diesel
https://qp.com.qa/ar/Pages/ConversionFactor.aspx
1 Barrel = 42 Gallon
1 Gallon of Diesel = 0.01018 Metric Tons CO_2
https://www.epa.gov/energy/greenhouse-gases-equivalencies-calculator-calcula
    tions-and-references
1 TOE of HFO = 1.04 Ton of Diesel
https://www150.statcan.gc.ca/n1/pub/57-601-x/00105/4173282-eng.htm
1 Ton of Fuel Oil = 6.7 Barrel of Fuel Oil
https://qp.com.qa/ar/Pages/ConversionFactor.aspx
It is also assumed that 1 TOE HFO = 1 Ton HFO.
1 Barrel of Fuel Oil = 0.43 metric tons of CO_2
https://www.epa.gov/energy/greenhouse-gases-equivalencies-calculator-calcula
    tions-and-references
1 MTOE of Natural Gas = 39.2 Mcf
https://www.energy-sea.gov.il/English-Site/Pages/Data%20and%20Maps/calc.aspx
1 Mcf of Natural Gas = 0.0548 Metric Tons of CO_2
https://www.epa.gov/energy/greenhouse-gases-equivalencies-calculator-calcula
    tions-and-references

If ethane, butane, and propane are the main constituents of DOTH_IND, then LPG is
the core factor and calculations should be based on LPG conversion factor.

1 TOE of Liquefied Petroleum Gas (LPG) = 0.887862914 Ton of LPG

https://www.seai.ie/data-and-insights/seai-statistics/conversion-factors/

1 Ton of LPG = 11.6 Barrels of LPG

https://qp.com.qa/ar/Pages/ConversionFactor.aspx

1 Gallon of LPG = 0.2357 Metric Tons of CO_2

https://www.epa.gov/energy/greenhouse-gases-equivalencies-calculator-calcula
tions-and-references

1 TOE = 11.63 MWh

https://www.unitjuggler.com/convert-energy-from-toe-to-MWh.html

1 MWh Electricity Generated in KSA = 0.645 Metric Tons of CO_2

The conversion factor is taken from a pdf document by the Clean Development
Mechanism Designated National Authority of KSA (https://cdmdna.gov.sa/
content/pdf/GEF.pdf).

1 TOE of Petrol = 0.952380952 Ton of Petrol

https://en.wikipedia.org/wiki/Tonne_of_oil_equivalent#:~:text=6%20External%20
links-Definitions,toe%20%3D%2041.868%20gigajoules%20(GJ)

1 Ton of Gasoline = 8.5 Barrels of Gasoline

https://qp.com.qa/ar/Pages/ConversionFactor.aspx

1 Gallon of Gasoline = 0.008887 Metric Tons of CO_2

https://www.epa.gov/energy/greenhouse-gases-equivalencies-calculator-calcula
tions-and-references

1 TOE of Jet Kerosene = 0.949397133 Ton of Jet Kerosene

https://www.seai.ie/data-and-insights/seai-statistics/conversion-factors/

1 Ton of Kerosene = 7.8 Barrels of Kerosene

https://qp.com.qa/ar/Pages/ConversionFactor.aspx

1 Gallon of Jet Fuel = 0.00957 Metric Tons of CO_2

https://www.eia.gov/environment/emissions/co2_vol_mass.php

1 TOE of Liquefied Petroleum Gas (LPG) = 0.887862914 Ton of LPG

https://www.seai.ie/data-and-insights/seai-statistics/conversion-factors/

1 Ton of LPG = 11.6 barrels of LPG

https://qp.com.qa/ar/Pages/ConversionFactor.aspx

1 Gallon of LPG = 0.2357 Metric Tons of CO_2

https://www.epa.gov/energy/greenhouse-gases-equivalencies-calculator-calcula
tions-and-references

References

Ackerman, Frank. 2002. Still dead after all these years: Interpreting the failure of general equilibrium theory. *Journal of Economic Methodology* 9 (2): 119–139.

Alam, M. Shahid. 1982. The basic macro-economics of oil economies. *The Journal of Development Studies* 18 (2): 205–216.

Aljerayed, Khalid Jerayed Hasan. 1993. *A macroeconometric model of an oil-based economy: Case study of Saudi Arabia*. PhD diss., University of Colorado at Boulder.

Al-Teraiki, Ahmed. 1999. *A macroeconometric model of Saudi Arabia for economic stabilisation and forecasting*. PhD diss., Loughborough University.

Arezki, Mr Rabah, and Reda Cherif. 2010. *Development accounting and the rise of TFP*. International Monetary Fund.

Arora, Vipin. 2013. *An evaluation of macroeconomic models for use at EIA*. U.S. Energy Information Administration. Washington, DC, USA.

Ballantyne, Alexander, Tom Cusbert, Richard Evans, Rochelle Guttmann, Jonathan Hambur, Adam Hamilton, Elizabeth Kendall, Rachael McCririck, Gabriela Nodari, and Daniel M. Rees. 2020. MARTIN has its place: A macroeconometric model of the australian economy. *Economic Record* 96 (314): 225–251.

Banerjee, Abhijit V. 1992. A simple model of herd behavior. *The Quarterly Journal of Economics* 107 (3): 797–817.

Bardsen, Gunnar, and Ragnar Nymoen. 2008. *Macroeconometric modelling for policy*. Working Paper, 30 April.

Bårdsen, Gunnar, Eilev S. Jansen, and Ragnar Nymoen. 2004. Econometric evaluation of the New Keynesian Phillips curve. *Oxford Bulletin of Economics and Statistics* 66: 611–686.

Bardsen, Gunnar, Oyvind Eitrheim, Eilev S. Jansen, and Ragnar Nymoen. 2005. *The Econometrics of macroeconomic modelling*. Oxford: Oxford University Press.

Bayoumi, Tamim, Hamid Faruqee, Douglas Laxton, Philippe D. Karam, Alessandro Rebucci, Jaewoo Lee, Ben Hunt, and Ivan Tchakarov. 2004. *GEM: A new international macroeconomic model*. International Monetary Fund, no. 239.

Beenstock, Michael, Peter Warburton, Paul Lewington, and Alan Dalziel. 1986. A macroeconomic model of aggregate supply and demand for the UK. *Economic Modelling* 3 (4): 242–268.

Bjerkholt, Olav. 1993. Reviews of macroeconomic modeling needs of the Ministry of Economy and Planning in the Kingdom of Saudi Arabia. *Research Department, Statistics Norway* 93: 25.

Blanchard, Olivier. 2017. Do DSGE models have a future. In *DSGE models in the conduct of policy: Use as intended*, ed. Refet S. Gürkaynak and Cédric Tille, CEPR Press. Washington, D.C., United States. 93.

© The Author(s) 2023

159

F. J. Hasanov et al., *A Macroeconometric Model for Saudi Arabia*,
SpringerBriefs in Economics, https://doi.org/10.1007/978-3-031-12275-0

Blanchard, Olivier. 2018. On the future of macroeconomic models. *Oxford Review of Economic Policy* 34 (1–2): 43–54.

Blazejczak, Jürgen, Frauke G. Braun, Dietmar Edler, and Wolf-Peter Schill. 2014a. Economic effects of renewable energy expansion: A model-based analysis for Germany. *Renewable and Sustainable Energy Reviews* 40: 1070–1080.

Blazejczak, Jürgen, Dietmar Edler, and Wolf-Peter Schill. 2014b. Improved energy efficiency: Vital for energy transition and stimulus for economic growth. *DIW Economic Bulletin* 4 (4): 3–15.

Blazquez, Jorge, Lester Hunt, and Baltasar Manzano. 2017. Oil subsidies and renewable energy in Saudi Arabia: A general equilibrium approach. *The Energy Journal* 38 (S11): 29–45.

Bodkin, Ronald G., Lawrence R. Klein, and Kanta Marwah. 1991. *A history of macroeconometric model-building*. Edward Elgar Publishing, number 51.

Bontemps, Christophe, and Grayham E. Mizon. 2008. Encompassing: Concepts and implementation. *Oxford Bulletin of Economics and Statistics* 70: 721–750.

Bradley, John, Leonor Modesto, and Simón Sosvilla-Rivero. 1995. HERMIN: A macroeconometric modelling framework for the EU periphery. *Economic Modelling* 12 (3): 221–247.

Brouwer, Gordon de, and Neil R. Ericsson. 1998. Modeling inflation in Australia. *Journal of Business & Economic Statistics* 16 (4): 433–449.

Buenafe, Sheila W., and Celia M. Reyes. 2001. Alternative estimation methodologies for macro model: ECM vs. OLS. *PIDS Discussion Paper Series*, No. 2001-22.

Bulligan, Guido, Fabio Busetti, Michele Caivano, Pietro Cova, Davide Fantino, Alberto Locarno, and Maria Lisa Rodano. 2017. *The Bank of Italy econometric model: an update of the main equations and model elasticities*. Bank of Italy Temi di Discussione (Working Paper) No 1130.

Calzolari, Giorgio, and Paolo Corsi. 1977. Stochastic simulation as a validation tool for econometric models. In *Published in Models for regional planning and policy-making: proceedings of the joint IBM/IIASA conference*, 359–369.

Campos, Julia, Ericsson R. Neil, and Hendry F. David. 2005. *General-to-specific modeling: An overview and selected bibliography*. Board of Governors of the Federal Reserve System, International Finance Discussion Papers, No. 838 August.

Cappelen, Ådne, and Knut A. Magnussen. 1996. The selection model. A general equilibrium model for Saudi Arabia. *Research Department, Statistics Norway* 96 (14).

Castle, Jennifer L., Jurgen A. Doornik, and David F. Hendry. 2011. Evaluating automatic model selection. *Journal of Time Series Econometrics* 3 (1): 8.

Castle, Jennifer L., Jurgen A. Doornik, and David F. Hendry. 2021. Robust discovery of regression models. *Econometrics and Statistics*. https://doi.org/10.1016/j.ecosta.2021.05.004

Christ, Carl. 1951. A test of an econometric model for the United States, 1921–1947. In *Conference on business cycles*. NBER, pp. 35–130.

Clements, Michael P., and David F. Hendry. 2011. Forecasting from Mis-specified models in the presence of unanticipated location shifts. In *Oxford handbook of economic forecasting*, ed. Michael P. Clements and David F. Hendry, 271–314. Oxford: Oxford University Press.

Cobb, Charles W., and Paul H. Douglas. 1928. A theory of production. *The American Economic Review* 18 (1): 139–165.

Colander, David. 2006. *Post Walrasian macroeconomics: Beyond the dynamic stochastic general equilibrium model*. Cambridge: Cambridge University Press.

Colander, David, Peter Howitt, Alan Kirman, Axel Leijonhufvud, and Perry Mehrling. 2008. Beyond DSGE models: Toward an empirically based macroeconomics. *American Economic Review* 98 (2): 236–240.

Collins, Susan M., Barry P. Bosworth, and Dani Rodrik. 1996. Economic growth in East Asia: accumulation versus assimilation. *Brookings papers on economic activity*, No. 2: 135–203.

Crump, Richard K., Stefano Eusepi, Domenico Giannone, Eric Qian, and Argia M. Sbordone. 2021. A large Bayesian VAR of the United States economy. *Federal Reserve Bank of New York Staff Reports*, no. 976.

Cusbert, Tom, and Elizabeth Kendall. 2018. Meet MARTIN, the RBA's new macroeconomic model. *Australian Reserve Bank Bulletin* March: 31–44.

Dagoumas, A.S., and T.S. Barker. 2010. Pathways to a low-carbon economy for the UK with the macro-econometric E3MG model. *Energy Policy* 38 (6): 3067–3077.

Davidson, James E.H., David F. Hendry, Frank Srba, and Stephen Yeo. 1978. Econometric modelling of the aggregate time series relationships between consumers' expenditure and income in the United Kingdom. *Economic Journal* 88: 661–692.

De Brouwer, Gordon, and Ericsson Neil. 1995. *Modelling inflation in Australia.* International Finance Discussion Papers 530.

De Santis, Roberto A. 2003. Crude oil price fluctuations and Saudi Arabia's behaviour. *Energy Economics* 25 (2): 155–173.

Desboulets, Loann David Denis. 2018. A review on variable selection in regression analysis. *Econometrics* 6 (4): 45.

Dickey, David A., and Wayne A. Fuller. 1981. Likelihood ratio statistics for autoregressive time series with a unit root. *Econometrica* 49: 1057–1072.

Doornik, Jurgen A. 2009. Autometrics. In *The methodology and practice of econometrics: A festschrift in honour of David F. Hendry*, ed. J.L. Castle and N. Shephard, 88–121. Oxford, UK: Oxford University Press.

Doornik, Jurgen A., and David F. Hendry. 2009. *Modelling dynamic systems: PcGive 13.* London: Timberlake Consultants.

Doornik, Jurgen A., and David F. Hendry. 2018. *Empirical Econometric Modelling, PcGive 15.* London: Timberlake Consultants.

Douglas, Paul H. 1976. The Cobb-Douglas production function once again: Its history, its testing, and some new empirical values. *Journal of Political Economy* 84 (5): 903–915.

Econometrics Cambridge. 2019. *E3ME technical manual v6. 1.* Version March.

Elshurafa, Amro M., Alatawi Hatem, Fakhri J. Hasanov, Goblan J. Alghatani, and Frank A. Felder. 2022. Cost, emission, and macroeconomic implications of diesel displacement in the Saudi agricultural sector: Options and policy implications. *Energy Policy* 168 (9): 113090.

Enders, Walter. 2015. *Applied Econometrics time series*, Wiley series in probability and statistics. Tuscaloosa: University of Alabama.

Enders, Walter, and Junsoo Lee. 2012a. A unit root test using a Fourier series to approximate smooth breaks. *Oxford Bulletin of Economics and Statistics* 74 (4): 574–599.

Enders, Walter, and Junsoo Lee. 2012b. The flexible Fourier form and Dickey–Fuller type unit root tests. *Economics Letters* 117 (1): 196–199.

Engle, Robert F., and Clive W.J. Granger. 1987. Co-integration and error correction: Representation, estimation and testing. *Econometrica* 55: 251–276.

Engle, Robert F., and David F. Hendry. 1993. Testing superexogeneity and invariance in regression models. *Journal of Econometrics* 56 (1–2): 119–139.

Engle, Robert F., and Byung Sam Yoo. 1987. Forecasting and testing in co-integrated systems. *Journal of Econometrics* 35 (1): 143–159.

Engle, Robert F., David F. Hendry, and Jean-Francois Richard. 1983. Exogeneity. *Econometrica: Journal of the Econometric Society*: 51 (2): 277–304.

Engle, Robert F., Clive W.J. Granger, and Jeff J. Hallman. 1989. Merging short-and long-run forecasts: An application of seasonal cointegration to monthly electricity sales forecasting. *Journal of Econometrics* 40 (1): 45–62.

Epprecht, Camila, Dominique Guegan, Álvaro Veiga, and Joel Correa da Rosa. 2021. Variable selection and forecasting via automated methods for linear models: LASSO/adaLASSO and autometrics. *Communications in Statistics-Simulation and Computation* 50 (1): 103–122.

Ericsson, Neil R. 1992. Parameter constancy, mean square forecast errors, and measuring forecast performance: An exposition, extensions, and illustration. *Journal of Policy Modeling* 14 (4): 465–495.

Ericsson, Neil R. 1993. On the limitations of comparing mean square forecast errors: Clarifications and extensions. *Journal of Forecasting* 12 (8): 644–651.

Ericsson, Neil R. 2021. Dynamic Econometrics in action: A biography of David F. Hendry. In *International finance discussion papers 1311.* Washington: Board of Governors of the Federal Reserve System. https://doi.org/10.17016/IFDP.2021.1311.

Ericsson, Neil R., and John S. Irons, eds. 1994. *Testing exogeneity*. Oxford University Press. Great Clarendon Street Oxford OX2 6DP, UK.

Ericsson, Neil R., and John S. Irons. 1995. The Lucas critique in practice. In *Macroeconometrics*, 263–324. Dordrecht: Springer.

Ericsson, Neil R., Julia Campos, and Hong-Anh Tran. 1990. PC-GIVE and David Hendry's econometric methodology. *Revista de Econometria* 10: 7–117.

Ezzati, Ali. 1976. Future OPEC price and production strategies as affected by its capacity to absorb oil revenues. *European Economic Review* 8 (2): 107–138.

Fair, Ray C. 1979. An analysis of the accuracy of four macroeconometric models. *Journal of Political Economy* 87 (4): 701–718.

Fair, Ray C. 1984. *Specification, estimation, and analysis of macroeconometric models*. Harvard University Press. 79 Garden Street, Cambridge, MA 02138, USA.

Fair, Ray C. 1993. Testing macroeconometric models. *The American Economic Review* 83 (2): 287–293.

Fair, Ray C. 1994. *Testing macroeconometric models*. Cambridge, MA/London: Harvard University Press.

Fair, Ray C. 2004. *Estimating how the macroeconomy works*. Cambridge, MA/London: Harvard University Press.

Fair, Ray C. 2019. *Some important macro points*. Cowles Foundation Discussion Paper no. 2165.

Fanchon, Phillip, and Jeanne Wendel. 1992. Estimating VAR models under non-stationarity and cointegration: Alternative approaches for forecasting cattle prices. *Applied Economics* 24 (2): 207–217.

Favero, Carlo A. 2001. *Applied macroeconometrics*. Oxford University Press. Great Clarendon Street Oxford OX2 6DP, UK.

Favero, Carlo, and F. David Hendry. 1992. Testing the Lucas critique: A review. *Econometric Reviews* 11 (3): 265–306.

Flaute, M., A. Großmann, C. Lutz, and A. Nieters. 2017. Macroeconomic effects of prosumer households in Germany. *International Journal of Energy Economics and Policy* 7 (1): 146–155.

Furuoka, Fumitaka. 2017. A new approach to testing unemployment hysteresis. *Empirical Economics* 53 (3): 1253–1280.

Giacomini, Raffaella. 2015. Economic theory and forecasting: Lessons from the literature. *The Econometrics Journal* 18: C22–C41.

Gervais, Olivier, and Marc-André Gosselin. 2014. *Analyzing and forecasting the Canadian economy through the LENS model*. No. 102. Bank of Canada.

Gonand, Frédéric, Fakhri J. Hasanov, and Lester Hunt. 2019. Estimating the impact of energy price reform on Saudi Arabian intergenerational welfare using the MEGIR-SA model. *The Energy Journal* 40 (3): 55–77.

Gramkow, Camila, and Annela Anger-Kraavi. 2019. Developing green: A case for the Brazilian manufacturing industry. *Sustainability* 11 (23): 6783.

Gürkaynak, Refet S., and Cédric Tille, eds. 2017. *DSGE models in the conduct of policy: Use as intended*. CEPR Press. Washington, D.C., United States.

Gürkaynak, Refet S., Burçin Kısacıkoğlu, and Barbara Rossi. 2013. Do DSGE models forecast more accurately out-of-sample than VAR models? *Advances in Econometrics* 32: 27–79.

Haavelmo, Trygve. 1943a. Statistical testing of business-cycle theories. *The Review of Economic Statistics*: 13–18.

Haavelmo, Trygve. 1943b. The statistical implications of a system of simultaneous equations. *Econometrica* 11 (1): 1–12.

Haavelmo, Trygve. 1944. The probability approach in econometrics. *Econometrica: Journal of the Econometric Society*: iii–115.

Hall, Robert E., and Charles I. Jones. 1999. Why do some countries produce so much more output per worker than others? *The quarterly journal of economics* 114 (1): 83–116.

Halvorsen, R., and R. Palmquist. 1980. The interpretation of dummy variables in Semilogarithmic equations. *American Economic Review* 70: 474–475.

Hansen, Peter Reinhard. 2000. *Structural changes in cointegrated processes*. Ph.D. thesis, University of California, San Diego.

Hara, Naoko, Hibiki Ichiue, Satoko Kojima, Koji Nakamura, and Toyoichiro Shirota. 2009. *Practical use of macroeconomic models at central banks*. Bank of Japan No. 09-E-1.

Harvey, David, and Paul Newbold. 2000. Tests for multiple forecast encompassing. *Journal of Applied Econometrics* 15: 471–482.

Harvey, David I., Stephen J. Leybourne, and Paul Newbold. 1998. Tests for forecast encompassing. *Journal of Business and Economic Statistics* 16: 254–259.

Hasanov, Fakhri J. 2021. Theoretical framework for industrial energy consumption revisited: The role of demographics. *Energy Reports* 7: 2178–2200.

Hasanov, Fakhri J., Moayad H. Al Rasasi, Salah S. Alsayaary, and Ziyadh Alfawzan. 2022. Money demand under a fixed exchange rate regime: The case of Saudi Arabia. *Journal of Applied Economics* 25 (1): 385–411.

Hasanov, Fakhri, and Frederick Joutz. 2013. *A macroeconometric model for making effective policy decisions in the Republic of Azerbaijan*. International Conference on Energy, Regional Integration and Socio-economic Development 6017, EcoMod.

Hasanov, Fakhri, Frederick L. Joutz, Jeyhun I. Mikayilov, and Muhammad Javid. 2020. KGEMM: A Macroeconometric Model for Saudi Arabia. *KAPSARC Discussion Paper*, No. ks--2020-dp04.

Hasanov, Fakhri J., and Razek Noha H.A. 2022. *Oil and Non-oil Determinants of Saudi Arabia's International Competitiveness: Historical Analysis and Policy Simulations*. USAEE Working Paper No. 22-559.

Hasanov, Fakhri J., Jeyhun I. Mikayilov, Muhammad Javid, Moayad Al-Rasasi, Frederick Joutz, and Mohammed B. Alabdullah. 2021. Sectoral employment analysis for Saudi Arabia. *Applied Economics* 53 (45): 5267–5280.

Hasanov, Fakhri J., Amro M. Elshurafa, and Lester C. Hunt. 2022a. *What contributes more to the macroeconomy: Deploying solar PV at the utility-scale or at the distributed scale?* forthcoming KAPSARC Discussion Paper.

Hasanov, Fakhri J., Bollino C. Andrea, and Olagunju Waheed. 2022b. Consumption function for Saudi Arabia. What is new? forthcoming KAPSARC Discussion Paper.

Hasanov, Fakhri J., Muhammad Javid, and Frederick L. Joutz. 2022c. Saudi non-oil exports before and after COVID-19: Historical impacts of determinants and scenario analysis. *Sustainability* 14 (4): 2379.

Hendry, David F. 1993. Econometrics: Alchemy or science. In *Essays in econometric methodology*. Oxford: Blackwell Publishers.

Hendry, David F. 1995. *Dynamic econometrics*. Oxford: Oxford University Press.

Hendry, David F. 2000. Epilogue: The success of general-to-specific model selection. In *Econometrics: Alchemy or science? Essays in econometric methodology*, ed. David F. Hendry, 467–490. Oxford: Oxford University Press.

Hendry, David F. 2018. Deciding between alternative approaches in macroeconomics. *International Journal of Forecasting* 34 (1): 119–135.

Hendry, David F., and Jurgen A. Doornik. 2009. *Empirical econometric modelling using PcGive: Volume I*. London: Timberlake Consultants Press.

Hendry, David F., and Jurgen A. Doornik. 2014. *Empirical model discovery and theory evaluation: Automatic selection methods in econometrics*. MIT Press.

Hendry, David F., and Søren Johansen. 2015. Model discovery and Trygve Haavelmo's legacy. *Econometric Theory* 31 (1): 93–114.

Hendry, David F., and Hans-Martin Krolzig. 1999. Improving on 'data mining reconsidered' by K.D. Hoover and SJ Perez. *The Econometrics Journal* 2 (2): 202–219.

Hendry, David F. 2001. *Automatic econometric model selection using PcGets 1.0*. London: Timberlake Consultants Press.

Hendry, David, and Grayham Mizon. 2000. Reformulation empirical macroeconomic modelling. *Oxford Review of Economic Policy* 16 (4): 138–159.

Hendry, David F., and Carlos Santos. 2010. *An Automatic Test of Super Exogeneity*. In Volatility and Time Series Econometrics: Essays in Honor of Robert Engle. Tim Bollerslev (ed.) et al. Oxford University Press.

Hendry, David F., and Mizon, Grayham E. 2014. Unpredictability in economic analysis, econometric modeling and forecasting. *Journal of Econometrics* 182 (1): 186–195.

Hendry, David F., and John N.J. Muellbauer. 2018. The future of macroeconomics: Macro theory and models at the Bank of England. *Oxford Review of Economic Policy* 34 (1–2): 287–328.

Hendry, David F., Adrian R. Pagan, and J. Denis Sargan. 1984a. Dynamic specification. *Handbook of Econometrics* 2: 1023–1100.

Hendry, David F., Adrian R. Pagan, and John D. Sargan. 1984b. Dynamic specification. In *Handbook of econometrics*, ed. Zvi Griliches and Michael D. Intriligator, vol. 2, 1023–1100. Amsterdam: North-Holland.

Hendry, David, Jennifer Castle, and Michael Clements. 2019. *Forecasting*. Yale University Press.

Herbst, Edward, and Frank Schorfheide. 2012. Evaluating DSGE model forecasts of comovements. *Journal of Econometrics* 171 (2): 152–166.

Herbst, Andrea, Felipe Toro, Felix Reitze, and Eberhard Jochem. 2012. Introduction to energy systems modelling. *Swiss Journal of Economics and Statistics* 148 (2): 111–135.

Hoover, Kevin D., and Stephen J. Perez. 1999. Data mining reconsidered: Encompassing and the general-to-specific approach to specification search. *The Econometrics Journal* 2 (2): 167–191.

Hoover, Kevin D., Soren Johansen, and Katarina Juselius. 2008. Allowing the data to speak freely: The macroeconometrics of the Cointegrated vector autoregression. *American Economic Review* 98 (2): 251–255.

Hurtado, Samuel. 2014. DSGE models and the Lucas critique. *Economic Modelling* 44: S12–S19.

IEA. 2021. International Energy Agency Database. https://www.iea.org/data-and-statistics

Jadwa Investment. 2021. *2022 Saudi Fiscal Budget*. December 2021. https://www.jadwa.com/sites/default/files/2022-01/20211213_2022-Saudi-Fiscal-Budget.pdf

Javid, Muhammad, and Hasanov Fakhri J. 2022. *Determinants of outflow remittance: The case of Saudi Arabia*, KAPSARC Discussion Paper. No. ks–2022-dp05.

Javid, Muhammad, Fakhri J. Hasanov, Carlo Andrea Bollino, and Marzio Galeotti. 2022. Sectoral investment analysis for Saudi Arabia. *Applied Economics*: 1–15.

Jelić, Ozana Nadoveza, and Rafael Ravnik. 2021. *Introducing Policy Analysis Croatian MAcroecoNometric Model (PACMAN): Croatian National Bank*, Publishing Department.

Johansen, Søren. 1988. Statistical analysis of cointegration vectors. *Journal of Economic Dynamics and Control* 12 (2–3): 231–254.

Johansen, Søren, and Katarina Juselius. 1990. Maximum likelihood estimation and inference on cointegration—With applications to the demand for money. *Oxford Bulletin of Economics and Statistics* 52 (2): 169–210.

Johansen, Per R., and Knut A. Magnussen. 1996. The implementation model. A macroeconomic model for Saudi Arabia. *Research Department, Statistics Norway* 96 (13): 1-96

Juselius, Katarina. 1992. Domestic and foreign effects on prices in an open economy: The case of Denmark. *Journal of Policy Modeling* 14 (4): 401–428.

Kennedy, P.E. 1981. Estimation with correctly interpreted dummy variables in Semilogarithmic equations. *American Economic Review* 71: 802.

Khan, Muhammad Arshad, and Musleh ud Din. 2011. *A dynamic macroeconometric model of Pakistan's economy*. Working Papers & Research Reports.

King Abdullah Petroleum Studies and Research Center (KAPSARC). 2017. *The KAPSARC global energy macroeconometric model*. https://www.kapsarc.org/research/projects/the-kapsarc-global-energy-macroeconometric-model-kgemm/

Klein, Lawrence Robert, Aleksander Welfe, and Władysław Welfe. 1999. *Principles of macroeconometric modeling*. Amsterdam: North-Holland.

Krolzig, Hans-Martin, and David F. Hendry. 2001. Computer automation of general-to-specific model selection procedures. *Journal of Economic Dynamics and Control* 25 (6–7): 831–866.

Kwiatkowski, Denis, Peter C.B. Phillips, Peter Schmidt, and Yongcheol Shin. 1992. Testing the null hypothesis of stationarity against the alternative of a unit root: How sure are we that economic time series have a unit root? *Journal of Econometrics* 54 (1–3): 159–178.

Laxton, Douglas, Hamid Faruqee, Peter Isard, Eswar Prasad, and Bart Turtelboom. 1998. *Multimod mark III: The core dynamic and steady state model*. International Monetary Fund, no. 164.

Lee, Soocheol, Unnada Chewpreecha, Hector Pollitt, and Satoshi Kojima. 2018. An economic assessment of carbon tax reform to meet Japan's NDC target under different nuclear assumptions using the E3ME model. *Environmental Economics and Policy Studies* 20 (2): 411–429.

Lehr, U., and C. Lutz. 2016. German Energiewende - quo vadis? European energy and climate security. In *Public policies, energy sources, and eastern partners*, ed. R. Bardazzi, M.G. Pazienza, and A. Tonini, 203–232. New York: Springer.

Lehr, U., C. Lutz, and D. Edler. 2012. Green jobs? Economic impacts of renewable energy in Germany. *Energy Policy* 47: 358–364.

Lin, Steven A.Y. 1994. Government spending and economic growth. *Applied Economics* 26 (1): 83–94.

Ljungqvist, Lars. 2008. Lucas critique. In *The New Palgrave dictionary of economics*, ed. Steven N. Durlauf and Lawrence E. Blume, 2nd ed. Palgrave Macmillan.

Looney, Robert E. 1986. Socio-economic tradeoffs in Saudi Arabia's third five year plan (1980–1985). *Socio-Economic Planning Sciences* 20 (4): 181–192.

Looney, Robert E. 1988. Saudi Arabia's fiscal options: 1986–1992. *Socio-Economic Planning Sciences* 22 (3): 109–123.

Lutz, C. 2011. Energy scenarios for Germany: Simulations with the model PANTA RHEI. In *Interindustry based analysis of macroeconomic forecasting. Proceedings from the 19th INFORUM World Conference*, Pretoria, pp. 203–224.

Lutz, C., D. Lindenberger, M. Schlesinger, and C. Tode. 2014a. Energy reference forecast and energy policy targets for Germany. *Die Unternehmung* 68 (3): 154–163.

Lutz, C., U. Lehr, and P. Ulrich. 2014b. Economic evaluation of climate protection measures in Germany. *International Journal of Energy Economics and Policy* 4 (4): 693–705.

Mizon, Grayham E. 1984. *The encompassing approach in econometrics*. Australian National University, Faculty of Economics and Research School of Social Sciences.

Mizon, Grayham E. 1995. Progressive modeling of macroeconomic time series the LSE methodology. In *Macroeconometrics: Developments, tensions and prospects*, 107–180. Dordrecht: Springer.

Mizon, Grayham E., and Jean-Francois Richard. 1986. The encompassing principle and its application to testing non-nested hypotheses. *Econometrica: Journal of the Econometric Society* 54 (3): 657–678.

Mohaddes, Kamiar, Mehdi Raissi, and Niranjan Sarangi. 2020. *Macroeconomic effects of global shocks in the GCC: Evidence from Saudi Arabia*. Economic Research Forum (ERF).

Musila, Jacob Wanjala. 2002. An econometric model of the Malawian economy. *Economic Modelling* 19 (2): 295–330.

Nakov, Anton, and Galo Nuno. 2013. Saudi Arabia and the oil market. *The Economic Journal* 123 (573): 1333–1362.

Nehru, Vikram, and Ashok Dhareshwar. 1993. Sources, methodology and results. *Revista de análisis económico* 8 (1): 37–59.

Nikas, A., Doukas, H., Papandreou, A. 2019. A Detailed Overview and Consistent Classification of Climate-Economy Models. In: Doukas, H., Flamos, A., Lieu, J. (eds) Understanding Risks and Uncertainties in Energy and Climate Policy. Springer, Cham.

OEGEM (2022). *Oxford Economics*. Global Economic Model. https://www.oxfordeconomics.com/service/subscription-services/macro/global-economic-model.

Pagan, Adrian. 2003a. Report on modelling and forecasting at the Bank of England/Bank's response to the Pagan report. *Bank of England. Quarterly Bulletin* 43 (1): 60.

Pagan, Adrian. 2003b. An examination of some tools for macro-econometric model building. In *METU Lecture, ERC Conference VII*, Ankara.

Pagan, Adrian. 2019. *Australian macro-econometric models and their construction-a short history*. Centre for Applied Macroeconomic Analysis (CAMA), Working Paper 50/2019.

Park, Joon Y. 1990. Testing for unit roots and Cointegration by variable addition. In *Advances in econometrics*, ed. G.F. Rhodes and T.B. Fomby, vol. 8, 107–133. Greenwich: JAI Press.

Park, Joon Y. 1992. Canonical cointegrating regressions. *Econometrica: Journal of the Econometric Society* 60: 119–143.

Perron, Pierre. 1989. The great crash, the oil price shock, and the unit root hypothesis. *Econometrica: Journal of the Econometric Society* 57: 1361–1401.

Perron, Pierre. 2006. Dealing with structural breaks. *Palgrave handbook of econometrics* 1 (2): 278–352.

Perron, Pierre, and Timothy J. Vogelsang. 1992a. Nonstationarity and level shifts with an application to purchasing power parity. *Journal of Business & Economic Statistics* 10 (3): 301–320.

Perron, Pierre, and Timothy J. Vogelsang. 1992b. Testing for a unit root in a time series with a changing mean: Corrections and extensions. *Journal of Business & Economic Statistics* 10 (4): 467–470.

Pesaran, M. Hashem, and Yongcheol Shin. 1999. An autoregressive distributed lag modeling approach to Cointegration analysis. In *Econometrics and economic theory in the 20th century: The Ragnar Frisch centennial symposium*, ed. S. Strom. Cambridge, UK: Cambridge University Press.

Pesaran, M. Hashem, and Ron Smith. 2011. *Beyond the DSGE straitjacket*. CESIFO Working Paper No. 3447.

Pesaran, M. Hashem, Yongcheol Shin, and Richard J. Smith. 2001. Bound testing approaches to the analysis of level relationships. *Journal of Applied Econometrics* 16: 289–326.

Phillips, Peter C.B., and Steven N. Durlauf. 1986. Multiple time series regression with integrated processes. *The Review of Economic Studies* 53 (4): 473–495.

Phillips, Peter C.B., and Bruce E. Hansen. 1990. Statistical inference in instrumental variables regression with I (1) processes. *The Review of Economic Studies* 57 (1): 99–125.

Phillips, Peter C.B., and Mico Loretan. 1991. Estimating long-run economic equilibria. *The Review of Economic Studies* 58 (3): 407–436.

Phillips, Peter C.B., and Sam Ouliaris. 1990. Asymptotic properties of residual based tests for cointegration. *Econometrica* 58 (1): 165–193.

Phillips, Peter C.B., and Pierre Perron. 1988. Testing for unit roots in time series regression. *Biometrika* 75: 335–346.

Roberto, Pedace. 2013. *Econometrics for dummies*. Hoboken: John Wiley & Sons, Inc.

Romer, Paul. 2016. The trouble with macroeconomics. *The American Economist* 20: 1–20.

Rudebusch, Glenn D. 2005. Assessing the Lucas critique in monetary policy models. *Journal of Money, Credit and Banking*: 245–272.

Saikkonen, Pentti. 1992. Estimation and testing of cointegrated systems by an autoregressive approximation. *Econometric Theory* 8 (1): 1–27.

SAMA. 2020. Saudi Arabian Central Bank. Yearly Statistics, 2020 release.

Saudi Vision 2030 (SV2030). 2017. *Fiscal Balance Program*. (FBP). https://vision2030.gov.sa/en/bb2020

Saudi Vision 2030 (SV2030). 2018. *Fiscal Balance Program, Kingdom of Saudi Arabia Vision 2030. 2018 Update*. http://vision2030.gov.sa/en/bb2020

Saudi Vision 2030 (SV2030). 2019a. *Fiscal Balance Program, Kingdom of Saudi Arabia Vision 2030. 2019 Update*. http://vision2030.gov.sa/en/bb2020

Saudi Vision 2030 (SV2030). 2019b. *National Transformation Program (NTP)*. https://vision2030.gov.sa/en/ntp

Soummane, Salaheddine, Frédéric Ghersi, and Franck Lecocq. 2022. Structural transformation options of the Saudi economy under constraint of depressed world oil prices. *The Energy Journal* 43, no. 3.

Soummane, Salaheddine, and Frederic Ghersi. 2022. Projecting Saudi sectoral electricity demand in 2030 using a computable general equilibrium model. *Energy Strategy Reviews* 39: 100787.

Soummane, Salaheddine, Frédéric Ghersi, and Julien Lefèvre. "Macroeconomic pathways of the Saudi economy: The challenge of global mitigation action versus the opportunity of national energy reforms." *Energy Policy* 130 (2019): 263-282.

Stiglitz, Joseph E. 2018. Where modern macroeconomics went wrong. *Oxford Review of Economic Policy* 34 (1–2): 70–106.

Stock, James H. 1987. Asymptotic properties of least squares estimators of cointegrating vectors. *Econometrica: Journal of the Econometric Society* 55: 1035–1056.

Stock, James H., and Mark W. Watson. 1993. A simple estimator of cointegrating vectors in higher order integrated systems. *Econometrica: Journal of the Econometric Society* 61 (4): 783–820.

Taher, Abdulaziz Adeeb H. 1987. *World oil price shocks and the Saudi Arabian economy: A macro econometric simulation*. PhD diss., University of Colorado at Boulder.

Tawi, Saleh Ahmed. 1984. *A macroeconometric model for the economy of Saudi Arabia*. Master's thesis, Iowa State University of Science and Technology.

Valadkhani, Abbas. 2004. History of macroeconometric modelling: Lessons from past experience. *Journal of Policy Modeling* 26 (2): 265–281.

Vogelsang, Timothy J., and Pierre Perron. 1998. Additional tests for a unit root allowing for a break in the trend function at an unknown time. *International Economic Review* 39 (4): 1073–1100.

Welfe, Wladyslaw. 2011. Long-term macroeconometric models: The case of Poland. *Economic Modelling* 28 (1–2): 741–753.

Welfe, Władysław. 2013. *Macroeconometric models*. Advanced Studies in Theoretical and Applied Econometrics, Springer, edition 127, number 978-3-642-34468-8.

Weyerstrass, Klaus, and Reinhard Neck. 2007. SLOPOL6: a macroeconometric model for Slovenia. *International Business & Economics Research Journal (IBER)* 6 (11): 81-94.

Weyerstrass, Klaus, Reinhard Neck, Dmitri Blueschke, Boris Majcen, Andrej Srakar, and Miroslav Verbič. 2018. SLOPOL10: A macroeconometric model for Slovenia. *Economic and Business Review* 20 (2): 269–302.

Wickens, Michael. 1995. Real business cycle analysis: A needed revolution in macroeconometrics. *The Economic Journal* 105 (433): 1637–1648.

Wren-Lewis, Simon. 2018. Ending the microfoundations hegemony. *Oxford Review of Economic Policy* 34 (1–2): 55–69.

Yoshida, Tomoo. 1990. On the stability of the Japanese money demand function: Estimation results using the error correction model. *Bank of Japan Monetary and Economic Studies* 8 (1): 1–48.

Zivot, Eric, and Donald W.K. Andrews. 1992. Further evidence of the great crash, the oil-price shock and the unit-root hypothesis. *Journal of Business and Economic Statistics* 10: 251–270.

Index

Printed by Printforce, the Netherlands